Employment and Work Relations in Context Series

CW00502752

Series Editors

Tony Elger and Peter Fairbrother

Labour Studies Group,

Department of Sociology,

University of Warwick

The aim of the Employment and Work Relations in Context series is to address questions relating to the evolving patterns of work, employment and industrial relations in specific workplaces, localities and regions. This focus arises primarily from a concern to trace out the ways in which wider policy making, especially by national governments and transnational corporations, impinges upon specific workplaces, labour markets and localities in distinctive ways. A particular feature of the series is the consideration of forms of worker and citizen organization and mobilization in these circumstances. Thus the studies will address major analytical and policy issues through case-study and comparative research.

THE DYNAMICS OF WORKPLACE UNIONISM

Shop Stewards' Organization in Three Merseyside Plants

Ralph Darlington

MANSELL

First published 1994 by
Mansell Publishing Limited, *A Cassell Imprint*
Villiers House, 41/47 Strand, London WC2N 5JE, England
387 Park Avenue South, New York, NY 10016–8810, USA

British Library Cataloguing-in-Publication Data
Darlington, Ralph
  Dynamics of Workplace Unionism: Shop
  Stewards' Organization in Three
  Merseyside Plants. — (Employment & Work
  Relations in Context Series)
  I. Title   II. Series
  331.8733094275

  ISBN 0–7201–2168–X Hardback
  ISBN 0–7201–2239 2 Paperback

Library of Congress Cataloging-in-Publication Data
Darlington, Ralph, 1954–
  The dynamics of workplace unionism: shop stewards' organization
  in three Merseyside plants/Ralph Darlington.
        p.   cm. — (Employment and work relations in context)
  Includes bibliographical references and index.
  ISBN 0-7201-2168-X
  1. Shop stewards—England—Merseyside. 2. Trade-unions—
  England—Merseyside—Case studies. I. Title. II. Series.
  HD6490.S52G73   1994
  331.87′33′094275—dc20   93–46397
                                                       CIP

Typeset by Colset Pte Ltd, Singapore
Printed and bound in Great Britain by
Biddles Ltd, Guildford and King's Lynn

CONTENTS

Preface and Acknowledgements

The intellectual and methodological approach adopted in this study was profoundly influenced by Huw Beynon's *Working for Ford*, a penetrating account of shop-floor workers' struggles and of the limitations and potential of plant-based shop stewards' organization. Even though its inspirational celebration of working class militancy of the late 1960s might seem, to some commentators, at odds with the 'new realism' of the 1980s and early 1990s, its pioneering contribution to the study of shop-floor control, resistance and consent has guaranteed its enduring contemporary relevance. Of course, Beynon's study is out of date (notwithstanding a slightly updated second edition published in the early 1980s) in the sense that it does not directly shed any light on the nature of the changes in workplace unionism amidst the new economic and political realities of contemporary Britain. Nonetheless, this work seemed an extremely useful starting point from which to base my own research. By conducting an historical and retrospective evaluation of the strengths and weaknesses of shop stewards' organization in three Merseyside manufacturing plants (including Ford Halewood) since the late 1960s and early 1970s, it would be possible to explore the significance of the changes and continuities that have characterized workplace union relations during the 1980s and early 1990s.

The paucity of shop-floor studies similar to Beynon's, by writers who explicitly identify with workers' struggles and socialist organization, was another factor encouraging my endeavour, although there have been some notable exceptions, including *Workers Divided* (Nichols and Armstrong, 1976), *Living with Capitalism* (Nichols and Beynon, 1977), *Girls, Wives, Factory Lives* (Pollert, 1981), *Women on the Line* (Cavendish, 1982), *Working the System* (Thompson and Bannon, 1985) and *Remaking the Working Class?* (Spencer, 1989). The study contained herein, the genesis of which lies in a doctoral thesis conducted within the departments of industrial relations and sociology at the University of Warwick, is an attempt to rectify this situation.

Indeed perhaps the most influential factor encouraging me to carry out such a study has been a long-held commitment to working class self-emancipation and the socialist transformation of society from below (rather than the socialism from above of Labour MPs and full-time trade union officials). This basic orientation to rank-and-file workers' self activity, which is in many respects exemplified by the political tradition of the Socialist Workers Party, helped to focus my specific attention on the capacity for independent action by shop stewards, frequently seen to be the embodiment of the 'challenge from below' presented to employers, government and official leaders of the labour movement alike. Within the world of academia such sympathies may have seemed, if somewhat extreme, at least understandable during the 1970s. But in today's changing world such ideas are often seen as being completely eccentric. The apparent atrophy of shop stewards' organization over the past 15 years, especially in manufacturing industry – its traditional bastion of strength – obliged me to attempt to confront systematically a whole number of contemporary questions and debates about the demise of shop-floor militancy, the bureaucratization of shop stewards' organization, the changing nature of workplace unionism and so on. This led me to critically engage with the academic literature on the subject, and in the process modify my own analysis and interpretation.

Unfortunately, the question of socialist organization and the role of various political groupings is an aspect of workplace unionism that many commentators tend to ignore or treat only with a certain disdain. But in the process of conducting my study what became glaringly obvious was the importance of the relationship between forms of shop-floor workers' organization, activity and consciousness and the ideological and political resources of shop stewards. Indeed, the overarching premise guiding my research has been that the key dilemma of trade unionism and shop stewards' organization is that it expresses the contradiction between capital and labour but not the means of resolving it. It is my view that a revolutionary socialist organization rooted inside the workplaces is needed to build a bridge between workers' immediate struggles and the need for a generalized political movement that can fight to change society.

Although there is an intimate connection between a social researcher's own political outlook and that person's academic studies many writers seem to try to hide behind a bogus 'neutrality'. But no intellectual pursuit within capitalist society can stand above the fundamental social division between exploiters and exploited. What follows openly and explicitly reflects my own political allegiances and must be judged accordingly.

Whilst many readers may not always find themselves agreeing with the arguments that are presented, I hope that they will acknowledge the attempt to offer a distinctive contribution to an understanding of the dynamics of workplace unionism that opens up a number of important issues for further analysis and comment.

The original doctoral study and its transformation into book form could not have been written without the influence and support of a variety of people. As my external PhD examiner, Huw Beynon provided me with some very valuable observations, as did Mike Terry, my internal examiner. A principal intellectual influence was the insightful Marxist analysis of workplace unionism provided by Richard Hyman, from which I freely borrowed for my own research purposes, albeit 'biting the hand that feeds me' by attempting to develop a critical assessment of his more recent work. I am extremely grateful to both Richard Hyman and Tony Elger (my PhD co-supervisors) for reading and re-reading drafts of the manuscript, consistently offering helpful comments on its contents and forcing me to defend, qualify and elaborate my views on the issues it raises. Special thanks must also go to Peter Fairbrother, Pat Egan, John Dobson and Dave Lyddon for their willingness to comment on and discuss various aspects of the study. I owe a very special debt of gratitude to my partner, Carole Donovan, for offering her comments, putting up with my enforced isolation during the writing process and generally providing me with a tremendous amount of loving support.

Of course, my greatest debt is to all the interviewees from the plants studied who spent many hours sharing their experiences and understanding of events with me, and who helped the manuscript to 'come alive'. Needless to say, any errors of fact or of interpretation are mine.

ABBREVIATIONS

AUEW	Amalgamated Union of Engineering Workers
BPCC	British Printing and Communications Corporation
BPIF	British Printing Industries Federation
CBI	Confederation of British Industry
EETPU	Electrical, Electronic, Telecommunication and Plumbing Union
EI	Employee Involvement
FoC	Father of the Chapel
GMB	General Municipal Boilermakers' Union
GMWU	General and Municipal Workers' Union
IR	Industrial Relations
JNC	Joint Negotiating Committee
JWC	Joint Works Committee
MSF	Manufacturing, Science and Finance
NGA	National Graphical Association
NGA '82	National Graphical Association (amalgamation of NGA and SLADE)
NJNC	National Joint Negotiating Committee
NUM	National Union of Mineworkers
SLADE	Society of Lithographic, Artists, Designers, Engravers and Process Workers
SOGAT	Society of Graphical and Allied Trades
TGWU	Transport and General Workers' Union
TUC	Trades Union Congress
TV	Television

1 INTRODUCTION

The 'Responsible' Steward?

This book provides a detailed study of trade union organization and activity at the workplace. The role of the key trade union representative at this level, the shop steward, is the principal focus of analysis. Based on case studies of shop stewards' organization from the 1970s to the 1990s within three Merseyside manufacturing plants, the book attempts to provide an understanding of the dynamics of workplace unionism over three decades, a period of radical change in employment relations. It examines in detail the relationships between shop stewards and management, members and full-time union officials, and addresses a number of important contemporary debates about the nature of workplace unionism. In particular, the study highlights the limitations of shop stewards' strategies in the 1980s that responded pragmatically to managerial restructuring by means of a 'flexible' bargaining approach compared with the tradition of workplace militancy of the 1970s, and assesses the implications for workplace unionism in the 1990s. One of the central arguments developed is that it is necessary to pay much greater attention than hitherto to the relationship between shop-floor workers' organization and activity and the ideological and political resources that underpin the leadership strategies of shop stewards.

During the 1980s and early 1990s an evaluation of the 'strength' or 'weakness' of shop steward organization in Britain tended to become divided between two diametrically opposed interpretations. On the one hand, many commentators argued that the powerful stewards' organizations which had been built up in the key sectors of manufacturing industry during the 1960s and 1970s had been fundamentally weakened and transformed. The hostile economic and political climate of Conservative rule shifted the balance of workplace power towards management, sapped shop-floor militancy and encouraged the spread of a 'new realism' (Hawkins, 1985; Bassett, 1986; Beaumont, 1987). Some even argued that although shop stewards continue to operate using formal bargaining procedures they have become increasingly marginal to managerial concerns in many companies (Chadwick, 1983). On the other hand, a number of studies suggested that whilst it would be mistaken to believe stewards had not experienced some reduction in their power and influence, the extent of the decline is often exaggerated. Both in terms of the formal institutional aspects of workplace trade unionism, and in terms of substantive measures of the power of shop stewards, what remains striking is the enduring stability of workplace industrial relations rather than its profound and irreversible transformation. It was argued stewards continue to do much the same job as before, 'nothing much has changed', even if during the latter part of the 1980s there was a sharp fall in the number of stewards within smaller workplaces (Batstone, 1984, 1988b; Daniel, 1987; MacInnes, 1987; Millward and Stevens, 1986; Millward *et al.*, 1992).

More recently, it has been acknowledged that the real situation is probably somewhere between these two positions, with a tremendous degree of corporate, sectoral and regional variation (Elger, 1990; Kelly, 1990; Morris and Wood, 1991; Kessler and Bayliss, 1992; Marsh, 1992; Martin, 1992). In part, such differential assessments can be accounted for by the varying research methods adopted – surveys versus case studies (Morris and Wood, 1991) – the different criteria used to measure shop steward 'strength' and 'weakness' – such as procedural and institutional versus process and outcome indices (Terry, 1986a) – and the significance attached to secular and cyclical trends (Kelly, 1990). But the analytical and political vantage point of the researcher and the set of assumptions held by those attempting to interpret the evidence are also important factors shaping such contrasting assessments. Unfortunately, many contributors tend to conflate the empirical evidence uncovered with the model of workplace trade unionism they themselves politically champion without drawing out the linkages and disjunctures between the two. Often the underlying theoretical assumptions and analytical premises that shape their interpretation of procedural and substantive measures of shop-floor power are only stated implicitly. Many studies have provided a mountain of factual data about what shop stewards actually do – in terms of the conduct of collective bargaining and stewards' functions, activities and attitudes (Pedler, 1973; Nicholson, 1976; Partridge, 1978; Nicholson *et al.*, 1980; Winch, 1980; Broad, 1983; Schuller and Robertson, 1983; Terry, 1983a, b; Terry *et al.*, 1978). But most offer no adequate conceptualization of the social dynamics of the shop stewards' role or general theoretical consideration of the underlying interplay between objective and subjective elements which influence the changing nature of shop stewards' organization.

Yet it is ironic that notwithstanding discrepancies in the interpretation of the relationship between change and continuity in workplace industrial relations, a number of contributors from across the spectrum of the debate, with some exceptions, including Fairbrother (1988, 1989, 1990), Spencer (1985, 1987, 1989) and Darlington (1993), have drawn similar practical conclusions about what has been seen as constituting the most effective model of shop-floor trade unionism, involving a so-called realistic, moderate and flexible bargaining stance *vis-à-vis* employers. Such a model of 'responsible unionism' (Fairbrother and Waddington, 1990) has been advocated in the writings of Flanders (1975) and, in the more recent and specific context of the 1980s and early 1990s, by Batstone (1984, 1988b), Batstone *et al.* (1977), Jones and Rose (1986), Kelly (1987) and Ackers and Black (1992). The new stream of Human Resource Management thinking has further underlined the efficacy of such an approach (Guest, 1987; Storey, 1988; Blyton and Turnbull, 1992). Essentially, it is argued that shop stewards' reliance on the actions and approach of yesteryear – with its 'old-fashioned' principles of strikes, picket lines and collective solidarity – is counter-productive; militant workplace trade unionism as traditionally conceived has become increasingly outmoded. Instead, these writers herald the new brand of 'responsible' shop stewards who are not restricted in the range of compromises they are prepared to accept in the form of flexible bargaining over changes in employment and work. Such a cautious 'pragmatic' acquiescence to change is viewed as being the most appropriate strategy for protecting established structures of workplace trade unionism.

Of course, this 'new realism' was reflected during the 1980s inside much of the trade union movement in Britain, when compromise and conciliation with employers became viewed as the best response given the prevailing political and economic environment. Mass redundancies, high unemployment, decline in union membership, increasingly assertive managerial styles and a hostile Conservative government all formed part of the environment in which unions had to operate (McIlroy, 1988). As Bill Jordan, the engineering workers' union leader, commented: 'The days of confrontation have to end. Both sides of industry can no longer have the luxury of knocking each other about while competitors steal our trade and jobs' (*Guardian*, 12 September 1992). Although union responses differed in some important respects – for example between the 'social partnership' approach of the AEU and EETPU, the 'market unionism' of the GMB and the more independent stance of the TGWU and NUM (Towers, 1989; Martinez Lucio and Weston, 1992; Martin, 1992) – the leadership of most unions, in one way or another, conceded they did not have the power to resist patterns of employer and government behaviour they found objectionable. This changed mood and approach was symbolized by the invitation to employers' leader Howard Davies of the CBI to speak at the TUC conference in 1992.

The Tensions of Workplace Unionism

Within this book it will be argued that shop stewards act within the context of the general tensions that characterize workplace unionism, of seeking to organize resistance to exploitation but confined within the limits of capitalist society. This means there is a central tension between, on the one hand, pressures towards bureaucratic and accommodative forms of shop stewards' organization and, on the other, those towards resistance, collective mobilization and democratic participation. As a consequence, the nature of shop stewards' organization is not a fixed, static phenomenon. The relative strength of the internal and external, material and ideological, forces bearing upon shop stewards shifts and fluctuates. The in-built contradictory nature of workplace unionism gives the process a constantly uneven, dynamic nature. In other words, in any study of the processes of workplace unionism the key question should be not merely whether shop stewards are 'strong' or 'weak', 'militant' or 'responsible', but what the balance is between these contradictory tendencies and what pressures are pushing in each direction at various times and in different contexts.

This book documents the results of case study research into three manufacturing plants in Merseyside: the Birds Eye food processing plant in Kirkby, the Bemrose printing plant in Aintree and the Ford car plant in Halewood. In the light of the above considerations there are four broad objectives. Firstly, to shed some further detailed light on our understanding of the 'state' of shop steward organization by offering not merely a snap-shot of contemporary developments, but also an exploration of the earlier reel of film. The changes and continuities within the three plants studied are outlined within the historical context of the past 20–25 years. This reveals how *present* shop stewards' organization is a product of *past* activity and relationships, and how these contain the potential for *future* change and development.

The study contrasts the very different period of the 1970s with that of the 1980s and early 1990s, the latter of which witnessed the extreme restructuring process characteristic of much of manufacturing industry. This restructuring has dramatic implications for shop-floor unionism confronted with the problem of resistance or acquiescence to the employers. Evidence is provided which suggests that, although the substantive strength of stewards' organization has undoubtedly been undermined in recent years, the process of change has been uneven and that the current weaknesses should not be regarded as being necessarily of a permanent nature.

A second objective is to refine a distinctive Marxist analytical and conceptual framework from which to understand the essential features of the contradictory nature of shop stewards' organization, activity and consciousness within capitalist society. Some writers have adopted conceptual usage of the dualities of resistance/accommodation, democracy/bureaucracy, and independence/dependence (Lane, 1974; Boraston *et al.*, 1975; Hyman, 1975, 1979; Clarke and Clements, 1977; Beynon, 1984; Fairbrother, 1984, 1986). I have attempted to build on and extend the use of these terms to devise a threefold analytical framework that focuses on the contradictory nature of shop stewards' relationships to management, members and full-time trade union officials in each of the three plants. It is through such an explanatory mechanism that the various factors that influence the changing balance of workplace power, located within their broader economic, social and political context, are explored.

The third objective is to develop a critical assessment of the work of Eric Batstone in particular (Batstone *et al.*, 1977, 1978; Batstone, 1984, 1985, 1986, 1988a, b). This is because Batstone was a foremost contributor to the analysis of the role of shop stewards in relation to workplace leadership and organization, especially in *Shop Stewards in Action* (written jointly with Ian Boraston and Stephen Frenkel in 1977), which has been widely acclaimed as establishing a new way of looking at shop stewards' organization and behaviour. Even now it continues to provide many industrial relations researchers with their theoretical starting point. However, it will be my contention that despite some useful, although partial insights, Batstone's attempt to make explicit an analytical vantage point, namely that of 'Labourism', an unequivocally reformist workplace trade unionism, contains considerable flaws. In essence, my aim is to put Batstone's resolute endorsement of a 'sophisticated' shop steward organization that engages in 'strong bargaining relations' with management to the test of empirical research through the prism of an alternative Marxist theoretical framework. The notion that the most cost-effective strategy for shop stewards is one that rejects militant activity in favour of 'pragmatic' bargaining is tested by examining the experience of the three Merseyside plants between the late 1960s and early 1990s. The implications for the nature of workplace unionism that emerged are assessed.

Focusing specific attention on Batstone's model of 'sophisticated' steward organization is justified not merely because of the pivotal contribution his analysis has made to the study of shop-floor unionism, but also because it illustrates in sharp relief the way in which the researcher's analytical and political assumptions can shape the interpretation of different measures of shop steward 'strength' and 'weakness' (for example, with differing conceptions of workplace union democracy). Furthermore, Batstone's work provides a useful basis from which to comment on some of the related debates concerning the 'bureaucratisation of the rank-and-file' thesis (Hyman, 1979), the role of union officialdom at national level in defining local union practice (Heery and Kelly, 1990), and the potential for workplace-based union 'renewal' towards more active and participative forms (Fairbrother, 1989, 1990).

The fourth objective is to explore the relationship between forms of shop-floor union organization, activity and consciousness and the ideological and political resources of shop stewards. Beynon (1984) revealed the dialectical interplay between the day-to-day struggle of shop-floor workers, on the one hand, and the distinctive form of 'factory class consciousness' developed by an experienced shop stewards' leadership, on the other, that generates a basic collectivism and opposition to management and through which effective workplace unionism is developed and sustained. This book further explores such themes, in particular highlighting the limitations of the stewards' political horizons in confronting corporate restructuring. The case studies signal an alternative revolutionary socialist strategy for rebuilding the strength of workplace unionism.

The Research

The research documented below involves a case study approach aimed at providing a more detailed observation of particular workplaces than is possible with large-scale surveys. Existing surveys (Brown, 1981; Daniel and Millward, 1983; Millward and Stephens, 1986; Millward *et al.*, 1992) provide a wealth of data on shop stewards' organization and are especially useful for providing material on patterns of institutional arrangements, but they usually confine themselves to reporting certain easily observable features of industrial relations and present them by means of averages and distributions. The complex elements which are such an important component of shop-floor behaviour and organization often go unrecorded in any detail. By contrast, the great strength of a case study approach is that it allows a detailed concentration on specific workplaces and makes it possible to identify, explore and understand the various interactive social processes at work, the underlying substantive outcomes as well as the procedural forms. In addition, a case study approach can facilitate a distinctive, and rarely used, *historical* exploration of the changes and continuities underlying the different patterns of workplace trade unionism stretching over a 20–25 year period. By exploring the strengths and weaknesses of shop steward organization in the 1970s a case study has helped illuminate the weaknesses and strengths of the 1980s and early 1990s – not in any simple way of 'lessons from the past', but as an historical overview of processes whose consequences are still apparent.

It should be noted that my case studies are firmly located within the traditional focus of much post-war British industrial relations research, concentrated on manual workers in private manufacturing industry. Of course, manufacturing has been in decline for many decades and during the past 20 years has undergone massive contraction. In 1973 there were 7.5 million workers in manufacturing (35 per cent of all employees in Britain). In 1979 this had fallen to just over 7 million. In the following two years, however, the figure was to drop by more than a million, and then by a further half a million between 1981 and 1983. The decline continued throughout the 1980s and accelerated rapidly again during the early 1990s economic recession. By mid-1993 the number of workers in manufacturing had fallen to just over 4 million, representing just over 15 per cent of all the country's jobs (IRRR, 1993). Yet despite recent claims of 'post-Fordism', Britain remains a major industrial economy with total industrial capacity still amounting to the sixth largest concentration of global production within the boundaries of any nation state. In 1993 there were still over 1000 manufacturing sites with more than 500 employees (Millward *et al.*, 1992). Moreover, notwithstanding the decline of manufacturing employment relative to the rest of the British workforce, its social weight still far outweighs its numerical size (both in terms of its importance to the state of the economy as a whole and in overall levels of industrial action) and its workers still wield enormous potential muscle due to their strategic position at the point of production. In the past, shop stewards' organization in manufacturing industry has exercised a major influence on workplace unionism in the newer, less well organized sections of the British working class movement, amongst white collar and service sector workers. There is no reason, short of complete de-industrialization, to believe this will cease to be the case in the future. On this basis, empirical research into shop stewards' organization within manufacturing industry constitutes an important benchmark by which to assess some of the dilemmas faced by British workplace unionism more broadly.

The distinctive Merseyside context within which the research was conducted is obviously of some significance (see Chapter 2). On the one hand, a regional economy characterized by major concentrations of semi- and unskilled manual workers employed in the plants of national and multinational corporations, post-war Merseyside became a breeding ground for a relatively cohesive class-based identity and consciousness (Beynon, 1984; Lane, 1987) – hence Merseyside's (usually rather over-exaggerated) reputation as a bastion of trade union militancy with a notoriously strike-prone workforce (Bean and Stoney, 1986). On the other hand, the region's historical dependence on a small number of very large multinational companies, with branch plants vulnerable to cyclical fluctuations in the national and world economy, contributed to the avalanche of redundancies and closures, and consequent very high levels of unemployment, with which the area has become synonymous (Parkinson, 1985). Those plants that remained open have undergone substantial restructuring, usually involving an attempt to reassert managerial control at the expense of shop-floor workers. Thus on both counts, Merseyside provides a fascinating context within which to explore the predicament faced by shop steward organizations within manufacturing industry in recent years, and to reconsider previous empirical case study research on workplace unionism conduced in the region by Beynon (1984), Thompson and Bannon (1985), Spencer (1989) and Coyne and Williamson (1991).

Case studies were conducted into three Merseyside manufacturing plants owned by foreign multinational companies (namely Unilever, News International and Ford) with established shop steward organizations and formal bargaining relationships with management stretching back over 25 years. All of them experienced substantial work reorganization involving large-scale redundancies during the 1980s. In two of the plants (Birds Eye and Bemrose) reorganization resulted in plant closure (in 1989 and 1991 respectively). The three companies reflect a range of manufacturing sectors with varied product markets and contrasting shop-floor union organizations and traditions: Bemrose and Ford sharing a predominantly male workforce composition, Birds Eye being mainly female. Taken together, the case studies provide fertile ground for comparative assessment.

The bulk of the data were gathered from extensive semi-structured and tape-recorded interviews between 1988 and 1993 with a variety of strategically placed informants from different sections of the three plants, including shop stewards, rank-and-file union members, plant managers and full-time union officials. Most had ten or more years' experience and active involvement in plant-based affairs and were able to draw upon their wealth of knowledge to place particular events and general trends within their historical context. The reason for choosing to interview 'activists' was not merely that such people had relevant personal experience to base their interpretations upon, but also that they were more likely to be able to understand and articulate that experience in the light of their practical involvement. However, interviews were also conducted with a number of shop-floor union members who were not active in formal terms in the stewards' committee or union branch but who nevertheless had some very useful insights to shed upon workplace relations. Such oral data were supplemented by detailed analysis of primary and archival documents (such as shop steward and union branch minute books, management bulletins, leaflets and collective bargaining agreements) as well as secondary sources (such as research studies and newspaper accounts).

Interviews were chosen as the primary method of data collection because they permitted both the establishment of a narrative account of workplace management–union relations and an analytical understanding of the underlying social processes, including the internal and external constraints on shop steward activity. They also facilitated an emphasis on the *subjective* aspects of shop-floor behaviour that complements more structural accounts. Unfortunately, there exists a long line of research which tends to view workers as the objects of history and attributes an essentially passive role to rank-and-file trade unionists. Prima facie this may be considered mistaken, given the active initiative, often involving bitter struggle, of workers who have established a degree of control on the shop-floor and have encroached on managerial prerogative in the first place. Interviews helped place the emphasis on shop stewards and their members not merely as the objective products of society but also as actors who subjectively react back to change it. In addition, interviews gave an opportunity for a diversity of standpoints to be recreated, allowing for a realistic reconstruction of the nature of social relationships within each workplace (see Appendices 1 and 2).

Obviously, in some respects the analysis of specific case studies of shop steward organization within three Merseyside plants provides only a limited basis from which to make wider generalizations, not least because of sectoral, regional and corporate variations. Certainly the individual workplaces at the heart of this study can hardly be regarded as a representative sample or even 'typical' of the area in which they are located. But in some respects, the very idea of a typical factory is an artificial construction of those commentators who conceive of only one mode of generalization: the extrapolation from sample to population. There is, however, as Buroway has explained, a second mode of generalization:

> which seeks to illuminate the forces at work in society as a totality rather than to reflect simply on the constancy and variation of isolated factory regimes within a society . . . this second mode . . . is the extension from the micro context to the totality which shapes it. According to this view every particularity contains a generality; each particular factory regime is the product of general forces operating at a societal or global level.
> (Buroway, 1985, p. 18)

Therefore, whilst accepting the limitations of making any wide generalizations, one can make some analytical generalizations. In this sense, the importance of the case studies lies less in their 'typicality' than in their theoretical relevance and in the broad insights which they can provide in highlighting the underlying patterns of shop stewards' organization and behaviour, particularly in manufacturing industry.

From the outset it is important to state that this book has been written within the general framework of a revolutionary socialist approach and is devoted to assisting those everywhere engaged in the battle to advance the struggles of labour against capital. Such partisan motives might be regarded as academically somewhat disreputable. No doubt, to consider how shop stewards might build up the strength of workplace union organization by challenging the structures of managerial control is to display an 'irresponsible bias' – which, rather ironically, is rarely noticed in managerially orientated studies (Hyman, 1989c). As C. Wright Mills (1966) remarked: 'I have tried to be objective, I do not claim to be detached.' Naturally, the readers of this book are not obliged to share the political assumptions underpinning the case study research, although they do have the right to demand that it should not simply be the defence of a political position, but rather an internally well founded portrayal of the actual underlying social processes of shop stewards' organization.

Trotsky's answer to objections of a lack of 'impartiality' in his writings on the Russian Revolution is pertinent to my own research:

> The serious and critical reader will not want a treacherous impartiality, which offers him a cup of conciliation with a well-settled poison of reactionary hate at the bottom, but a scientific conscientiousness, which for its sympathies and antipathies – open and disguised – seeks support in an honest study of the facts, a determination of their real connections, an exposure of the causal laws of their movement. That is the only possible historic objectivity, and moreover, it is amply sufficient, for it is verified and tested not by the good intentions of the historian, for which only he himself can vouch, but by the natural laws revealed by him of the historic process itself. (Trotsky, 1977, p. 21)

It will be up to the reader to judge how far I have met this criterion. The aim is not just a simple narrative of events and developments, although that in itself is of historical interest, but a rigorous analysis, interpretation and assessment of the underlying social processes involved which seeks to contribute to the strengthening of workplace unionism and socialist organization. Nonetheless, my attempt to link theoretical, methodological and policy perspectives will be open to critical scrutiny from alternative vantage points of analysis, not only by students of industrial relations but also by management and trade union front-line practitioners 'in the field'.

Structure

The structure of the book is as follows: Chapter 2 considers the dynamics of shop stewards' organization by means of a critique of Eric Batstone's interpretation and an outline of an alternative Marxist analytical framework. Chapter 3 locates the three shop steward organizations in the specific geographical context within which they are embedded, namely the distinctive labour and cultural traditions of Merseyside. Particular consideration is given to the problem of workers' resistance to the tidal wave of redundancies in the region during the 1980s. Chapters 4, 5 and 6 document the results of the case study research into workplace trade unionism within the Birds Eye, Bemrose and Ford plants. Chapter 7 provides a comparative assessment of the social relations underlying the different patterns of workplace unionism. Recurring themes within the research material are explicitly addressed in the light of the issues raised in this introduction. An attempt is made to draw some general conclusions and implications about the dynamic nature of shop stewards' organization.

2 THE DYNAMICS OF WORKPLACE UNIONISM

Introduction

Although many commentators argued that shop-floor trade union power in large-scale manufacturing industry declined sharply during the 1980s, this view was refuted by Eric Batstone's surveys of personnel managers and shop stewards (Batstone, 1984, 1985, 1988b; Batstone and Gourlay, 1986), which underlined the continuities between the 1970s and 1980s. He claimed that steward organizations remained durable and resilient, with no indication that stewards had been co-opted by management or had become ineffective in pursuing workers' interests (although he suggested the more 'sophisticated' stewards' organizations were likely to be most effective). Such evidence provided some justification for assuming that the basic *institutions* of steward organization remained fundamentally intact during the 1980s, and in this respect, his notion that 'nothing much has changed' (1988b) had the merit of countering some of the more pessimistic assessments provided by other commentators. However, it is quite conceivable that, whilst the machinery of workplace collective bargaining and the institutions of shop-floor trade unionism were maintained, the all-important *substantive* content was simultaneously considerably transformed, undermining the self-confidence and power of shop stewards' organization compared with the 1970s. Whilst Batstone explicitly attempted to refute such an interpretation his evidence and arguments on this matter appeared distinctly less convincing than on others.

Unfortunately, an evaluation of such issues was considerably hampered by Batstone's underlying analytical framework. This is not to imply that the procedural and substantive indices of shop steward power and influence he utilized were completely worthless. On the contrary, if we want to talk about the balance of workplace power then we have to use the indicators and measures that are on hand, and in doing so Batstone provided some notable, if partial, insights into the strengths and weaknesses of workplace unionism. However, it is necessary to bear in mind that all such indices are open to diverse interpretations depending upon the vantage point of the observer. Arguably, Batstone's mainstream Labourist/reformist prism of analysis not only blinkered his assessment of such measures but also resulted in a distorted analysis of the dynamics of shop stewards' organization more generally. Labourism and reformism can be understood as a theory and practice which create defensive barriers against the naked exploitation of capitalism but at the same time accept the possibility of social change within the existing framework of capitalist society, rather than seeking through revolutionary means to overthrow it (Saville, 1973). Whilst the chief focus is the achievement of piecemeal reform from above, mainly via Parliament and the Labour Party, collective bargaining by trade union officials and stewards can also play a role. Reformist workplace trade unionism is characterized by the attempt to reconcile the interests of management and workers and tends to view rank-and-file workers as essentially passive.

This chapter outlines and then critically assesses Batstone's reformist analysis of workplace unionism and provides an alternative revolutionary socialist analytical framework from which to understand the nature of shop stewards' relationship to management, members and full-time union officials. It also discusses the various factors that affect the balance of workplace power within the context of society as a whole, and their significance and implications for the vitality of shop-floor unionism.

Batstone's 'Sophisticated' Stewards' Organization

Despite the multifaceted nature of Batstone's contribution to the analysis of workplace unionism, it is useful to focus attention on three distinct components which highlight the overarching themes of his notion of shop steward 'sophistication'; namely, the emphasis he placed on the key role played by 'leader' stewards; on the 'strong bargaining relations' such 'leader' stewards establish with management; and on his rebuttal of the dangers of the 'bureaucratization' of stewards' organization. Each of these elements is explored in more detail.

Firstly, Batstone *et al.* (1977, 1978) were most concerned with the institutional, organizational and ideological features of the work situation which encouraged shop steward leadership, and its consequences for the dynamics of workplace industrial relations. At the heart of Batstone's analysis was the notion of a 'sophisticated' shop stewards' organization, a centralized organizational structure which has the resources to take into account the interests of union members as a whole, and co-ordinate the activities of sectional groups and formulate the most cost-effective strategy in the light of the union's relative power position. The focus of attention was placed on the relatively small number of 'leader' stewards, the most important of whom were referred to as the 'quasi-élite'. These are a cen-tralized network of stewards who seek to shape a strategic plant-wide perspective supportive of 'trade union principles' of unity and collectivism and who act in a 'representative' role on behalf of a fragmented and sec-tional membership. Such 'leader' stewards have close informal contacts with management and are able to improve their members' conditions through pragmatic bargaining, with little need to resort to strike action or risky confrontations. Through their network of relations with members and the 'mobilization of bias', 'leader' stewards exercise a decisive degree of power and influence both within the stewards' body and over a volatile union membership. They are able to mould the definition of individual and group grievances, to control their progress through the joint machinery, and to secure favourable outcomes (Batstone *et al.*, 1977, pp. 33–5).

Other, less centrally positioned, 'populist' stewards were also identi-fied by Batstone. Possessing rather tenuous contacts with management, 'populist' stewards lack sophisticated bargaining awareness and are more susceptible to managerial attempts to gain the advantage. Without firm links with their members they confine themselves to a 'mouthpiece' (populist) role, placing greater emphasis on the pursuit of sectional interests, and are more likely to adopt the strike tactic to advance their grievances. It follows that such 'populist' stewards are far less effective in representing their members than the 'leader' stewards. Batstone also identified two subsidiary types of steward: 'nascent leaders' who are committed to trade union principles but fail to gain the support of other stewards or from the shop-floor, and 'cowboys' who play a representative role in promoting the short-term interests of their members but do not adhere to union principles (Batstone *et al.*, 1977, p. 35).

Secondly, Batstone also focused on what was termed stewards' 'strong bargaining relations' with management. Whilst acknowledging a basic conflict of interest between employers and workers, Batstone did not believe this represented a fundamental antagonism; such conflicting goals are compatible with and dependent upon some form of accommodation. Without losing sight of the fact that a rational calculation of advantage in a context of power relations is always at stake, there was an assumption that conflict can be resolved through compromise and concession within a mature system of workplace bargaining, which both sides find acceptable and mutually advantageous. Batstone emphasized how 'leader' shop stewards and managers tend to press for their own competitive advantage in such a way that no group is completely dominant or able to have its own way on every occasion. Instead, there is often something approximating a rough balance of power. 'Strong bargaining relations' involve 'leader' stewards in close contact with managers, adopting a tough but cautious bargaining approach of give-and-take, a process of marginal incremental adjustment that maintains a more or less stable equilibrium within a generally agreed framework of formal and informal rules and procedures. 'Strong bargaining relations' mean that 'both stewards and managers are on the same wavelength. Bargaining occurs on the basis of shared understanding and definitions' (Batstone *et al.*, 1977, p. 174). It is the philosophy of 'you win some, you lose some', with stability being the keynote.

From this perspective, by moderating their goals shop stewards can achieve more for their members than they possibly could through a more adversarial or militant perspective. This might mean that in specific instances the gains won by stewards would be less than they might be, but equally there would be other occasions when procedural routes achieve gains (or minimize losses) where outright conflict would suffer resounding defeats. Thus, the moderation of demands involves a rational estimate of the chance of success. The key question becomes the overall balance of gains and losses and the formulation of the most cost-effective strategy. Whilst some stewards might have rather ambitious goals and be prepared to adopt an adversarial stance to pursue them, Batstone envisaged a much narrower horizon of restricted, readily negotiable and mutually advantageous trade-offs which do not seriously obstruct managerial objectives. A frontal challenge to the existing framework of power and control would only be possible at disproportionate cost to the maintenance of established workplace union structures.

The third principal component of Batstone's work (Batstone, 1984, 1988b; Batstone and Gourlay, 1986) was his systematic criticism of the tendency identified by some commentators towards a 'bureaucratization' of shop stewards' organization arising from the implementation of the Donovan Commission recommendations. According to this view (Cliff, 1970, 1979; Lyddon, 1977; Hyman, 1979; Terry, 1978, Willman, 1980; Beynon, 1984), during the 1970s, shop stewards' organizations' became much more hierarchical and centralized, with a layer of senior shop stewards becoming isolated from their members through their full-time status, the provision of facilities by management and their involvement in plant-level bargaining. The fuller integration of stewards into the larger national union also increased their exposure to a higher degree of official control by union leaderships. To explore this question Batstone made a detailed assessment of available survey evidence and various indices of 'bureaucratization' such as the increase in the number of senior stewards (particularly full-time stewards), the regularity of stewards' meetings, stewards' tenure of office, the extent to which stewards' positions are contested in elections, and the provision of facilities. He concluded there was a very real danger of exaggerating the scale, nature and sources of bureaucracy within shop steward organizations. Despite an overall rise in the number of senior stewards and full-time stewards relative to employees, many of the features of bureaucracy existed prior to the Donovan reforms (particularly in engineering industry) and were not noticeably enhanced during the 1970s and 1980s. He insisted that what is often interpreted as 'bureaucratization', or the expression of the interests of a centralized layer of senior shop stewards, might in fact reflect considerations of efficiency and effectiveness. 'Sophisticated' structures of stewards' organization (bureaucratic or not) may permit coherent policy formulation, which takes into account the interests of the membership as a whole and facilitates a more critical assessment of the stewards' relative power position.

These then are the three principal components of Batstone's contribution to an analysis of the nature of workplace unionism. In so far as it provided a detailed examination of shop steward organization and behaviour his work has helped transform an understanding of shop-floor union life. However, it will be my contention that his overriding conception, analysis and vigorous defence of the notion of 'sophisticated' shop stewards' organization contained very real limitations and flaws. Such a critique can be most usefully explored by an interrogation of the key terms Batstone utilized, namely 'power', 'strong bargaining relations', 'interests', 'leadership', 'trade union principles' and 'bureaucracy'.

To begin with, there was his usage of the term 'power'. Batstone was primarily interested in the exercise of power where it could be readily 'observed', concentrating his attention on decision making within the shop stewards' body and stewards' day-to-day bargaining relationship with management. Whilst this highlighted the uneven distribution of power and influence that exists within stewards' organization it also tended to segregate workplace industrial relations as an arena of analysis from the broader social and historical context within which it unfolds, thereby providing only a partial and insufficient picture. Thus, Batstone appeared to take the existence of shop stewards' 'action' (their ideas, beliefs and goals) as given rather than attempting to explain their source and origin (at least beyond specific organizational and institutional factors within the workplace) in the underlying social 'structure' and relations of production within a capitalist society. He took for granted an existing system of workplace relations where shop stewards are motivated to act in terms of social norms which serve to generate their commitment to rules which do not seriously obstruct managerial objectives. He also took for granted the substantive inequality of power and rewards that results from the command of the economy by capital and which structures the whole agenda of collective bargaining in a manner conducive to employers' interests.

What Batstone ignored or underestimated is the fact that the 'frontier of control' (Goodrich, 1975; Batstone, 1988a) in the workplace is necessarily conditional precisely because it operates within an economic and structural context which can be expected to persist only so long as an employer is able to extract an acceptable level of profit from workers' labour. This means that not only does control over higher-level policies and decisions set rigorous limits to workplace controls, but the employers and the state are in a position to use their immense economic and social power to threaten the very security and survival of shop steward organization that does not agree to work by the 'rules of the game'. Yet playing the rules of the game means not pressing demands 'too far' or directly challenging the 'rights of capital' but accepting the compromises imposed by capitalist economic and political logic. It is within this framework that we can see how stewards' subjective 'meanings' are systematically influenced in the interest of maintaining control over the structure of society through the exploitation of labour.

The essential point being made here is that it is because shop stewards are faced with these broader material and ideological pressures, and not just organizational factors within the workplace, that they are encouraged to engage in 'strong bargaining relations' with management. It follows that this cannot be interpreted as anything other than an accommodation to external power, a theme which reveals why Batstone's underlying assumption of convergent and reconcilable interests between shop stewards and managers, obtained through mutually advantageous trade-offs, is woefully inadequate. This does not mean that 'strong bargaining relations' cannot achieve some limited concrete gains for sections of workers, but it does mean that the scope for such give-and-take bargaining is strictly circumscribed by the wider structural context of capitalist social relations. It is conditional on company and capitalist stability in which there is a considerable margin available for employers to make concessions to workers. Yet competitive pressures and/or economic recession are not necessarily an opportune context for the orderly accommodation of opposing interests. Indeed, in such conditions, social and economic antagonisms are often sharpened and the processs of give-and-take can become a manifestly zero (or even negative) sum game.

A related problem with Batstone's focus on stewards' bargaining power was that it failed to take adequate account of the way many of the most important limitations on managerial prerogative derive not from the bargaining skills of the quasi-élite of 'leader' shop stewards but from the unilateral regulation of employment through forms of informal, sponta-neous and independent action taken by rank-and-file workers themselves (Goodrich, 1975). Of course, the power of workplace union organization is built through effective steward negotiation, but at the end of the day it comes from what workers are prepared to do collectively to set limits to the power of management. Stewards have little else to fall back on the when the crunch comes. The frontier of control constantly shifts as workers' determination not to have their conditions of work entirely dictated to them often expresses itself in their struggles to establish some element of counter-control. In this sense, the power of workplace union organi-zation is not the personal property of the steward, but only really comes from the daily shop-floor battles over pay and conditions, sometimes led by shop stewards, but often organized independently of their initiative. Arguably, it is these shop-floor controls which are the basis upon which real material improvements in workers' positions are achieved, rather than solely, or even primarily, through the channels of collective bar-gaining. 'Invasion, not admission should be the trade unionist's watch-word' is a sentiment with deep historical roots in the British labour movement (Goodrich, 1975).

This raises the question of 'interests'. Because Batstone conceived conflict between workers and managers as narrowly bound within workplace institutional forms, he made a sharp distinction between what he appeared to regard as workers' 'realistic' subjective interests, which arise from their lived experiences of work, and so-called unrealistic objective 'radical' interests that might challenge the capitalist system. Ironically, whilst he acknowledged that the material situation and ideological influence of 'leader' stewards makes workers' subjectively expressed interests ambivalent, Batstone did not clarify his definition of interests. Yet he provided a false dichotomy that fails to take account of the fact that within capitalism both employers and workers are forced to act in certain ways that express contradictory and mutually antagonistic interests, irrespective of what they may consciously articulate at any point in time. It is in this respect that Batstone's analytical starting point, the specific work situation, stands in complete contrast to Marx's own understanding of the totality of class relations within society.

Marx's evidence for a 'class in itself', generating conflict and giving the working class objective interests, can only be understood if the nature of inter-capitalist competition external to the workplace is taken into consideration. In order to remain competitive, employers are compelled to drive up the rate of exploitation, thereby demonstrating that their interests (profit) fundamentally conflict with those of workers. Equally, workers are often driven to take action to defend their wages and conditions precisely because employers refuse to satisfy their basic aspirations and needs (Draper, 1978). In these circumstances immediate forms of workers' struggle and consciousness can actually seek to embody, in however fragmentary and partial forms, 'radical' needs which cannot be met within exploitative relations of production and which as a result can lead workers to consciously act on those 'objective' interests. In this sense, workers' activity within capitalism shows the potential, notwithstanding the very real obstacles involved, for transcending capitalist production relations (Thompson, 1983).

Workers' leaders emerge as a feature of the organizational forms of workers' struggle. Significantly, Batstone tended to treat leadership as a generalized property of certain (usually senior) stewards, rather than as a pattern of behaviour all stewards adopt when dealing with particular issues in certain situations. As noted above, he identified two distinguishing features of a 'leader' steward: namely, their 'representative' role in relation to members (as opposed to 'populist') and their commitment to 'trade union principles' of unity and fairness (Batstone *et al.*, 1977, pp. 23–53). The problem with such a characterization is the assumption that leadership is essentially a one-way relationship between 'leader' shop stewards and their members. Although he acknowledged the influence of other key figures on the shop-floor who transmit their concerns upwards (namely, the 'opinion-leader' and 'griever') Batstone saw the 'leader' steward as pivotal in amending and squashing issues, and knowing what was 'best' for the members. But this conception to a large extent simplifies and underestimates the complexities involved in what is a dynamic interaction. Of course, day-to-day experience of shop-floor bargaining and conflict with management can help shop stewards to develop distinctive insights into workplace industrial relations. Moreover, the stewards' committee provides crucial resources and support for stewards to develop and test their perspectives. Nonetheless, whilst they retain a degree of autonomy, stewards are under constant pressure not to become too isolated from the practical needs of their members, and in order not to face a challenge to their position they are often forced to respond to such rank-and-file demands.

In other words, the 'leadership' relationship is a two-way interaction between the members and shop stewards, between day-to-day resistance to management and building effective workplace trade union organization. It involves stewards both sharing their members' experience and being responsive to their immediate interests whilst simultaneously 'giving a lead' and attempting to transcend their limitations. In fact, the internal factional conflict that sometimes takes place amongst 'leader' stewards, and which Batstone partially identified, concerns in part arguments about what this involves and reflects differing currents of concern and activity amongst rank-and-file members (although Batstone provided no real indication of the way in which some internal faction-fighting may be related to differences in the *political* sympathies and allegiances of various stewards). On this basis, it would be an oversimplification to term a shop steward either a 'leader' or a 'populist'; stewards may behave differently in varying situations and circumstances, depending on the issue and the work group involved, the strength of shop-floor confidence, management's strategy, the role of union officials and so on (Pedler, 1973; Willman, 1980; Broad, 1983). Batstone's distinction is far too sharply polarized, exaggerating the difference between the roles; in practice, stewards usually display characteristics from both extremes.

In many respects, Nichols and Beynon's description (1977, pp. 147–60) of the ChemCo shop stewards, Alfie and Greg, confirms the way Batstone's distinction between 'leader' and 'populist' is too overdrawn. Alfie is a shop steward, active in the union and committed to trade union principles. Using Batstone's term he is a 'leader' steward in that he has 'strong bargaining relations' with management and a 'representative' role in relation to his members. At the same time, however, contrary to Batstone's characterization, he has little contact with his members, over whom he has little influence. Given his unwillingness to deal with rank-and-file grievances with sufficient militancy, his members think he is too soft with management, and withhold their loyalty because of his inability to achieve satisfactory improvements in working conditions. By contrast, Greg is a shop steward, not active in the union, but committed to 'trade union principles'. Using Batstone's terms he is more inclined to act as a 'populist' in that he does not have close links with management and because he takes up and militantly pursues his members' sectional grievances. Yet, again at variance with Batstone's characterization, because of his willingness to represent the rank-and-file, Greg has good contacts with his members, who provide him with their loyal support. Moreover, not only is he able successfully to deliver real improvements in their conditions, but also he attempts to bridge the day-to-day sectional concerns of his members with a longer-term strategy aimed at building up strong and collective plant-wide union organization.

Moreover, as Willman (1980) has argued, Batstone's typology does not allow for the impact which management may have through promoting the stewards' role as part of the formalization of workplace industrial relations. Thus, steward organizations may display quite different policy characteristics depending on the degree to which they are 'independent' or 'management sponsored'. Using Batstone's typology, one could conceive both of these types of steward organization as having both 'leaders' and 'populists'. But it would be impossible to distinguish between them in terms of the policies pursued because such a vague definition does not allow it. Crucially, it is necessary to take account of the contrasting traditions of accountability, and forms of membership contact, characteristic of different steward organizations, something which Batstone's framework merely obscures.

All of these arguments relate to more recent debates between those commentators who have drawn attention to the contrast between 'participatory' and 'representative' forms of democracy in shop stewards' relationship with their members and who emphasize the apparent transformation of the directly accountable shop stewards of the 1950s and 1960s to the more 'professional' and centralized stewards' organizations of the 1970s and 1980s (Hyman, 1979; Terry, 1983a). This is a view disputed by Batstone on the basis that stewards' organization is as 'sophisticated' as it ever was in the past. But even if it is the case that tendencies towards democracy and bureaucracy co-existed with one another throughout both periods an exploration of the balance between these two contradictory tendencies and the pressures pushing in each direction remains critical.

Meanwhile, Batstone's use of the term 'trade union principles', which he defined in terms of generalized subjective value concepts such as 'unity' and 'justice', poses a problem (Batstone *et al.*, 1977, p. 27). The problem with this definition is that it makes it difficult to relate 'trade union principles' to the specific actions or policies adopted by shop stewards. Success in leadership is something which requires judgement in relation to the achievement of more specific-related policies (Willman, 1980). Indeed, the precise manner in which 'trade union principles' may be operationalized can vary. By way of example, take the issue of sectionalism. Batstone's framework assumed that not only were 'trade union principles' and sectional interests incongruent, but that left to themselves the members tend to pursue only sectional interests. It requires the quasi-élite of 'leader' shop stewards to mobilize collective responses and behaviour on the shop-floor by encouraging sentiments of solidarity.

Undoubtedly there is an uncertain relationship between the immediate day-to-day grievances of rank-and-file members and the desire of shop stewards to provide a long-term strategy to protect the interests of all workers across the plant. Nonetheless, sectional interests and collective attitudes are not necessarily incompatible. Members may have immediate sectional grievances which are potentially directly relevant to other workers in the plant (as well as the working class movement generally) but which are blocked by shop stewards' narrow organizational interests in not upsetting stable relations with management. For example, the victory of a sectional strike to resist changed working practices could help boost the strength of union organization in every section of a factory. However, if stewards utilized so-called 'trade union principles' (in the way Batstone envisaged) to restrain sectional militancy and to prevent it spreading, it could amount to a self-defeating policy of weakening union organization generally.

Certainly, there is the problem about the meaning of 'trade union principles'. Batstone's fleeting recognition of the existence of 'hard-liners' within the quasi-élite of 'leader' senior stewards (Batstone *et al.*, 1977, p. 89) who hold a militant perspective illustrates how it is possible to have quite different assessments of the costs and benefits involved in workplace union activity. Again, Nichols and Beynon's study (1977, pp. 147–60) provided an example of an alternative type of shop steward role in the application of 'trade union principles'. Greg represents the type of steward who recognizes both the strengths and weaknesses of sectional rank-and-file activity and attempts to accentuate the positive and overcome the negative. Crucially, this involves making a conscious effort to build up the level of organization and consciousness of shop-floor workers by fighting against management, rather than engaging in backroom compromise deals (even if in the absence of a wider group of stewards he is not able to progress very far). In other words, Batstone's 'trade union principles' is rather an omnibus category under which a variety of styles or strategies could be adopted.

Batstone argued against the view that his model of trade unionism was that of a bureaucratized set of relations; but it is of major significance that his interpretation was predicated on a Labourist/reformist analytical framework. This meant his evaluation was based on a set of theoretical assumptions (about 'sophisticated' stewards' leadership) which conspicuously failed to view members' activity as being absolutely central to workplace unionism. Instead, he effectively looked at stewards' organization through the prism of the 'quasi-élite' and developed a theory derived from and for the 'quasi-élite', a 'top-down' view of stewards' relationship to the members. From his vantage point, the key to 'sophisticated' union organization is the 'leader' stewards' bargaining expertise and contacts with management. The members are viewed as essentially passive agents, whom stewards might occasionally mobilize into activity, whilst ensuring any independent initiative is strictly controlled.

Arguably, such a conception of the relationship between stewards and their members is, paradoxically enough, a recipe for the very type of 'bureaucratized' workplace union organization Batstone claimed does not really exist. It can be contrasted with a 'bottom-up' attempt by stewards to act not merely on their members' behalf but to encourage them to act for *themselves*. From this vantage point, rank-and-file self-activity, the collective participation and involvement of members in decision making, and their collective mobilization through struggle against management, is crucial to building strong shop steward organization. Only when such contrasting interpretations of workplace union organization are taken into account is it possible to evaluate adequately the differing assessments made about steward 'bureaucratization'.

To illustrate the point, we can examine such measures of steward bureaucratization as tenure of office and the granting of extensive time off work. Whilst he acknowledged the quasi-élite of 'leaders' stewards might become divorced from their shop-floor members, Batstone insisted there was no real evidence that their stability in office or 100 per cent time off from work leads to the reinforcement of a pattern of bureaucratic power. A lengthy tenure of office may simply reflect membership satisfaction in their performance. By stewards being readily available to their members it can facilitate the development of a 'sophisticated' union organization, able to channel members' views and formulate co-ordinated strategy and tactics. Clearly, Batstone was justified in challenging any simple identification between these features and steward bureaucratization, particularly when it should be borne in mind that time off has sometimes only been granted by management as a result of shop-floor pressure. But the issue can be most fruitfully explored by placing such features within the context of the contrasting analytical vantage points outlined above, and the wider substantive circumstances in which they are located.

Thus, if the emphasis is on the quasi-élite of 'leader' stewards who engage in 'strong bargaining relations' with management, then it seems logical to view extensive time off work and a lengthy tenure of office as welcome features likely to encourage the development of more experienced, 'sophisticated' and 'bargaining aware' senior stewards, albeit acting on behalf of an essentially passive membership. But if the emphasis is on workers' self-activity, combative union organization and directly accountable shop steward mechanisms, then it is apparent that the closer the links between stewards and their members, and the more steward positions are contested in elections, the more likely a vibrant form of workplace union democracy will be enhanced. From this alternative perspective, the danger is of senior stewards becoming divorced from the shop-floor, spending much of their time in the union office and engaged in activities which act as a substitute for the active involvement of their members. Of course, this is not an inevitable development. Moreover, as Winch (1980) has suggested, the danger of the stagnating and anti-democratic effects of a low turnover in stewards' positions, and the bureaucratization of workplace union organization, has to be balanced by the necessity of having a good level of experience within the stewards' body for the effective representation of members' interests. Certainly, refusing to accept any time off whatsoever is likely to be a recipe for disaster, although its extent and scope are much more problematic. Nonetheless, it would appear that in many workplaces its extensive provision was seen by managers as a way of encouraging the formalization of steward bargaining with the long-term aim of encouraging more co-operative relations (Willman, 1980; Terry, 1983b).

Whether it has this effect can be seen to a large degree to be affected by the level of workers' confidence, strength and activity *vis-à-vis* management. Thus, where there is a relatively high degree of shop-floor struggle, it is likely that quite a large proportion of a steward's facility time will be spent in dealing with members' grievances; there can also be some encouragement for the contesting of steward positions by different potential candidates. By contrast, in conditions where workers lack the confidence to fight the employers and are relatively passive, there is likely to be much less pressure from the rank-and-file that could act as a democratic check on the activities of stewards who have a large degree of time off. In these circumstances there is more likelihood of steward elections having only one (incumbent) candidate with existing personnel becoming a permanent feature. It is my argument that the essential link missing in Batstone's analysis is a concrete examination of the way in which the ebb and flow of workplace power and shop-floor struggle can dramatically alter the nature of stewards' organization. Moreover, this missing link is also critical to an understanding of the significance of stewards' integration within national union structures, which Hyman (1979) identified and Batstone (1988b) disputed, on the basis that such integration as has occurred has tended to impose greater checks on full-time officials rather than on stewards.

A Marxist Analytical Framework

Trade unions are profoundly contradictory institutions, struggling both *against* capitalism and *within* it (Lane, 1974; Hyman, 1975; Clarke and Clements, 1977; Beynon, 1984). On the one hand, they are the means whereby workers begin to organize and act independently as a class to combat capitalist exploitation. They mobilize workers' collective strength and stop the employers riding roughshod over them, and through their experience of trade union struggle workers can develop the confidence, organization and political consciousness necessary to overthrow capitalism. Engels (1974) suggested: 'As schools of war the unions are unexcelled.' On the other hand, trade unions operate within the framework of capitalism. They seek not to overthrow it, but to improve workers' position within the existing system; they are concerned with improving the terms on which labour power is exploited, not with ending that exploitation. As Marx (1970) commented: 'They deal with effects, not the causes of those effects.'

The self-limiting nature of British trade unionism manifests itself in a variety of ways (Coates, 1984). A first feature of this trade unionism is sectionalism. Thus, whilst uniting workers into distinct groups, 'trade unions', as the name implies, separate them from workers in other unions through the different wages, conditions and traditions pertaining in different industries. Secondly, British trade unionism has been characterized by a debilitating separation between economics and politics. Unions push the notion that for political change workers must look to the Labour Party, while they mainly confine themselves to the narrow horizon of economic issues, such as wages and conditions. This false divide is used to prevent workers' mobilizing their vast potential industrial strength against the power of the capitalist class concentrated in the state. It also reinforces the politics of reformism – of negotiating piecemeal improvements in workers' conditions through collective bargaining and Parliament rather than fighting for the revolutionary transformation of society through militant class struggle. Thirdly, because trade unions limit their horizons to those set by capitalism, every struggle, however militant, must end up in a compromise and it is this situation which gives rise to a permanent apparatus of full-time trade union officials, who form a classic bureaucracy and who constitute a distinct and relatively privileged social layer with interests different from and contrary to those of rank-and-file union members (Callinicos, 1983; Cliff and Gluckstein, 1986).

It is precisely because shop steward organizations arise directly from the daily struggles in the workplace and are much more responsive to rank-and-file members' needs and interests that they can be distinguished from full-time union officials, with whom they are sometimes in conflict. Even though shop stewards' organizations are themselves usually sectional and reformist they tend to provide a significant counter-weight to the bureaucratic structures of official trade unionism, representing what Flanders (1975) termed the 'challenge from below'. Nonetheless, workplace trade unionism under capitalism is itself shot through with contradictions, as will become evident if we consider the dynamics of shop stewards' organization through the threefold conceptual framework of stewards' relationships to management, members and full-time union officials.

Shop Stewards' Relationship to Management

The shop stewards' relationship to management is characterized by a tension between *resistance* and *accommodation*. Thus, stewards display the general contradictory tendencies involved in trade unionism (Lane, 1974; Hyman, 1975; Clarke and Clements, 1977; Beynon, 1984). On the one hand, stewards are a manifestation of the need for the collective defence of workers' interests against the management exploitation which capitalist production requires. By co-ordinating workers' collective strength, and on occasions directing this towards militant action, shop stewards can win significant improvements in their members' pay and conditions, as well as building up the strength of workplace trade union organization. Such shop-floor resistance, although often sectional and limited in character, contains the potential for a radical challenge to both employers' prerogative and the capitalist system. On the other hand, the inherent threat posed to the security of shop steward organization that does not agree to work by the 'rules of the game' encourages the development of a stable and compatible bargaining relationship in which stewards channel workers' grievances into accommodatory procedures that operate within the boundaries of managerial authority and existing relations of production. Whilst their members, constantly subject to the exploitative relations of capitalist wage-labour, are always liable to overturn some aspect of this *modus vivendi*, the shop steward is under pressure to 'keep the faith' with management, to regard each conflict as a 'problem' to be resolved, rather than as disputed ground in a continuing relationship of conflict.

Turner, Clack and Roberts in their detailed study of the car industry in the mid-1960s stressed that in becoming established, stewards had developed:

> a dependence on management itself. In a sense the leading stewards are performing a managerial function, of grievance settlement, welfare arrangement and human adjustment, and the steward system's acceptance by management (and thus in turn, the facility with which the stewards themselves can satisfy their members demands and needs) has developed partly because of the increasing effectiveness – and certainly economy – with which this role is fulfilled. (Turner *et al.*, 1967, p. 214)

The response of shop stewards to such pressures towards 'responsibility' is often ambivalent. As Hyman has explained:

> They were often conscious of the threat involved in such employer strategies, and at times resisted fiercely. Yet they were also conscious of a common interest with employers in establishing an 'industrial legality', in creating order and regularity; partly because union security seemed dependent on some formal accommodation with the power of capital; partly because they had more faith in employer's goodwill than membership combativity as a source of improvements in employment conditions; partly because their own control was consolidated by the new machinery. (Hyman, 1975, p. 158)

This is the central paradox of the shop stewards' relationship with management: expressing rank-and-file members' grievances but seeking to limit their manifestation to forms over which they can exert control and which do not jeopardize the overall bargaining arrangements developed with management. The key task of the shop steward is to mediate these conflicting pressures between resistance and accommodation.

Shop Stewards' Relationship to Members

The shop stewards' relationship to members is characterized by a tension between *democracy* and *bureaucracy*. On the one hand, stewards are a profoundly democratic, authentic expression of members' experience and aspirations; elected regularly they work alongside, receive the same wages and conditions and are directly accountable to the changing needs and expectations of their members. Lane has contrasted a male steward with a parliamentary MP:

> The shop steward . . . did not once elected pack his bags and move off to carry out his representational duties in an institution alien to the experience of his constituents. Neither was his constituency so large that he could remain personally anonymous to the overwhelming majority of his electors . . . The steward spent the bulk of his time at work alongside those who had elected him . . . He was highly visible, subject to the same experiences at work as his comrades, and subject to the same group pressures. (Lane, 1974, p. 198)

The shop stewards' (male and female) regular contact with management, other stewards and the wider official union often gives them a breadth of knowledge and experience not readily available to their members and invests them with some authority and respect on the shop-floor (although this does not mean stewards' recommendations are uncritically accepted). If stewards are to lead, they must be responsive to the changing needs and expectations of their members, for failure to respond can lead to a challenge to their position. They may be forced to resign by an *ad hoc* vote of constituents or replaced informally, if not by loss of office, by others who command wider support. This democratic accountability does not mean stewards are subject to the beck and call of every demand placed upon them. Nonetheless, the power of any shop steward is largely dependent upon the continuing support of his or her members and the ability to carry them in any course of action (Goodman and Whittingham, 1973).

On the other hand, as with 'official' trade unionism, the pressures towards bureaucratization clearly operate at the level of the workplace itself (Lyddon, 1977; Terry, 1978; Hyman, 1979; Cliff, 1979). The problems of organization, specialization and concentration of decision making can create a gap that separates stewards from their members. Particularly within larger workplaces a distinct hierarchy can emerge with a number of senior shop stewards and convenors tending to spend a great deal of their time on union business. Provided with a union office and involved in joint management–union committees they can become divorced from the shop-floor and encouraged to think in terms of the interests of the company rather than their constituents. Moreover, because of their extensive networks of information, negotiating ability and influence with management, the senior stewards' 'machine' of formal and informal sanctions can be utilized to discipline and bureaucratically stymie workers' militancy. As the Donovan Commission stated:

> It is often wide of the mark to describe shop stewards as
> 'troublemakers'. Trouble is thrust upon them . . . Quite commonly
> they are supporters of order exercising a restraining influence on
> their members in conditions which promote disorder.
> (Royal Commission on Trade Unions and Employers' Associations, 1968,
> p. 28)

Thus the predicament of the shop steward, whose relationship to rank-and-file members is torn between the pressures towards democracy and those towards bureaucracy.

Shop Stewards' Relationship to Full-Time Union Officials

The shop stewards' relationship to full-time union officials is characterized by a tension between *independence* and *dependence* (Boraston *et al.*, 1975; Hyman and Fryer, 1975). On the one hand, shop steward organization has an autonomy to it, often possessing the resources and experience necessary to handle a variety of grievances and negotiations internally rather than relying on the external official union machine. Stewards can act as an important counter-balance to the often cautious or different pre-occupations of full-time union officials, putting pressure on officials in negotiations with employers, encouraging them to call industrial action and occasionally taking the initiative to act independently. On other hand, because stewards are the key link between the unions as an organization and the membership, they are inevitably dependent upon a whole range of services from the external representatives of the official union apparatus. This may include information, assistance in collective bargaining, help in legal backing and securing support in strikes, without which they could not function. Often full-time officials can wield enormous authority and influence over stewards' organization, transmitting leadership policies downwards onto the shop-floor. Moreover, when the confidence of shop stewards to mount an effective fightback against employers and government is lacking they tend to become relatively much more dependent on the officials. Thus the contradiction between independence and dependence in stewards' relationship to full-time union officials.

Although, as Hyman (1979) has stressed, shop stewards are by no means immune from the accommodative and bureaucratic pressures diagnosed at the level of official trade unionism, they remain, in general terms, qualitatively different from local and national full-time union officials in their potential responsiveness to rank-and-file pressure. Indeed, stewards have several advantages from the point of view of working class democracy because, despite their sometimes full-time status inside the workplace, there are major links cementing them to other stewards and shop-floor workers. Shop stewards are usually paid the average wage of the workers they represent – at a level determined by the strength of trade union organization in the workplace – unlike union officials, whose salary is paid by the union and is usually considerably greater. Most shop stewards spend most of their working day alongside their members and are usually subject to annual or bi-annual election by their constituents. Because they can be removed by the members they provide an instrument that can be subordinated to the rank-and-file in a way that no relatively remote union official (operating on a geographical basis, often appointed rather than elected and usually holding office for five years or more) ever could be. Shop stewards are liable to be victimized in any management offensive and lose their jobs if redundancies are imposed or if the workplace is closed down, again setting them apart from full-time officials, whose position is generally more secure.

It follows that the dichotomy within trade unions between the 'rank and file' (shop stewards and their members) and the 'trade union bureaucracy' (a stratum of full-time trade union officials) is a meaningful generalization of a real contradiction (Callinicos and Simons, 1985). Of course, some qualifications to such a picture need to be noted. Because elements of bureaucracy pervade trade union practice at every level of the representational structure (Hyman, 1984) it is possible in some circumstances, notably inside some of the largest workplaces, for the senior shop stewards' organization to have become so centralized and hierarchical that the contrast between the 'union bureaucracy' and the 'rank-and-file' becomes somewhat blurred (Lyddon, 1977). Thus, in some extreme cases there can be a greater similarity between full-time workplace convenors and full-time union officials than between either of them and shop-floor workers, although this can change over time depending upon the pressures from internal and external forces. This raises the fact that the term 'rank-and-file' provides only a broad categorization of a union membership that contains some differentiation between full-time convenors and senior shop stewards, lay sectional stewards, union activists and the mass of shop-floor union members (Cronin, 1989; Hyman, 1989b; Price, 1989; Zeitlin, 1989a, b). Equally there is considerable internal differentiation within the ranks of full-time union officialdom both between local and national levels of the hierarchy and within the higher echelons (Kelly, 1988; Heery and Kelly, 1990). Interesting tensions and splits can arise from the different conditions and traditions pertaining within different industries, from the varying pressures faced and from ideological divisions between left and right-wing officials. However, whilst all of these complexities may qualify the central argument presented above they in no way invalidate it. They do not alter the fundamental cleavage of interests that exists between full-time union officials and rank-and-file members within trade unionism under capitalism.

As we have seen, there is a radical tension in the nature of shop steward organization – between *resistance* and *accommodation* in stewards' relationship to management, between *democracy* and *bureaucracy* in stewards' relationship to members, and between *independence* and *dependence* in stewards' relationships to full-time union officials. There are powerful tendencies or forces within capitalist society which push in opposite and mutually incompatible directions. However, the different elements are not always of the same weight. Each of these polar oppositions must be understood not as a fixed proposition in terms of an 'either/or' logic but constantly in motion reflecting and at the same time changing the social conditions of which it is part. The result is a continuum of possible and overlapping shop steward responses, each dominant to a greater or lesser degree at particular points of time. In other words, each of the relationships are extremely *dynamic*. Also, the three contradictory tendencies and counter-tendencies have to be understood as being relative and not absolute. For example, if shop stewards' accommodation to management was absolutely missing, workers would seize control of production and take over the running of the workplace. That this does not happen and could not within the confines of trade unionism indicates that each tendency has to be measured *relative* to its counter-tendency. Moreover, each of the three stewards' relationships cannot be viewed as entirely separate phenomena that occur irrespective of developments in the other. On the contrary, they are inextricably *linked* to each other, with each of the relationships directly influencing and being influenced by the other. Finally, it follows that the pressures operating in one specific workplace cannot be viewed in isolation from those operating within other workplaces and within society more *generally*.

Thus, in different contexts, the balance struck between these contradictory tendencies and counter-tendencies within the shop stewards' position will vary considerably. Indeed, the history of shop stewards' organization has been a history of the shifting balance between resistance and accommodation, democracy and bureaucracy, independence and dependence. In other words, the nature of shop stewards' organization and workplace unionism is not a static phenomenon. As Antonio Gramsci wrote:

> The trade union is not a predetermined phenomenon. It becomes a determinate institution; it takes on a definite historical form to the extent that the strength and will of the workers who are its members impress a policy and propose an aim that define it. (Gramsci, 1977, p. 265)

The Balance of Power in Society and the Workplace

It is the changing balance of class forces between capital and labour that has a profound impact on the nature of shop stewards' organization and its relationship to management, members and full-time union officials, in terms of which side is more confident, stronger and successfully pushing the frontier of control to their advantage. The balance of power between management and workers in any specific workplace is only an expression of this more basic power relation between the capitalist class and the working class, although there is considerable variation in the distribution of power in different workplaces and sectors of industry (as will be explored below). This balance depends upon the pressure on, and confidence of, the capitalist class to make workers pay for increased profits, and the ability and confidence of the working class to fight back. Every day in thousands of shop-floor disputes the wrestling for advantage goes on. Hence time-and-motion and productivity deals, go-slows and overtime bans, strikes and lock-outs, pickets and anti-union laws and all the other tactics and stratagems used by the contending classes in the industrial struggle. Whilst the balance of class forces in society is affected by a variety of economic, political and social factors, some of which go far beyond what happens in the workplace, it is the struggle on the shop-floor which is usually of most significance.

Of course, in some respects, it is not straightforward to talk of the 'balance of class forces' because on the whole the correlation of forces is such as to give the capitalist class power over the working class. Whilst some sections of workers may be stronger in individual parts of the battle-field, overall they are weaker than their opponents. If this were not the case, the rule of the capitalist class would be long past. Nonetheless, work-place union organization does provide workers with the collective strength to act as a powerful counteracting power to that of the employers which, although rarely equivalent, is capable of setting significant limits to managerial authority through a permanent process of pressure and mobilization of sanctions. Arguably, the most important factor pushing the balance of class forces in favour of the working class is their self-activity, organization and independent initiative through collective struggle in the workplace. It follows that the development of cohesive and self-confident shop steward organizations, able to apply pressure directly at the point of production, is a crucial factor in shifting the balance of workplace power and permitting further inroads into the prerogatives of capital.

This is not to suggest that workers are hell-bent on permanent struggle and that shop stewards adopt a permanently antagonistic attitude towards management. Industrial relations under capitalist conditions are a battle-field; but the battlefield is relatively quiescent for long stretches of time, particularly when economic and political conditions are unfavourable to militant action, as during the 1980s. In addition, the employment relationship is characterized by aspects of co-operation between workers and management. Management rely on the initiative and motivation of their workers in the detailed performance of its various tasks; and workers are dependent on the company or organization for their liveli-hood. Such considerations set some limits on each side's intransigence towards each other, ensuring elements of co-operation. Nevertheless, because managers are driven by virtue of their position in the productive process and the inner dynamic of that process of seeking ways to keep down wage costs, of improving productivity and affirming their control upon which the fulfilment of these aims depends, pressure is built into the managers' role just as resistance is built into that of their workers (Miliband, 1989).

Within this day-to-day conflict the level and character of strike action is one important measure of workers' power. Of course, it should be noted that the lack of strike action by some strategically placed groups of workers (particularly in manufacturing industry) might reflect their strength, not their weakness, in that employers may feel obliged to concede union demands to avoid conflict. Also, the number of strikes might also reflect employers' policies as well as union strength (although of course employers' policies are formulated partly on the basis of workers' strength). In addition, strikes are only the most obvious means of exerting power and might on occasion be less effective than overtime bans or a 'work to rule' (Martin, 1992). But the fact remains that most strikes only take place when workers feel strong enough to challenge manage-ment and – after taking into consideration whether they are offensive or defensive, victorious or defeated – they are a particularly salient barometer of the nature and extent of shop-floor power.

Another important point is the way workers' consciousness is pro-foundly affected by their sense of confidence in what they can achieve in relation to the employers. On the one hand, workers who discover their ability to fight together and win against management can potentially develop all sorts of ideas based on their new-found solidarity. Even small victories can give workers new confidence and new understanding.

Undoubtedly there are very substantial material and ideological limitations and dilemmas for any translation of the radical potential of workplace
unionism into a wider movement, including the deep sectional divisions
based on skill, gender and race, as well as the influence of reformism and
Labourism (Nichols and Beynon, 1977). However, this does not mean
that when there is a real upsurge in struggle there cannot be a politicization
of quite wide layers of workers (Luxemburg, 1977; Kelly, 1988). In such
circumstances the belief that trade union officials and Labour Party
politicians can substitute their own efforts for the struggle of the mass of
workers can be undermined and a minority attracted to revolutionary
socialist ideas. But this is by no means an automatic process; it depends
on the general objective situation in society and material constraints, how
effective reformist leaders are in blocking action, the intervention of
militant socialists, and so on; the potential in certain exceptional circumstances for periodic upsurges of revolutionary consciousness among
millions of workers was demonstrated in Russia 1917, Germany 1919–23,
Spain 1936 and Portugal 1974–75 (Barker, 1987).

On the other hand, even workers with a traditionally strong sense of
class solidarity can have their whole position undermined, for example by
employers' defeats of key sections of the working class movement and/or
by the impact of mass unemployment. Every defeat of workers can spread
some degree of demoralization, hopelessness and acquiescence to the
status quo. If workers fail to use their collective power to fight successfully
against management, that lack of confidence will be reflected in their
political ideas. In such periods the majority of workers can forget it was
struggle that won their gains in the first place, and the idea holds sway that
everything derives from the efforts of union officials and Labour Party
politicans. Ideas which tell them the rule of capital is inevitable and that
'uneconomic' factories must close will seem reasonable since it reflects
their real-life experience.

The key point being made here is that the nature of shop stewards'
organization and workplace unionism is deeply affected by the balance of
class forces in society and in particular the fighting strength and
consciousness of the working class in the workplace. A variety of factors
directly affect the balance of class forces including the state of the
economy, employers' strategies, government policies, the judicial context,
the character and size of the class struggle, the level of workers'
organization, the nature of the political leadership inside the working class
(combined with other social and political developments within society

generally). Of course, the 'state' of shop stewards' organization – its strength, cohesiveness and independent initiative – is itself an index of the balance of class forces, which will have a major influence on the pendulum of advantage between capital and labour. Nonetheless, the balance of class forces cannot be reduced to shop stewards' organization. It describes something much broader than this complex sphere of workplace unionism which affects its dynamic nature, its limits and potential. As one element in a equation, the state of shop stewards' organization is both a cause and effect of the balance of class forces.

However, as noted above, it is clear that there are significant variations in bargaining leverage and in the terrain of management–shop steward relations within different workplaces, and across different industries and localities. The balance of workplace power can be used to describe the specific pendulum of advantage between management and workers in any particular workplace, something which is affected by such 'micro-level' factors as the state of product and labour markets, the size of employment unit, the nature of the production system and the relationship of workers to it, management strategy and the structure of collective bargaining arrangements, workers' collective cohesion, the role of full-time union officials, the nature of shop steward leadership and the influence of political activists (Hill, 1974; Batstone, 1988a; Martin, 1992). Obviously there is a continuous and overlapping interrelationship between the balance of class forces generally and balance of workplace power specifically. For example, the state of the British economy can have a direct bearing on product and labour markets in a particular geographical area, which in turn affects an individual plant management's strategy towards shop steward organization and workers' willingness to fight. In other words, in evaluating the nature of shop steward organization in any single workplace it is necessary to locate any consideration of the distinctive 'micro-level' factors affecting the balance of workplace power within its much broader 'macro-level' context of the balance of class forces in society.

The relevance of all this to the earlier focus on the contradictory nature of shop stewards' relationship to management, members and full-time union officials will become apparent if we consider the general background premise guiding the case study research below. Thus, some commentators have identified two broad phases of the class struggle between capital and labour in Britain over the past 20 years, namely the *upturn* in workers' struggles during the late 1960s and early 1970s in which the balance of class forces swung in favour of the working class, and the period of *down-turn* which set in from the mid-1970s and continued throughout the 1980s in which the pendulum swung back in favour of the capitalist class (Cliff, 1979; Coates, 1989). The Labour government's Social Contract, with its spirit of class collaboration between government, employers and trade unions, and the recession of 1974–75 were crucial in making the switch (Coates, 1989). Certainly, the struggles under the Heath Conservative government were qualitatively different from those that occurred under the Thatcher administrations, with a notable contrast between the 1972 and 1974 miners' strikes on the one hand, and the 1984–85 strike on the other. However, this is obviously only a general characterization which, whilst an important overarching influence, does not preclude considerable differentiation in its actual impact across specific industries and different workplaces, particularly during the late 1970s when, although its character was usually rather different from that of the early 1970s, the level of workers' struggle was quite high. Moreover, although in general terms the downturn preceded the 1979–82 recession the very rapid rise in unemployment during the 1980s exacerbated the situation dramatically; its impact was much more easily discernible at the level of the individual workplace.

Despite the complexities of the interrelationship between the general 'balance of class forces' and the specific 'balance of workplace power' it is possible to draw a broad contrast between the period of the 1970s and that of the 1980s and to identify its overall impact on workplace unionism.

Thus, during the 1970s the high level of shop-floor struggle and victory of some workers inspired others to take action. Strong, self-reliant shop stewards' organizations emerged that were relatively combative in their relationship to employers and the government. The confidence of shop-floor members provided the steam for the engine of shop steward strength, ensuring a relatively close and democratic relationship, as stewards articulated members' grievances and proved highly responsive to the demands of the rank-and-file. Moreover, shop-floor strength *vis-à-vis* employers encouraged stewards to act relatively independently of full-time union officials, sometimes in defiance of their wishes. Finally, sectionalism, both within and between sections of workers, became less central, at least amongst a minority of workers and shop stewards, who began to broaden their horizon and go beyond the boundaries of the workplace to engage in generalized activity of considerable political content.

By contrast, during the 1980s, the level of struggle was very low and the confidence of shop stewards to mount an effective fightback against the employers and government was very much on the defensive, a process reinforced by factors such as the hostile economic and political climate, major defeats suffered by sections of the working class movement and the encouragement of new 'flexible' bargaining strategies and the TUC's 'new realism'. Equally, sectionalism tended to predominate with little political generalization amongst those in struggle or between those fighting and those not. The result was an atrophy of shop stewards' organization, which in turn had an enormous impact on workers' consciousness. Management ideas about 'competitiveness' and 'effi- ciency' were reinforced as being the only practical ones. The outcome of all this was that shop stewards became generally much less confident and combative in their relationship with management as the balance tilted towards a more accommodative relationship. There was an undermining of the close accountability of shop stewards to their rank-and-file members, as the tendencies towards bureaucratization intensified and stewards became more inclined to restrain than to lead shop-floor militancy. At the same time stewards generally lacked the confidence to take action irrespective of the influence of full-time union officials, with the pendulum swinging towards a relative dependence on them.

Nonetheless, apart from the differentiation that existed between industries and workplaces, there were also important countervailing pressures and informal workplace sanctions to those acting solely to weaken and bureaucratize shop stewards' organization during the 1980s. The retreat was punctuated by public sector strikes, protests and the poll tax riot over the effects of government policy, and the hard-fought struggles from the (1980) steel strike through the (1984–85) miners' to the (1986–87) print workers' strike. The latest Workplace Industrial Relations Survey has shown that, despite the fall in union membership and collective bargaining, where manufacturing plants remained open the basic struc- ture of workplace unionism appears to have survived the economic and legal assault and is still largely intact, with around 250 000 shop stewards nationally. Moreover, there is no justification for assuming that the present weaknesses of shop stewards' organization will be either per- manent or irreversible. Not only could the balance of class forces in Britain also be reversed at some stage in the future but the balance struck between the general contradictory tendencies within shop stewards' relationships to management, to members and to full-time union officials could also be radically altered.

Therefore, to repeat the central tenet of the background premise guiding the research: the nature of shop stewards' organization is not a fixed or static phenomenon, but largely depends on the ebbs and flows of the class struggle reflected in the balance of class forces and the balance of workplace power. The relative strength of the internal and external, material and ideological, forces bearing upon shop stewards shifts and fluctuates. The in-built contradictory nature of workplace unionism gives the process a constantly uneven, dynamic character. The case study material that follows contains an examination of the specific factors contributing to the changing nature of shop stewards' organization within three workplaces on Merseyside over the past 20–25 years within a broader analysis of the 'political economy' in which they are embedded. The analytical framework above – with its focus on stewards' relationship to management, members and full-time union officials – has not only structured the interpretation of the empirical evidence but has also shaped the mode of its written presentation for each of the three workplaces examined. Although it is only by making the connections between these relationships that a fully rounded understanding of workplace unionism can be obtained, it is helpful to separate them conceptually for reasons of presentation and accessibility to the reader. It is also useful to separate the decades of the late 1960s and 1970s from those of the 1980s and early 1990s, because in general terms there is a marked contrast between the two periods with respect to the contradictory tendencies at work.

Finally, some comments on terminology in the text. The term 'shop steward' is used to describe the voluntary workplace union representative who has a sectionally based constituency of members. The term 'shop stewards' organization' is used to describe the collective plant-wide form of union representation established by the stewards' committee as a whole. Using broad brush-strokes, the term 'shop stewards' can be understood as embracing 'senior shop stewards' and 'convenors', both of whom conduct major negotiations with management and represent the interests of the workforce across the plant. Although many senior stewards often spend more of their time on union business than most ordinary stewards they retain their representational role *vis-à-vis* a specific constituency of members, from whom they are elected and to whom they are directly accountable. Whilst convenors, particularly those who hold a full-time position, do not always carry out the functions of a sectional steward they retain their link with the specific constituency of members who periodically elect them as a union representative, and the stewards' committee which elects them as convenor. However, whilst the term 'shop stewards' formally includes sectional stewards, senior stewards and convenors, within the text there is sometimes a more specific differentiation drawn between the different positions and the varying activities of their occupants.

A distinction is also made between 'shop stewards' (whether sectional stewards, senior stewards or convenors) and 'full-time union officials' (whether at local or national level). The term 'full-time union official' is used to describe those individuals who, instead of being workers who sell their labour power to an employer, are the paid functionaries of a trade union organization. This includes local or district officials, regional officials and the national leadership of trade unions. In this sense, a distinction is drawn even between full-time factory convenors and full-time union officials.

As far as the term 'rank-and-file' is concerned, as has already been mentioned this should formally be taken to include all those sections of workers below the level of full-time union officials whether at local or national level. However, for the sake of clarity the term 'rank-and-file' is used within the text more narrowly to refer specifically to the mass of ordinary shop-floor workers and union members, as opposed to all those who hold a representative function within the workplace such as shop stewards, senior stewards or convenors. Finally, the term 'the left' can be broadly defined as including both those militant trade unionists who hold a basic socialist and class commitment without any fixed political affliation and those influenced by either Labour left or revolutionary socialist ideas, although the distinctions between these positions are by no means ignored.

3 THE MERSEYSIDE CONTEXT

Introduction

Merseyside, and the city of Liverpool in particular, has a worldwide reputation and seems to prompt more extreme reactions, good and bad, than most other places in Britain (Lane, 1986, 1987; McIntyre Brown, 1991). This polarization of the city's image is reflected in the way many people have a firmly held view on the city – regarding it either as the worst or as the best place imaginable. Either way, to judge by the national publicity the area attracts, it is a powerful magnet for journalists and television producers, who, whilst finding it 'different' in ways they find difficult to describe, are constantly fascinated by its rich multilayered character. During the 1960s and 1970s the region became synonymous with 'militancy', reflected most notably in the shop-floor defiance against employers in its car plants and docks; and during the 1980s the confrontation between Liverpool Labour Council and the Conservative government maintained this reputation for militancy.

It is necessary to locate the three case study workplaces within their Merseyside context in order to appreciate fully the broader economic, political, social and cultural influences on the character of workplace unionism in the region. This can most appropriately be explored by briefly outlining firstly, the historical development of the local economy, secondly, the distinctive cultural and political tradition of the Merseyside trade union and labour movement, and thirdly, the limits and potential of workers' resistance to the restructuring process that occurred in the region during the 1980s.

Historical Development of the Local Economy

All cities have special characteristics and Liverpool is no exception. Its geographical position, which marked it out in the past as one of Britain's most important seaports, shaped its complex economic and social history, thereby moulding the character of the city and the surrounding area. The slave trade, combined with the cotton and tobacco trade, provided the initial source of the city's great wealth and opulence enjoyed by a thriving merchant class throughout the seventeenth and eighteenth centuries (Fryer, 1984). The terrible Irish famine of the 1840s provided the impetus for the thousands of immigrants who came into Liverpool. By the nineteenth century Liverpool was a major shipbuilding centre and the city's port emerged as second only to London, with one-third of Britain's raw material exports and one-quarter of its imports passing through the city's docks. It also became the main port for mass emigration from Northern and Western Europe to America (Aughton, 1990). Such developments had serious long-term consequences for the labour market, with the emergence of a working class consisting largely of seafarers, unskilled workers and casually employed dock labourers. A high percentage of these were immigrants, particularly Irish Catholics. Unlike in other cities, a core of skilled workers did not develop to any great extent, because the pattern of capitalist development was not primarily into manufacturing industry but into port, shipping and related activities. However, between 1850 and 1913, amidst a dramatic growth in Britain's gross national product, Liverpool's national and international importance was indisputable (Merseyside Socialist Research Group, 1980).

The unbalanced character of Liverpool's economy did not seem important until shortly after the turn of the century, when British capital found itself no longer in a monopoly position in terms of international trading relationships and there was a critical deterioration in Britain's rate of growth. All traces of optimism evaporated as the collapse of the international economy and the depression that occurred after World War I led to massive redundancies in Merseyside's shipbuilding, shipping and associated distributive industries. By the early 1930s unemployment in Liverpool remained persistently above 18 per cent, double the national average (Belchem, 1992). This was worsened by the fact that little developed to counteract the decline in the traditional labour-intensive industries. There was some development of manufacturing industry during the 1920s and 1930s – with companies such as Jacob's, Crawford's and Hartley's in the food and drink sector, and Plessey in the engineering sector. But these tended to rely extensively on recruiting female labour, and the absence of a pool of skilled labour, outside shipbuilding in Birkenhead and ship-repairing in Liverpool, left little scope for expansion by engineering firms. Unlike in some other areas of the country, the most notable fact about the inter-war emergence and growth in manufacturing employment (in consumer durables, light electrical engineering, motors and chemicals) was their location outside the depressed area of Merseyside. Although some new manufacturing jobs did emerge in the 1950s, mainly in the food processing industry, they were not enough to offset the effects of factory closures and the continuing loss of jobs in the port. The city's basically unfavourable industrial structure remained unchanged.

Only in the 1960s did there appear the prospect of an improvement in the economic structure of Merseyside when government policy to redistribute industry appeared to break the pattern of long-term decline. A number of multinational companies were encouraged to invest in the area, largely as a result of the government's regional policy and also by the existence of a large reservoir of unemployed and unorganized labour. For the first time in its history manufacturing became a growth sector in Merseyside with the opportunity for factory work on a large scale. This was most graphically evidenced by the construction of three new car plants – Ford at Halewood, Vauxhall at Ellesmere Port and Standard Triumph at Speke – employing a total of 25 000 workers, and the simultaneous development of new industrial estates in Kirkby, Speke and Halewood.

By the end of the 1960s, despite some reservations there was a feeling that the area was finally on the road to recovery. Unfortunately, such high hopes proved to be misplaced because of a continuing decline of the traditional industries that were once the life-blood of the Merseyside maritime economy. This process was accelerated by the wholesale restructuring of the dock industry that accompanied the shift of traffic to the east coast and by the containerization of cargo handling. Equally important was the significant reduction in the numbers employed within the new manufacturing industry as industrial combines decided to close down their Merseyside operations once development aid and other short-term advantages had been exhausted. Numerous plants were hit by redundancies and closures during a period of profound rationalization of firms that occurred during the late 1960s and 1970s. Between 1966 and 1977, 350 plants closed or transferred production elsewhere with the loss of 40 000 jobs and by 1979 unemployment in Merseyside was over 12 per cent, the highest in Britain (Parkinson, 1985).

The already devastated area reeled under the Thatcher-induced economic recession of the early 1980s as a whole host of multinational companies with plants in Merseyside (such as BICC, British Leyland, Courtaulds, Dunlop, GEC, Massey-Ferguson, Meccano, Lucas, Spillers, Tate & Lyle and Thorns) either imposed mass redundancies or closed down altogether. Between 1979 and 1985 a total of 449 factories closed with the loss of another 40 000 manufacturing jobs, one-third of Merseyside's total. The rate of unemployment in the region, historically higher than in other conurbations, rocketed to 27 per cent, double the national average. Even the so-called 'Lawson boom' of the late 1980s passed Merseyside by, with the region subsequently suffering the hammer blows of another economic recession during the early 1990s, which included the closure of the Cammell Laird shipyards in Birkenhead.

The crucial problem of Merseyside's economic development during the post-war years was its dependence on a small number of extremely large nationally and internationally based multinational companies. For example, at the beginning of the 1980s 57 per cent of manufacturing jobs were in plants employing over 1000 workers compared with the national average of only 29 per cent. In 1979 less than 1 per cent of the city's firms provided nearly 40 per cent of total employment and by 1985 seven large firms – Ford, Plessey, Dunlop, United Biscuits, General Electric Company, Bemrose and Glaxo – controlled almost half of all the manufacturing jobs in the city. Between them, these companies shed 30 per cent of their workforce during the period 1981–85 (Parkinson, 1985). Moreover, the vast majority of the largest manufacturing companies in the region have tended to be branch plants of national or multinational corporations rather than locally controlled, making them particularly vulnerable to the loss of jobs and transfer of operations elsewhere as companies restructure according to cyclical fluctuations in the national and world economy and with no particular commitment to Merseyside or its workforce. Meanwhile, public service employment continued during the 1970s as the one area of growth until cuts in central government support in the early 1980s threw the city's finances into prolonged crisis that left the city council struggling to balance the budget from one year to the next.

Although national figures show similar underlying trends, economic decline in the Merseyside region during the 1980s produced a range of social problems more serious than in many other areas of Britain. Annual surveys of the economic health of 63 areas in England, Wales and Scotland during the late 1980s and early 1990s were carried out by the Royal Bank of Scotland. These surveys analysed measures such as unemployment rate, employment change, population change, number of cars per 1000 population, and household disposable income, and consistently found that Merseyside was the poorest area of Britain (*Daily Post*, 23 April 1992). The deprivation and poverty have been particularly associated with high unemployment, insufficent benefit levels, inadequate housing, poor quality health and education provision, and discrimination. In 1981 an inner-city riot errupted in the Toxteth area of Liverpool, born out of years of frustration at the economic devastation. Tear gas had to be used by police for the first time on the British mainland. Meanwhile, Merseyside's population shrank by 276 000 to fewer than 1.4 million between 1971 and 1991, the most rapid rate of contraction in Britain during that period (*Financial Times*, 26 February 1993).

A Distinctive Labour Tradition

Looking back over the twentieth century it is clear that Liverpool could never be regarded as a typical industrial city, not least because of its unusual occupational structure. It had a relatively large proportion of unskilled and casual labour centred on the port, and a small skilled labour force. But there have been other peculiarities, including the religious divide between immigrant Irish Catholic and Protestant working class communities, which helped shape the contours of local representational politics. The Labour Party did not win a parliamentary seat in Liverpool until a by-election in 1923 and did not win an overall majority on the council until as late as 1955. Throughout the decades of the British labour movement's 'turning point', socialists, syndicalists and official trade union activists either kowtowed to sectarian prejudice or failed to face the religious and political questions dominating the working class. As a result, they effectively left Liverpool politics in the hands of 'Tory Democracy, the Irish nationalists and right-wing trade union organisers' (Smith, 1984, p. 42). By the time Labour did gain a firmer base in the 1950s and early 1960s it had become dominated by a right-wing political machine that operated on the basis of patronage, corruption and bossism (Merseyside Socialist Research Group, 1980).

Yet Labour failed to become the natural party of power in the city, not least because of growing disillusionment with its massive urban renewal and slum clearance programme which broke up working class inner-city communities and sent thousands of people to the high-rise flats on the overspill estates of Speke, Kirkby and elsewhere. Instead, there was the extraordinary rise of the Liberal Party, which took votes and seats from both major parties and between 1973 and 1983 exercised effective control within minority and coalition council administrations. Only in the 1980s did Liverpool Labour Party, under the influence of supporters of the 'Militant Tendency' who managed to capture control of a moribund party machine, transform its traditional right-of-centre position. Significantly, from the late 1970s onwards a number of new left-wing activists had joined the local constituency parties dissatisfied with the past failures of both the Liberal council and the Labour government, as well as in reaction to the incumbent Thatcher administration. After the 1983 local government elections supporters of the Militant Tendency gained a decisive influence within Liverpool city council, with popular support from both blue and white collar public sector trade unions for their defiance of government ratecapping (Crick, 1984). But Labour's rightward drift under the leadership of Neil Kinnock and Militant's primary orientation on operating inside the party rather than building an independent political organization on the shop-floor saw its support quickly wane by the late 1980s.

But if Merseyside lacks a militant *political* tradition, at least until recently, this cannot be said about its *industrial* past. Not surprisingly, the economic and cultural influence of the port, with its casual labour force and seafaring tradition, bequeathed to Liverpool distinctive forms of trade union organization and militant struggle. As Belchem (1992, p. 18) has commented: 'Militancy, it would seem, is a symptom of decay and collapse, of the belated and abortive attempt at structural change.' Of major significance was the Liverpool transport strike of 1911, involving dockers, seafarers and railway workers, which was led by the famous syndicalist agitator Tom Mann. The strike successfully defied two gunboats on the Mersey and the violent break-up of a mass demonstration by police and troops, to establish mass trade unionism in the region, notably in the form of what later became known as the Transport and General Workers' Union (TGWU). In fact, syndicalist ideas of industrial unionism flourished on Merseyside during the pre-war years (Holton,

1973). Meanwhile, in 1919 there was a police strike in Liverpool (and London) over the issue of union recognition; in 1926 Merseyside played an active role in the General Strike, and in 1932 the anger of the unemployed boiled over into riots which erupted in Birkenhead.

During the 1950s and 1960s the issue of union democracy became a prominent concern amongst dockers and seamen, some militant sections of whom attempted to break the stranglehold of autocratic full-time union officials associated with the port. This was pursued by organizing rank-and-file opposition movements, such as the Port Workers' Committee and the National Seamen's Reform Movement. Merseyside seafarers were involved in unofficial strikes in 1947, 1955 and 1956, as well as the national strike of 1966. This latter strike, Labour Prime Minister Harold Wilson claimed, was led by Communist Party members, some of whom were based in Liverpool. There were major unofficial stoppages on the docks in 1951, 1954 and 1967 and the development of powerful local union organization (Heffer, 1991). A similar picture existed on the shipyards in Birkenhead.

Moreover, although the port that had created Liverpool declined in significance and suffered a gradual reduction in jobs, the assertive and collective nature of the trade unionism it had spawned continued to linger on, and even spread elsewhere. The large numbers of seafarers who went ashore during the 1960s to work in the new manufacturing industries, such as the car plants, took with them their grassroots trade union experience and helped to influence a new generation of factory workers in the virtues of collective action. The concentration of very large numbers of workers in the plants of externally owned multinational companies, often on repetitive assembly line work with its attendant factory discipline and managerial prerogatives, encouraged the growth and consolidation of strong workplace trade union organization and shop steward structures. Thus, the early years at Ford Halewood were characterized by the emergence of a shop stewards' committee which built its strength through workplace militancy over issues of control and authority. At the unrivalled trade union showpiece – the Dunlop Speke plant – there was a demand for full-time union officials to have only an advisory role in plant-level negotiations.

Meanwhile the straitjacket imposed on the local labour movement by the Labour Party's right-wing political machine generated further tensions which spurred on the 'unofficial' tradition of shop-floor unionism. Thus, in the late 1960s the joint Liverpool Trades Council and District Labour Party mounted political campaigns to co-ordinate working class resistance to the Labour government's economic policies and anti-union legislation, much to the annoyance of local and national leaders who sought to distance the troublesome trade union contingent from the party. Yet despite a formal split between the local industrial and political wings of the labour movement, the Trades Council continued to be central to the mobilization of political action in Merseyside during the 1970s. This was particularly the case over the Conservative government's housing and industrial relations legislation. Although unemployment rates remained well above the national level, stoppages on Merseyside between 1967 and 1969 reached almost seven times the national average, in many ways appearing to contradict conventional theories about the automatic negative relationship between strikes and unemployment.

Yet, perhaps more than anything else, it was the style of Liverpool trade unionism that succeeded in attracting such constant media attention during the 1960s, reflecting a mood which has been described as brash, mocking and irreverent (Lane, 1987). Beynon captured this feature in his description of shop stewards at the Ford Halewood plant:

> The stewards were young men. They wore sharp clothes; suits with box jackets. They thought of themselves as smart, modern men; and this they were. They walked with a slight swagger, entirely alert and to the point of things. They walked, talked and looked as they were. They knew what their bit of the world was about and they were prepared to take on anybody who challenged it. (Beynon, 1984, p. 80)

Such confidence was undoubtedly encouraged by the simultaneous cultural notoriety and success of the Beatles pop group, the 'Mersey Poets', numerous comedians and Liverpool football club. But its foundation lay in the working class nature of the city, its relatively close-knit communities, and the sense of bitter injustice at economic and social deprivation experienced. Trade unionism seemed to represent, besides its economic and protective functions in the here and now, the struggles fought by workers over generations. This was a living tradition based on collectivist values of unity and solidarity.

Merseyside remained in the news headlines during the 1970s because of its special contribution to the growing levels of industrial unrest across the country. There were prolonged rent strikes mounted by thousands of council tenants in opposition to the Housing Finance Act, culminating in the imprisonment of some Kirkby tenants and a one-day strike by dockers, building workers and others. When the Fisher Bendix plant in Kirkby was threatened with closure in 1972, workers marched into the boardroom, threw out the management and announced a sit-in. Occupiers were divided into six-hour shifts to ensure round-the-clock control of the site. Committees were formed to deal with security, propaganda, the press, welfare, finances and discipline. Delegations were sent out constantly to raise support and win backing, with the strikers' families also involved in the struggle. The four-week sit-in and months of organized solidarity activity across Merseyside ended in victory: the plant was saved by a new owner, albeit only temporarily (Marks, 1974). A similar occupation took place at the motor components CAV Lucas plant employing 1600 workers, which only went down to defeat for lack of effective official union support. At the same time, the car factories and docks were the sites of periodic industrial relations disputes as workers struggled to establish counter-controls to those of management. During the 1978/79 'winter of discontent' public sector revolt against the Labour government, the area received widespread media attention as a bastion of union militancy, exemplified by the picket lines mounted by striking grave-diggers. Other traditionally less well-organized groups of workers in the city also began to take direct action, with drawn-out strikes by social workers and council typists in the early 1980s.

Of course, the popular image of 'Merseyside militancy', particularly during the 1960s and 1970s, can undoubtedly be overdrawn. As Lane (1978, 1987) and Bean and Stoney (1986) have argued, in some respects there was nothing exceptional about the labour movement in the region during this period. Thus, it is pointed out that Merseyside's alleged strike-proneness could be attributed to the fact that it was overrepresented in terms of industries like cars, shipbuilding and docks which were nationally relatively active; and to a large degree militancy in the region was a reaction to national and international restructuring. Although the Merseyside strike record was higher than that of Britain in general, even allowing for differences in industrial structure, the highly publicized work stoppages in specific sectors such as the car industry and the docks tended to distort and exaggerate the propensity of workers to engage in strike action. Large sections of workers across the region were not involved in disputes, and even in those plants that were affected, more conciliatory relations between shop stewards and management were often the norm, with the drip-drip of redundancies and plant closures proceeding apace. More-over, even in Ford Halewood, the strategy of shop-floor union militancy and its associated 'factory class consciousness' (Beynon, 1984) was not concerned with social or political change above the level of the work-place. This type of trade unionism proved to have severe limitations when confronted with the task of attempting to resist the extensive redundancies and factory closures that swept the region during the 1980s.

Nonetheless, it remains the case that the peculiar nature of the Mersey-side local economy and its social and cultural influences did help produce a particularly distinctive form of collective trade union organization and consciousness, even if it is a collectivist tradition that has come under severe pressure in more recent years.

The Limits and Potential of Workers' Resistance during the 1980s

The dramatic closure of British Leyland's No. 2 car plant in 1978 and the Dunlop tyre plant in 1979 (with a combined loss of over 4000 jobs) was subsequently followed, in the economic recession of the early 1980s, by a massive acceleration in the level of redundancies and closures at some of the city's largest, long-established union-organized plants. It was no coincidence that the 1981 TUC People's March for Jobs commenced in Liverpool (attracting 150 000 demonstrators), where 20 per cent of the labour force were unemployed at the time. Whilst relatively strong collec-tive trade union organization had provided the first line of workers' defence over wages and conditions, the sheer scale of the job losses during this period posed problems of a totally different order. Fighting a factory closure is very different from organizing a strike for more wages or better conditions, where the loss of a strike usually means a return to work. By contrast, in opposing a closure workers stand to lose everything; they are forced into a situation where anything less than total victory entails at least a partial defeat. Yet the 'frightening' impact of job loss in Merseyside in the early 1980s (Beynon, 1987) made it a very difficult task, although by no means an impossible one, to convince workers that they had the ability and potential to resist successfully.

Despite the nature of the obstacles they faced, many groups of workers *did* seek to challenge employers' attacks on their livelihoods, even if their struggles were fragmented and ephemeral. In the process workers adopted a variety of campaigns and tactics. At the Courtauld's and Jacob's Aintree plants they organized strike action. At the Dunlop Speke plant they staged a series of shop-floor actions and used the tactic of the community picket to galvanize local support. At Meccano, Massey-Ferguson, Tate & Lyle, Scotts bakery and Cammell Laird's shipyard, workers occupied the premises and sought support from other trade unionists. When 37 Cammell Laird workers were jailed for defying a court injunction against their sit-in there was a massive day of solidarity across Merseyside. At KME (ex-Fisher Bendix) workers set up a workers' co-operative. At CAV Parsons and United Biscuits shop stewards advocated alternative plans. At Birds Eye they organized huge local demonstrations. Elsewhere, at firms such as Bemrose and Kraft, they relied more on Labour MPs' protests. Virtually nowhere, except in very small workplaces, was there a completely resigned acceptance, even if in most cases such resistance proved ultimately unsuccessful, and even if the 'victories' were usually partial and perhaps temporary. But in many instances at least some gains were registered, a degree of morale sustained, union organization held together and a tradition of resistance maintained for others to emulate another day.

Meanwhile, Liverpool's Labour council became engaged in a major confrontation with the Conservative government over local government spending. Despite promises after the 1981 riots, the city was starved of central government funds and the widespread disillusionment with the Liberal/Tory local council's 1983 budget of further cuts and redundancies was reflected in the election of the first majority Labour administration for ten years. Although the new 'Militant' council, and its flamboyant leading figure Derek Hatton, were accused by the Conservative government of being irresponsible and hell-bent on destruction, their policy of no cuts and no rate rises, the creation of 1000 jobs and a massive new house-building project inspired a fighting spirit of resistance across the city and received widespread popular support (Liverpool City Council, 1984, 1986). Mass meetings of the council's 32 000 workforce, delegate shop stewards' meetings, public rallies and city-wide one-day strikes and demonstrations took place throughout 1984 and 1985, involving tens of thousands of people and including many of the city's major workplaces. Liverpool, the 'city that dared to fight' (Taaffe and Mulhearn, 1988), acquired a reputation for political belligerence to match its 'strike-prone' industrial image. Yet the refusal of national Labour and trade union leaders to back the council, combined with a number of tactical mistakes by the council itself, paralysed the movement's potential. The crisis came to a head in 1985 when 47 local Labour councillors were surcharged and disqualified from office for refusing to set a rate over a period of three months. The District Labour Party was suspended by the national executive and nine leading Liverpool Militant supporters were expelled from the Labour Party (Taaffe and Mulhearn, 1988).

For many outside media commentators the city council's defiance of the Conservative government seemed to symbolize the spirit of workers' belligerency with which Merseyside has become renown. But it is clear that as far as manufacturing industry in Merseyside is concerned a number of critical dilemmas were raised during the 1980s concerning shop-floor union responses to restructuring, redundancies and closure, as they were elsewhere across the country (Levie *et al.*, 1984; Dickson and Judge, 1987; Beynon *et al.*, 1991). In some respects the absence of a generalized and nation-wide fightback against unemployment left those who raised the banner of militant shop-floor resistance at the level of the individual workplace extremely isolated. But isolation did not mean that opposition campaigns, sit-ins or strikes were simply acts of protest or despair, or were inevitably doomed to defeat. Whilst it made any decisive breakthrough or change in the overall drift of events much more difficult it did not necessarily preclude effective workers' opposition forcing important chinks in the employers' armour. For example, 'old-fashioned' threats of national strike action in Ford UK in 1993 (which were endorsed at the Halewood plant) successfully forced a withdrawal of compulsory redundancy plans. Such continuing resistance in many respects contradicts the commonly held assumption that the contraction of manufacturing industry, the historically low strike levels and the alleged cultural changes that have occurred in regions like Merseyside during the 1980s have led to the demise of solidaristic trade union traditions.

Nonetheless, even though in all the three case studies reported on in succeeding chapters the shop stewards organized protests against the particular restructuring process they encountered, there is no doubt the advocacy of militant workers' resistance – in contrast to more 'flexible' and 'pragmatic' responses – *was* often seen as being totally inappropriate and counter-productive given the the sheer scale of the job losses on Merseyside and the lack of any broader national mobilization. Whilst in the circumstances such a 'responsible' approach was understandable, the impact of adopting this more conciliatory stance on the nature of shop stewards' organization, particularly when contrasted with the rather different period of the 1970s, was severe. Despite the immense obstacles confronting the stewards at Birds Eye, Bemrose and Ford the account below explores the very real possibilities that existed for pushing the limits of workers' resistance and considers the relationship between the ideological and political resources of shop stewards, socialist organization and the outcome of workers' struggles.

4 BIRDS EYE

Introduction

During the 1950s Birds Eye, encouraged by regional grants and the promise of an accessible workforce, located its frozen food plant on an industrial estate in Kirkby, on the site of a redeveloped wartime munitions works. By the 1960s Birds Eye had become a subsidiary of Unilever, the giant Anglo-Dutch multinational, whose consumer products stretch from Persil washing powder to Blue Band margarine and Lipton's tea. During the 1970s and 1980s other Birds Eye plants operated in Lowestoft, Yarmouth, Hull, Grimsby, Eastbourne and Gloucester, although the Kirkby plant remained one of the largest in the combine. In 1989, during the same month that Unilever announced the closure of its Merseyside plant, allegedly because of the refusal of its 1000 workers to accept new working practices, it reported record profits of £1516 million (*Financial Times*, 11 March 1989).

The product range varied considerably over the 36 years the plant was operational. During the factory's heyday in the early 1970s it primarily made the 'Captain Birds Eye' frozen fish range of products, beefburgers, steaklets, pies and pastries. Change in people's eating habits during the 1980s towards more varied and health-conscious tastes led to the equally successful 'MenuMaster' frozen TV dinner ready meal range (including vegetable meals, spaghettis, curries, and cauliflower cheeses). Such changes in product range produced a corresponding transformation in the organization of work in the plant. During the early 1970s the machinery was very antiquated and the work process was intensive and extremely repetitive, with a quite marked sexual division of labour. Most female workers were concentrated on the assembly lines whilst most male workers did heavy manual work, supplying ingredients to the women on the production lines and operating the machinery. This sexual division of labour was even more evident in particular departments within the factory, which were almost exclusively either male or female. A massive influx of capital investment and 'state of the art' new technology into the plant in the late 1970s transformed what had previously been a very labour-intensive operation into a more capital-intensive one, but did not alter the basic sexual division of labour.

The growing popularity of Birds Eye frozen food products led to a sustained increase in employment during the 1960s, and at its peak in the early 1970s the factory employed about 1650 production workers (plus electricians, engineers, supervisors and white collar staff). Throughout the 1970s, the figure stabilized at about 1400 production workers, until redundancies in 1978 reduced the workforce to 1000 during most of the 1980s. Whilst across the workforce as a whole there were more male than female employees, amongst the production workers, who formed three-quarters of the workforce, there was always a majority of women workers. Situated on a sprawling estate and housed in two main buildings, the plant during the 1970s was organized into a number of departments, all with their own managers and financial budgets, including:

- the cooked foods department – known as the pie room (200 mainly female workers);
- the chicken-stripping department (130 mainly female workers);
- the butchery department (80 male workers);
- the steaklets/beefburger department (160 male and female workers, although predominantly female);
- the cold store department (60 male workers);
- the freeze-and-case department (30 male and female workers);
- the fish department – known as the 'cod-in-sauce' (30 mainly female workers);
- the boilerhouse (20 male workers);
- and in addition, a number of different craftsmen worked on the site, with an 80-strong engineering department.

Following an 18-week lock-out of the workforce in 1978 the factory underwent a major restructuring exercise involving large-scale redundancies, the introduction of new technology and the closure of a number of departments. The most important development was the complete renovation of an adjacent building complex on the site, known as 'Unit 2', where new types of automated assembly lines were installed to produce the new MenuMaster range of products and to which the old pie room operations were transferred. The largest department within Unit 2 (cooked and prepared foods) employed about 600, predominantly female, workers. In addition to Unit 2, there was a completely new chicken-stripping department (employing 130 mainly female workers); the old butchery department (employing 80 male workers); the old cold store (now employing only 30 male workers); and the old freeze-and-case department (now employing only 15 male and female workers). There was also a small engineering department. By 1987, after further cutbacks, the only major part of the plant left functioning was Unit 2, where all the production lines were situated.

During the 1970s most women worked a single day shift (8 am–4.30 pm) although a substantial number of women worked a twilight shift (5.30 pm–10 pm) on the main production lines either in the cooked foods or the beefburgers/steaklets departments. Meanwhile, most men worked a double day shift (6 am–2 pm and 2 pm–10 pm, alternating weekly), apart from a handful who were on single day shift or permanent night work. For example, in the beefburger/steaklet department there was a mixed, although predominantly female, workforce, operating and servicing the assembly lines, with 20 men each on a double day shift, 60 women on a single day shift, 60 women on a twilight shift and a number of single day shift and permanent night shift male workers. By contrast, in the cooked foods department – known as the 'pie room' – it was an overwhelmingly female workforce, with 100-plus women on a single day shift and 100-plus women on a twilight shift, with only a handful of men working in the department. Elsewhere in the factory, it was virtually either all women, as in the chicken-stripping department, or all men, as in the butchery and cold store departments.

After 1978, and until the factory's closure in 1989, the vast majority of female workers (except those in the new chicken-stripping department) went onto a double day shift operation as the old twilight shift was disbanded. Meanwhile, a new three-shift operation was started for male workers in the preparation side of the cooked foods department of Unit 2 (which at its height employed 84 men). Thus, in Unit 2, the major department in the factory during the 1980s, there was a concentration of over 600 workers, approximately 400 women and 200 men, mainly on a double day shift, plus 80 male workers on a three-shift system. By contrast, the other two major departments in the factory were virtually either exclusively female, as in the new chicken-stripping department, or exclusively male, as in the old butchery and cold store departments.

Trade union recognition was formally recognized in the plant only after repeated skirmishes between shop-floor workers and management led to a closed shop agreement in 1960 with the Transport and General Workers' Union (TGWU). Even so, management refused to grant the shop stewards any facilities and there continued to be periodic conflicts over time off work to attend to members' grievances. All plant-wide negotiations were conducted through the single channel of a (lay) shop stewards' convenor. However, during the late 1960s a number of changes occurred in line with the Donovan Commission's recommendations for the reform of workplace industrial relations. The plant convenor was granted full-time status and provided with a union office and telephone, and the shop stewards were allowed greater leeway in the time off available to them. Later, in 1971, a plant-wide negotiating committee was set up – composed of the convenor, a deputy convenor and three other senior stewards – to bargain over major conditions of work. At national level, an agreement between Birds Eye and the TGWU established a Joint Negotiating Committee (JNC) through which annual wage negotiations were conducted by top-level corporate managers and full-time national union officials. By 1973 convenors from each of the four plants were also allowed to attend JNC meetings and by 1984 the deputy convenors had also become part of the negotiating forum. At local level, stewards continued to negotiate over job evaluation, bonus schemes and condition rates; that is, until the introduction of measured day work in 1978.

The shop stewards' committee throughout the 1970s and 1980s numbered between 27 and 30 members and was always a male-dominated body. Stewards were elected every two years by secret ballot in each department of the plant, usually on a shift basis. Larger departments had greater steward representation. The stewards' committee met monthly during working hours and every two years elected the five senior stewards on the plant's negotiating committee. Most day-to-day negotiations with management were conducted directly by the convenor, the only steward with full-time facility status. The TGWU 6/505 union branch was organized on a factory basis and meetings were held monthly to discuss, amongst other things, the convenor's report on developments within the plant. A branch committee, composed of a mixture of 15–20 shop stewards and rank-and-file union activists, also met monthly, usually in working hours, and was elected annually at a branch meeting. A Birds Eye shop stewards' combine committee, linking up with the other plants in Gloucester, Grimsby and Lowestoft, became firmly established only in the late 1980s, although there had been some attempts to set up a combine committee during the 1970s.

Chronology of Major Events

1968   Convenor granted full-time status.

1969   One-day factory strike against withholding of pay.

1971   Three-day factory strike over lay-off pay.
TGWU branch policy on lay-offs adopted.
Negotiating committee formed.

1972   One-day factory strike over lay-offs.

1973   Cold store inquiry.
One-day factory strike over May Day holiday.

1974   One-hour factory strike against canteen price increases and national pay offer.

1975   Resignation of Martin Roberts and negotiating committee.

1976   Birds Eye Five Year Plan.

1977   Martin Roberts re-elected convenor.
Two-day factory strike over payment for 'racque' line.
Four-week factory strike over automation bonus payment.
Management lock-out of workforce begins.

1978   Lock-out ends.
Factory overtime ban over short-term contracts.

1979   Two-day factory strike over suspension of two workers.
Jack Boyle elected as convenor.
Two-week factory strike over demarcation in three-shift area.

1980   One-day factory strike in support of TUC Day of Action over anti-union legislation.

1982   One-day factory strike across all Birds Eye plants over pay.
One-day factory strike in support of TUC Day of Action for NHS workers.

1984   One-day factory strike in support of Liverpool City Council.
One-day factory strike across all Birds Eye plants over redundancies in Great Yarmouth.

1989   Factory closed.

Stewards' Relationship to Management: The 1970s

The Early 1970s: The Stewards' Strengths and Weaknesses

By the early 1970s a very well organized shop steward structure had been established inside the Birds Eye Kirkby plant, with a relatively oppositional form of workplace union organization and activity. Indeed, in 1972–73 the relationship between the stewards and local management was considered so strained that the chairman of Birds Eye personally visited the Merseyside plant to 'lay down the law' to the workforce under the threat of factory closure. The explanation for why the balance of workplace power was weighted to the advantage of shop-floor workers, and for the strength of the stewards' organization during this early part of the 1970s, is to be found in a variety of both objective and subjective features of work relations.

One factor enhancing stewards' bargaining leverage appears to have been the rapid expansion of the market for frozen TV dinner convenience foods, which led to a dramatic increase in factory output and a steady influx of new labour. Such favourable product and labour market conditions formed the backcloth against which workplace industrial relations was conducted. Another important factor which acted to build up the strength of workplace unionism was management's relatively confrontational stance. In general terms, management strategy tended to oscillate between vigorous clashes over particular issues and congenial acceptance of shop-floor arrangements based on custom and practice. In part, this reflected a disparity between the attitude adopted by plant managers as opposed to those at departmental level. Within the departments day-to-day relations between managers and shop stewards were usually relatively consensual, although this tended to vary from one section to another, whilst at plant level relations were much more conflictual, sometimes encouraged by corporate Birds Eye management intervention. Thus, major changes in Birds Eye's product range on occasion led to lay-offs of hundreds of workers within the plant and outright confrontation over the issue of the 'guaranteed working week'. Such challenges tended to reinforce workers' commitment to strong collective union organization.

The influence of key individuals was another factor helping to build the strength of union organization in the plant. By 1968 Birds Eye had finally granted full-time status to the convenor and provided facilities such as a union office and telephone. No doubt it was hoped that by creating a single, authoritative figure in the Kirkby plant the convenor's control over what was becoming an increasingly more assertive workforce would be reinforced. However, Martin Roberts, elected the new shop stewards' convenor at the beginning of 1971, played a quite different role to those who had been previously in office.

Ray started working at Birds Eye in 1973, was elected to a shop steward's position in the cooked foods department (which he retained for 13 years), and served for a period of time on the factory negotiating committee. He outlined the influential, combative and also political role that Martin Roberts played in the plant:

> He was a very influential figure in as much as Birds Eye hated him. He worked in the plant for 20 years and was a very charismatic person, articulate, an orator. He could hold an audience, Martin could, speak on any subject until the cows came home. He was a fairly militant convenor all right. There were a lot of disputes in the early '70s and Martin Roberts would always get involved, and in my experience of things nine times out of 10 he would win . . . He was very much politically minded. He was a member of the Labour Party but a real socialist, and he allied his politics to his job. It was through Martin Roberts's influence that we got the type of policies we did.

Nonetheless, it should be noted that such a socialist outlook and combative approach towards management do not appear to have been matched by most of the other senior shop stewards in the factory during the early 1970s.

The day-to-day shop-floor wrangling with management was an additional factor helping to forge the strength of the Birds Eye stewards' organization. In part, these tussles were on the question of wages. Basic wages were negotiated at national level by full-time officials and the convenors from the four Birds Eye plants with TGWU representation. Invariably, when the company announced its pay offer, the Merseyside stewards' committee would recommend rejection, sometimes imposing an overtime ban, only to find themselves left isolated by the unwillingness of the other less well union-organized plants to take any action. However, in 1974 the stewards organized a one-hour factory-wide stoppage of work to bolster the bargaining leverage of full-time national union officials involved in wage negotiations, and to protest at local canteen price increases. There was also a significant element of local pay determination via job evaluation inside the Kirkby plant. Ray remembered:

> One of the things you used to measure the stewards by was how well they performed in writing up job descriptions and getting the claim submitted through a job evaluation panel. It was a fairly easy system to understand and even easier to make sure you got an award out of it. If you look at national pay awards we didn't do very well but we did fairly well in local negotiations within the factory. Basic pay was about £35 at the time – the top rate on job evaluation was £4.35.

Job evaluation was not the only way stewards could get money into the wage packets of their members. Bonus schemes were also an important feature of union activity and concerns.

Peter, a left-wing member of the Labour Party who worked at Birds Eye for 26 years (mainly in the butchery department) and held the TGWU branch secretary's position for 15 years, explained the importance of bonus schemes:

> They were set up on a weekly basis – in some departments on an individual basis and in others on a group basis. In theory, they were subject to review every twelve months but in practice most of them would be altered whenever there was a dispute. Often it would be geared to a machine. But if the machinery broke down and people lost their bonus there'd be a dispute and the shop stewards would renegotiate it. There were little innovations all the time. The bonus was worth up to about £1.30 per week, so it was a fair chunk of money.

In addition to job evaluation and bonus schemes, there were condition rates, negotiated by stewards in particularly hazardous departments of the factory such as the cold store – which were worth up to £2.50 a week.

Perhaps the principal factor helping to sharpen the stewards' strength was the high level of disputes in the factory, disputes usually provoked by management's confrontational approach. In March 1971, the company imposed lay-offs on hundreds of workers for four weeks (Branch minutes, 13 March 1971). As a result, one of the first policies adopted by the shop stewards' committee under Martin Roberts's leadership was the 'one-out, all-out' policy aimed at forcing the company to concede lay-off pay or a 'guaranteed working week'. It took two major plant-wide all-out strikes, lasting three days in 1971 and one day in 1972, before management finally granted a lay-off agreement (Branch minutes, 13 March 1971, 26 March 1972). The stewards' willingness to take vigorous action in the face of management intransigence was further successfully demonstrated with another one-day plant-wide stoppage in 1973, this time over the company's refusal to grant workers a May Day holiday (Branch minutes, 20 May 1973). There were also quite a few sectional disputes, although there was a significant variation in stewards' bargaining leverage between different departments in the factory.

By far the best organized section was the cold store department, the final assembly area where the finished manufactured products were stacked on to pallets ready for transportation. The cold store workers' strategic position meant they wielded tremendous shop-floor power. Ray recalled:

> It was a well organized part of the factory – no two ways about it. There was a walk-out practically every week. They were forever getting into trouble. A lot of it transpired from the fact that they had this large meandering workforce within the cold store that knew its strength in the factory as far as its industrial power was concerned. Their key tool was the high-reach forklift truck. No one else in the factory was trained to drive them, so if there was a stoppage in the cold store nothing could be done; the factory would virtually come to a standstill there and then. They held a monopoly of power in that sense . . . A lot of the disputes were just parochial issues that just concerned the cold store itself. But the stewards were very capable stewards. They used to gain bonus payments double what the rest of the factory got. It was the most militant part of the factory. Actually, they used to say that if one of the stewards broke wind in the cold store they'd all walk out.

The next best organized section of the plant was the butchery department, where the 80-strong male workforce cut the massive carcasses of meat. Because management relied upon a continuous flow of production, with little space to store the raw material meat, the butchers' stewards were often able to press home their advantage and were always assured of receiving a top bonus; for example, in November 1974 they took successful industrial action to win improved condition rates (Branch minutes, 23 November 1974). By comparison, in the other areas of the factory, where the assembly lines were situated, such as the cooked foods and beefburger/steaklet departments, shop-floor workers did not have the same kind of crucial relationship to production; the work regime was more controlled, the discipline stricter and there was greater flexibility of labour.

As a result, the steward organization was much weaker. Nonetheless, there were still a number of disputes in these areas, usually arising when the breakdown of antiquated machinery curtailed workers' weekly bonus payments.

A contributory factor spurring on the militancy of shop-floor workers was the inspiration of the high level of struggle inside the British working class movement generally. As Ray recalled:

> The union organization was at its height in the early '70s – no two ways
> about that. A lot of the time we had the company on the run. Because
> what you've got to remember about the early '70s is that there was this
> huge wave of euphoria the unions were carried away on at the time. You
> know, the industrial relations legislation was in force at the time and
> there was a massive upswell against that. There was a general air of
> confidence on the shop-floor in terms of what people thought they could
> win. It was a situation where you felt that if you did go into dispute you
> were going to win.

In December 1971, when 600 workers occupied the nearby Fisher Bendix plant in Kirkby and launched a highly successful campaign for the 'right to work' throughout Merseyside, Birds Eye workers were centrally involved in solidarity work (Branch minutes, 6 February 1972). Running parallel with this campaign during 1972–73 was the battle spearheaded in Kirkby against the Conservative government's Housing Finance Act, when thousands of Tower Hill council tenants, including many Birds Eye workers, went on rent strike (Stewards' committee minutes, 10 December 1973).

But notwithstanding its undoubted strengths, the shop stewards' organization in Birds Eye also had significant weaknesses during the early 1970s. To begin with, there was the break-up of its bastion of strength in the cold store department. In 1973 the plant's Personnel Manager set up an internal inquiry into the shop-floor industrial relations situation in the department. The convenor, Martin Roberts, and two other senior stewards from the negotiating committee agreed to participate in its deliberations because they were concerned that the future of the plant was being threatened by periodic stoppages disrupting production. Despite the indignant protests of the cold store stewards, the inquiry report recommended a reduction of the department's 60-strong workforce and the dispersal of some of its pallet-moving operations throughout the rest of the plant. Management subsequently offered a much enhanced voluntary redundancy deal aimed at enticing those not willing to be redeployed to leave the factory. To the union's horror 26 cold store workers, including some of the militants and shop stewards, took the money, which at £800 was a considerable lump sum at the time. This left the cold store department with only about 30 workers. The break-up of the cold store, even though it retained some of its potential industrial muscle, dealt a severe body blow to the strength of the stewards' organization in the plant and highlighted the underlying ambivalent attitude taken by Martin Roberts towards sectional stoppages. As the shop stewards' minute books reveal, the number of disputes markedly declined in the aftermath of this event.

Another factor weakening steward organization was the sexual division of labour in the plant. During the late 1960s, at a time when the food-processing industry was expanding at a rapid pace, Kirkby's Birds Eye management welcomed women workers who ideally fitted their need for young and flexible labour. Although women welcomed this new employment, they were at a distinct disadvantage as compared with male workers. A sharply defined sexual division of labour ensured that certain jobs remained effectively closed to women. Their reproductive functions, and the fact that women's work was likely to be interrupted through childbirth, if not curtailed, meant they were considered much less likely to work permanently. Thus, marriage and motherhood effectively 'deskilled' women, preparing them for only unskilled or semi-skilled work on the assembly lines. Male workers tended to be offered work which was either skilled or which offered the opportunity of substantial overtime, or both. As a consequence, the earnings women received were well below those of male workers. Whilst the basic pay structure remained the same for everyone (after an equal pay deal in 1972) the factory's job evaluation scheme introduced in 1971, which slotted people into job rates according to skill, entrenched a significant pay differential between men and women. The result could be the difference between a woman day shift assembly line worker on a job rate of 90p compared with a male shift worker operating machinery on a job rate of £4.35.

Moreover, this division of labour was compounded by some stewards' attempts to protect the bargaining position of men's jobs. For example, the pallet-moving job at the end of an assembly line was traditionally carried out by a man because it usually involved some heavy labour. But this had a double-edged effect, as Marion, a TGWU union member who worked for many years in the beefburger/steaklet department, described:

> If management happened to be short of male labour they'd quite often
> look towards the women. So what the shop stewards did was get them
> to agree that whenever that situation arose they would always put two
> women onto one man's job. Obviously, that suited the women because
> they could share out the work between them and the men were happy
> because they knew they would always be able to walk back into the job.
> You never got a take-over position. It would only be a temporary
> arrangement.

This sexual division of labour weakened the shop-floor unity of male and
female workers by reinforcing a 'them and us' set of relations.

Some male stewards were prepared, alongside the relatively few women
on the stewards' committee, to make attempts to alleviate the disadvan-
tageous conditions women workers faced. For example, Martin Roberts
negotiated an equal pay agreement and formally pursued with the company a claim for paid maternity leave (Branch minutes, 19 May 1974).
Moreover, the periodic stoppages of work, both within departments and
across the plant as a whole, facilitated a breakdown of barriers by
emphasizing the interdependence of male and female workers *vis-à-vis*
management. As Marion explained:

> If the men who did all the heavy physical jobs decided they were refusing
> to do a job because it was too dirty or something, they'd go to the
> women and say: 'Will you support us? We know it'll affect your bonus,
> but we need your support.' And the women would say: 'OK, yeah, we'll
> support you.' And the same thing would happen if the women walked off
> the job and went to the men. They'd say: 'We can't work with that
> machine.' And the men would back them up, even if it meant they lost
> their bonus as a result. There was no real animosity when it came down
> to it in that sense.

Thus, there was an ongoing struggle to obtain unity between male and
female workers on the shop-floor. But many individual shop stewards *did*
accept the in-built demarcation between men's and women's jobs, thereby
undermining the potential cohesion of the stewards' body as a whole.

Another underlying weakness of the Birds Eye stewards was that the
senior stewards did not share Martin Roberts's strategic and combative
stance towards management, although the formation of a negotiating
committee in 1971 had the effect of ensuring a more collective style of

leadership than the completely convenor-dominated approach of the past. The senior stewards preferred a rather more 'strong bargaining relations' stance and their willingness to engage in militant activity was more pragmatically based and contingent on varying sectional pressures. They also tended to perceive him as being 'too political'. Peter outlined the different approach:

> Martin was always looking for progression, improvements in one thing or another, if you know what I mean. But with the others on the negotiating committee nothing happened unless the company made it happen.
> Rather than go to the company and say: 'We'll be seeking this, that and the other', it would be the company who came up with an idea for change and them reacting to it: 'Yes, we'll go along with it,' or 'No, we won't'.

The negotiating committee stewards were often reluctant to give their unequivocal backing to Martin Roberts's occasional requests for industrial action across the whole plant aimed at strengthening his hand in negotiations with management over particular issues. After being rebuffed on a number of occasions Martin Roberts gradually became more and more frustrated, until the issue came to a head in late 1975. Peter related what happened:

> I remember there was a run-up to a stoppage and he called a special stewards meeting. He told them: 'I'm going to try this and if you don't back me then I'm going to resign and you can go it alone without me.'
> At the time, they said: 'OK, we'll back you.' But then when it came to it, they didn't.

In response, Martin Roberts took the dramatic step of resigning from his position as convenor (although remaining a departmental steward), whereupon the five other senior stewards, including the deputy convenor, Jack Boyle, resigned from the negotiating committee (although most remained as departmental stewards). It was an extremely serious loss to the cohesion of the stewards' body and led to the second major phase of shop-floor struggle that can be identified, during which the balance of workplace power inside the Birds Eye plant tilted towards the advantage of management.

The new convenor, Simon King, was much older than Martin Roberts, and as a moderate Labour Party member he was from a completely different political background. His main concern appeared to be to build up a new conciliatory relationship with management. Ray outlined his different approach:

> Simon was very much a mediator. He wouldn't take a hard line on anything – he always tended to take the soft option. And he was apolitical. Those were the main differences with Martin. Simon was one of those fellas who would sit down with the management and say: 'I'm a professional and you're a professional – can't we do a deal?' It was that type of relationship with the company . . . There was all kinds of wheeling and dealing going on at the time. He'd have one story for the stewards' committee and then his actions with the company were completely different.

Meanwhile, the new *deputy* convenor found himself obliged to resign his position within weeks of his election in the most embarrassing of circumstances. A card check revealed he had failed to pay union subscriptions since starting work in the factory a number of years before.

Somewhat traumatized by such events the stewards' committee lost much of its self-assurance in its relationship with management during 1976, and the latter began to press home their advantage. Ray explained what this meant for the stewards:

> We had a position where some managers mounted a challenge for supremacy. They succeeded in a number of little issues. In some departments if you had an argument with the company then you could be sure that five minutes afterwards they would send the supervisors down and there'd be a lot of finger-wagging. They'd come out quite openly and say to people, 'If you take any notice of your steward then we'll take disciplinary action against you.' And they began to win the propaganda war. We felt they began to take control of the site. The union took a bit of a nosedive during this period.

According to the stewards' and union branch minute books, there was not one single dispute inside the factory during 1976. Of course, it would be wrong to assume this reflected a complete collapse of confidence on the shop-floor and a willingness of all stewards to acquiesce in managerial prerogative. Over the previous two years a handful of younger and more political union activists (including Ray) had already begun to transform the TGWU branch into a lively forum for argument and debate, and having been newly elected as stewards they were also able to make important shop-floor gains in some areas of the factory. For example, on the permanent night shift in the cooked foods department, the stewards pushed their members from the lowest band within the job evaluation scheme (£1.00) to the highest band (£4.35) through sectional bargaining backed up with the threat of industrial action.

Nonetheless, it was only to be the lull before the storm. During 1976 the full implications of the threat posed to workplace union organization at the Kirkby plant gradually became apparent when Birds Eye corporate management unveiled their 'Five Year Plan'. This threatened a major reorganization of production affecting all the company's frozen food plants with the long-term aim of introducing new technology. Despite promises of a massive investment programme in the Kirkby factory, the company stated its intention of transferring production of some of its major product ranges – steaklets, beefburgers and all fish-based products – to other sites within the group, as well as introducing drastic changes to established working practices, which included the introduction of a new double day shift. Growing discontent with the bargaining ineffectiveness of the new convenor, combined with the threat posed to the Kirkby site by the company's Five Year Plan, resulted in a vote of no confidence at a stewards' committee meeting and, at the end of 1976, the return of Martin Roberts to the convenors position. At the same time, two of the 'old guard' senior stewards, who had previously resigned from the negotiating committee, were re-elected, along with a couple of younger, more militant stewards.

1977–1979: Offensive and Counter-Offensive

The changed composition of the shop stewards' leadership ushered in the third phase of the struggle inside the Kirkby plant. As Peter recalled:

> Whereas people hadn't supported Martin before, they wanted him back because he was the only one who could do the job properly. Then you saw a change of tactics, because Martin now got more support than ever. It made a hell of a lot of difference. In his mind, Martin was as militant as he always was, prepared to use industrial muscle to achieve things. He was shrewd enough to know when to push the stewards into action or not. But his ability to get things done was vastly improved. For

instance, he instigated negotiations for a maternity agreement for the
women. Previously he would have had difficulty in getting support for
that through the stewards' committee – because it was male chauvinist.
But after the experience of Simon King they backed him on it.

Certainly, Martin Roberts's return at the beginning of 1977 appears to
have revitalized the self-esteem and authority of the stewards' organization in general and the younger, more political stewards in particular.
Moreover, it seemed to unleash the latent discontent over wage restraint
that existed on the shop-floor.

During the first few weeks of the new year, a sudden wave of sectional
strike activity swept the plant, with stoppages in the butchery, chicken-
stripping and freeze-and-case departments. The union organization began
to reassert its power and regain some of the ground it had lost. The
disputes were of an offensive nature with stewards demanding extra job
rates or bonus payments. In February, a new bout of militancy erupted
on the 'racque' pie line in the cooked foods department. Management had
introduced new automated meat dispensing machinery, which had led to
a redeployment of a number of women workers elsewhere in the factory.
The racque line was viewed as being symbolic of the production changes
sought by the company as outlined in its Five Year Plan and, under
Martin Roberts's leadership, the stewards' organization prepared its
strategic response: to fight for increased bonus payments to compensate
for the extra job responsibilities required. It took a two-day plant-wide
strike before management conceded an agreement to increase payments
to female workers (Branch minutes, 17 February 1977).

But the deal was never implemented in practice and, after months of
management evasion, the issue finally exploded in August 1977 when the
stewards' committee called an all-out strike, linking the issue of a £7 bonus
for running the new racque line with the wider question of the threat posed
to the Kirkby plant by the centralization of products and Five Year Plan.
Whilst pickets manned the gates in Kirkby, a delegation of strikers lobbied
the two other Birds Eye plants that were part of the same national pay
negotiating set-up, appealing for solidarity action. Yarmouth agreed to
impose an immediate overtime ban. When Lowestoft shop stewards
refused to offer support, the Kirkby strikers mounted a 'flying picket' on
the factory gate. The production workers traditionally had a very weak
union organization and ignored the appeal for solidarity, but the blockade
had an immediate and dramatic effect when Unispeed lorry drivers, also

members of the TGWU, refused to cross the picket lines. Unable to move anything in or out, the factory was effectively paralysed and after two weeks Birds Eye finally backed down, agreeing to make a £5 productivity payment to the Kirkby strikers in order to secure an immediate return to work. This was a significant victory and the stewards' committee was jubilant with the outcome.

However, it proved to be a false dawn. The workers' offensive was met with a Birds Eye counter-offensive. The counter-attack followed a walk-out by the Kirkby plant's 80 AUEW engineering craftsmen a couple of weeks later, after unilateral suspension of all negotiations on their annual pay claim. TGWU stewards were approached by the company and informed that if they allowed supervisors and managers to take over the striking engineers' jobs, the company would attempt to provide work for at least some of their members, although most would be laid off without pay. The company assumed that as the engineers had refused to respect the TGWU's picket lines in their own recent dispute, then TGWU members would be willing to act likewise. But following an emergency meeting the stewards' committee voted unanimously not only to support the engineers' strike, but also to invoke union branch policy on lay-offs of 'one out, all out'. The stewards mounted the picket line alongside the engineers and appealed to their members not to cross. In an impressive display of solidarity only 197 out of some 1300 TGWU rank-and-file members broke the union's ranks to go into work.

The company responded two days later by announcing a complete shut-down of the plant and the lay-off of the entire workforce pending a resolution of the engineers' strike. The lock-out proved to be only the start of a long, drawn-out and bitter dispute with the company that was to last for no less than four-and-a-half months, between October 1977 and March 1978, before finally ending in workers' ignominious defeat. Ray recalled the predicament the stewards found themselves in:

> We thought it would last a week or two. But after a while it became obvious the engineers had walked into a closed door. Five weeks into the strike the company called the engineers to a meeting and produced a five-point plan for the resumption of work. The engineers took it away and agreed to accept three of the points and went back to the company suggesting compromise on the other two. But the company then produced a seven-point plan. And that's how their negotiations went. Every time they met the company they'd get so far and then no further

because the company would add something else on. It was a deliberate ploy to prolong the dispute.

The TGWU and AUEW shop stewards formed a 'joint liaison committee' which met weekly to coordinate activities, organize picketing of the plant by both unions' members, and campaign for financial support throughout the Merseyside labour movement. A number of mass meetings, and a huge trade union and community solidarity demonstration in Kirkby, reaffirmed shop-floor union members' support for their stewards' defiant stance (Branch minutes, 11 October 1977; 1 February 1978).

As the months went by without a settlement of the engineers' dispute, it became apparent that corporate Birds Eye management would only consider reopening the plant after completely new contracts of employment for both TGWU production workers and AUEW strikers had been signed. Despite the continued defiance of the joint liaison committee, tremendous pressure to recommend acceptance of the company's terms was placed on the stewards by national full-time TGWU and AUEW officials. After holding secret meetings with the company in London, the national union leaders eventually foisted an agreement on the Kirkby workforce that conceded their unconditional surrender to the company in exchange for an immediate return to work. The capitulation included, amongst other things: 340 redundancies amongst TGWU production workers (as well as the loss of a third of the engineers' jobs); the relinquishing of the previously agreed bonus payment for the racque line; the replacement of the women's twilight shift by compulsory double day shift working; the introduction of a new three-shift system for some male workers, and the substitution of all bonus schemes by a new 'balanced pay structure' involving measured day work.

It is difficult to confirm whether Kirkby management had deliberately provoked the engineers into taking strike action as many people subsequently claimed. But there is no doubt that the lock-out provided Birds Eye with the perfect opportunity not only to speed ahead with its Five Year Plan transfer of particular products from Kirkby to other sites, but also to prepare the ground for a complete restructuring of production within the Merseyside plant. Peter related how management took advantage of the situation:

It might have been fortunate that the engineers entered into a wage dispute but it allowed management a good few months when they could shut production down and get the plant ready for the new investment. When we got back into the factory we saw the extent of the building work that had been started. And for the first eighteen months after the dispute we actually worked in a food factory which was also a building site. They were pulling down walls everywhere, building a whole new area.

This was the start of a new era for the Kirkby factory, the introduction of a massive new investment programme in which the nature of production was transformed from the old manually operated system to brand new automated assembly lines, with 'multi-vacuum' self-sealing packaging machinery. In the process, the beefburger/steaklet and fish departments were completely closed down and the chicken-stripping department was transferred to a new area of the factory. But the most important development was the transfer of the old cooked foods department to a completely renovated building complex known as 'Unit 2', where new high-technology assembly lines were installed. Employing over 600 men and women, all of whom now worked a rotating double day shift, it became the largest department on the site.

Although formally the shop stewards' organization remained intact (having continued to meet and organize throughout the period of the lock-out), it had suffered a severe setback. The return-to-work package concluded by the national union officials placed severe constraints on stewards' negotiating capacities, giving management *carte blanche* to reorganize production. Despite the fact the 350 redundancies were eventually agreed voluntarily, the balance of workplace power now swung right back in favour of management. Peter remembered the stewards' loss of confidence:

From the outset we went back very much with our tail between our legs. The morale was fairly low, obviously after a major defeat like that. From the T and G point of view there was a lot of acquiescence for about the first six months. Management were quite cocky. In certain departments the supervisors were dictatorial. They'd say: 'Well, if you don't like it you know where you can go.' But stewards had to step back from the brink, because we'd lost a lot of members, people had been out of work for four months, you knew they couldn't be motivated into action. To a great extent the company were laughing at us for a few months.

This was the beginning of a reassertion of management control over the workforce and an attempt to marginalize the stewards' committee.

Management exploited the stewards' bargaining weakness by allowing the short-fall in labour created by the redundancies to be overcome by moving workers from one department to another at their discretion. Many of the stewards found themselves unable to resist this new offensive. Ray described the dilemma they faced:

> There were a lot of arguments within the stewards' committee as to how much flexibility the company should get. I think the environment that we had in the factory at the time tended to lend itself to the majority of stewards saying: 'Well, there's not a great deal we can do about 100 per cent flexibility – is it really that wrong?' Some of us argued that covering the gaps was a block to the recruitment of new labour. But a lot of the stewards put the argument: 'Can we actually fight it?' obviously people were scared of getting pushed out the gate so soon after coming back. The whole position was tenuous to say the least.

This was a dilemma which was not easy to resolve.

Birds Eye also ended the element of local pay determination in the factory, introducing what it termed a 'balanced pay structure' that combined job and basic rates and had the effect of significantly widening the differentials amongst male and female workers, from between £3 to as much as £17 a week between a day shift female worker and a three-shift male worker. Under what became a new national benchmark, rather than being locally determined, it proved very difficult to move from one level to another within the pay structure.

Even though the stewards' organization was initially seriously disarmed by the reorganization of production in the plant, it was gradually able to recover some of its bargaining strength in some areas of the new Unit 2 cooked foods department, where the installation of the new technology and assembly lines proceeded apace. Stewards in this department were able to capitalize on management's predicament of being faced with 'state of the art' machinery that proved difficult to operate on the manning levels originally imposed by successfully increasing the numbers employed on the new 'multi-vac' assembly lines. Perhaps the best agreements were negotiated by stewards representing the three-shift male workers in the new prepared foods section of Unit 2, where they were able to push up the manning levels from nine to nearly 30 workers per shift.

The presence of two or three of the most militant and political stewards in the factory within this particular area was instrumental in securing the new labour.

Of course, management clearly envisaged that such an arrangement would only be a short-term measure until all the machinery was firmly in place and working smoothly; and to cover the transition period they recruited new labour into the plant on the basis of six-week fixed-term contracts. Although the shop stewards' committee expressed its opposition to this stop-gap measure in favour of the employment of a permanent workforce, they were overruled by full-time union officials. But after a few months' experiment the stewards' body took the initiative and imposed a factory-wide overtime ban to force management to abandon the use of short-term contracts. Within 24 hours the company had backed down and given an assurance that only permanent labour would henceforth be taken on (Branch minutes, 3 December 1978).

Thus, it was the enormous new investment programme and accompanying increased factory output that strengthened the stewards' bargaining leverage and gave them the confidence to act in such a defiant fashion. Plant management's concern to keep production running – amidst the launch of the MenuMaster range – actually meant that ever greater numbers of new workers were hired and manning levels increased to practically their pre-1978 lock-out level. By February 1979 the stewards' committee even felt strong enough to organize a two-day plant-wide stoppage over a demarcation dispute, involving two union members suspended for refusing to do engineers' jobs (Branch minutes, 24 February 1979). It was a further illustration of the way the stewards' body slowly began to recover its strength. Of course, the balance of workplace power still lay overwhelmingly in the hands of management, but the stewards' organization (in some sections of the factory) gradually began to retrieve some of the ground it had lost.

However, the period of recovery was short-lived. Martin Roberts again resigned as convenor at the end of 1979, this time to take up a full-time district official's position within the Merseyside Region of the TGWU. It marked another new phase in the fortunes of the Birds Eye stewards' leadership and its relationship to management, with the 1980s witnessing a distinct shift from a militant leadership style to a much more 'responsible' approach.

Stewards' Relationship to Management: The 1980s

The Early 1980s: 'Don't Rock the Boat'

Although the stewards' organization slowly began to recover some of its strength, for the majority of workers, the legacy of the lock-out still weighed heavily on shop-floor confidence. This sense of uncertainty was significantly enhanced during the early 1980s by the wave of redundancies and factory closures that swept through Merseyside, with unemployment levels rocketing in the Kirkby area. When Birds Eye itself began to issue veiled threats to shut down the plant unless efficiency was dramatically improved, it helped to reinforce further a siege-like mentality amongst many shop-floor workers. It was against this background that Jack Boyle, elected as the new convenor, promptly abandoned the relatively militant and political leadership style adopted by Martin Roberts in favour of a new 'co-operative' approach towards management. He felt that it was only by keeping their heads down and trying to make the plant as viable as possible that workers could hope to retain their jobs in the long term. This involved, in exchange for seeking some demonstrable improvements in working conditions via a 'strong bargaining relationship' with management, the exercise of a more 'responsible' leadership role than previously.

Ritchie, a steward in the 1980s on the three-shift system in the prepared foods section of Unit 2, the largest department in the factory, described the new convenor's consensual approach towards management:

> There was very definitely a more co-operative relationship with the management. Don't get me wrong: Jack was never weak with management. He would go in and negotiate and get rewards. But he didn't have to go in like Martin Roberts with his entourage behind him, banging the table and calling people out. He would do it quietly. He'd say: 'This is what people want and we can come to some sort of arrangement on it.'

Ray, who also worked in the three-shift area of Unit 2 during the 1980s, echoed this description:

> Jack's air of co-operation was a lot greater than Bob's ever was. Jack was a pragmatist. He was the type who would say: 'Listen, you've got to be realistic about this.' There was a mutual love society that seemed to develop between the union and the company. They would give us

certain things and we would give them certain things. Jack would bend to certain pressures, of course. He would always push an issue. But the basic difference was how far an issue should be pushed. If we had an issue that we thought was strong enough and we should push, Jack would say: 'No, what we'll do is keep it in procedure.' Jack was a great procedure man. There were plenty of times we could have had a major dispute but we used to step back because Jack wasn't a fighter in that sense. Any issue that looked as if it was going to lead to a dispute was fairly quickly circumvented. He'd get involved and say: 'You're not doing that.' The saying for Jack Boyle, especially among the three-shift workers, was: 'Don't rock the boat.' That's what he'd say all the time.

The main political difference between Jack Boyle and Martin Roberts was pointed out by another union branch activist and independent socialist, Terry:

Martin Roberts was very much a political figure, a Labour Party man. Under his stewardship the branch took on a definite political shade, to the left. He would allow a fair amount of political discussion. Jack Boyle tended to divorce politics entirely from trade union organization. With him it was purely an industrial, trade union business. He went in, did his job and went home, and that was it. So under Jack Boyle there was a political vacuum . . . The stewards from the '70s had never been political in terms of party politics but they had been politically motivated in terms of industrial politics. But that type of politics gradually disappeared.

Within a few weeks of assuming the convenor's position Jack Boyle attempted to stamp his new-found authority and restraining influence on any glimmer of shop-floor militancy, particularly within the three-shift area of the new Unit 2 cooked foods department. With Birds Eye's new products coming on stream this was an area constantly changing and under pressure from departmental managers hell-bent on imposing less 'restrictive' working practices. Flexibility of labour and job demarcation lay at the heart of the persistent disputes between the three-shift stewards and management. As the first stage in the production process it effectively became the 'new cold store' in reverse, with workers wielding enormous potential industrial muscle and becoming the centre of militancy in the factory. Instead of being tied to an assembly line, the all-male work-force operated as a close-knit self-contained unit in a 'free working' environment and, with the help of two or three militant stewards, were able to build up strong sectional trade union organization.

But from the outset Jack Boyle made it clear he would not countenance disputes. At a heated emergency stewards' meeting in October 1979, called to discuss a walk-out by the three-shift workers in a confrontation over manning levels, the new convenor argued vigorously for the strike to be called off. This was despite the fact that management's unilateral imposition of new working arrangements represented a direct challenge to union negotiating rights. As it happened, the company's sudden imposition of selected lay-offs pulled the carpet from under his feet and the stewards' committee invoked their 'one out, all out' union policy, completely closing the factory down for two weeks before a compromise settlement was eventually agreed (Stewards' committee minutes, 29 October 1979). The new convenor was more successful in March 1980 when he used his casting vote at a stewards' meeting against supporting another walk-out in the three-shift area over demarcation.

This approach was very disappointing to many stewards. Ray recalled the frustrations he felt as a departmental steward in the three-shift area:

> Basically, they would negotiate, co-operate, do everything other than call a dispute. To give you examples, I would be here all day long, there were that many. So many times we stepped back from the brink and said 'No'. A lot of the issues were to do with flexibility. They wanted to move us to other areas – but we wouldn't budge. When we used to put the arguments on flexibility to Jack in the context of having a dispute over it, Jack would always say: 'You're not going to win that because we've got a factory-wide agreement that gives them 100 per cent flexibility. What makes you think you're so bleeding different in the three-shift area?'

This assessment was backed up by Carole, who also worked at Birds Eye during the 1980s, on the multi-vac assembly lines in Unit 2. She explained how the 'don't rock the boat' philosophy equally applied to the less well organized sections of the factory:

> There were a number of times when the women would walk off the lines, nine times out of ten because of the cold. We were handling frozen meat and it was freezing. They wouldn't even give us jackets to wear. They were kind of spontaneous stoppages but we were always slapped like naughty girls: 'Get back to work.' The stoppage would last until the

convenor came down and said: 'Right, get back to work girls and I'll go and sort it out.' But he never would do, really.

There was a very marked decline in the number of sectional stoppages during the early 1980s, only about four or five a year across the whole plant compared with an average of about ten previously. Despite the relative strength of the three-shift area and the occasional stoppage on the lines in Unit 2, disputes appear to have been generally much more volatile, short-lived and unsuccessful compared with those of the 1970s. Of course, this was a consequence of the legacy of the lock-out, of Birds Eye's threats of plant closure, of the general shake-out of jobs in the region, and of the negative impact of the major defeats suffered by sections of the British working class movement, notably the miners in 1984–85. As Ritchie acknowledged:

> The effect was apathy amongst the workers. They saw very
> well-organized groups of workers being defeated and the attitude that
> became inbred was 'we cannot win'. Because of Thatcher you started
> hearing rumours that the trade union movement was finished. You had to
> argue with your own membership and convince them that trade unionism
> was still alive and kicking.

But the convenor's disapproval of strikes inside the Birds Eye plant also contributed to this lack of confidence on the shop-floor. Pouring cold water on the isolated sparks of workers' resistance that occasionally ignited only further reinforced the belief that 'we cannot win'. Although the handful of shop stewards in the three-shift area had gained a reputation across the factory for their militancy, they were in a distinct minority on the stewards' committee as a whole, which never really questioned Jack Boyle's stance. Indeed, the negotiating committee's role was gradually transformed from a body that made collective decisions on bargaining and strategy, to essentially no more than a vehicle through which management transmitted its ideas. Ritchie explained:

> In the early '80s the negotiating committee didn't function. It was there
> in name only. The company would send for them if they wanted to
> introduce third-party meat into the factory, introduce new products or if
> there was a serious failure to agree on a factory-wide basis. They got
> involved in departmental disputes to tell people they were out of

line – they were 'wildcatting'. But apart from that it played a very
low-key role. Otherwise the company just went direct to the convenor.

As the general economic situation outside the plant deteriorated the
politics of survival inside it under Jack Boyle's leadership proved a
more unifying factor than any alternative which the left stewards, marginalized within the three-shift area, were able to provide. The convenor
was able to keep in check those elements within the stewards' body
who were more active and wanted to fight by relying on the majority
who were more passive and less antagonistic to management. Terry
commented:

> I think it inherently weakened the stewards' organization overall. If you're
> not allowed to use the last weapon in your arsenal at any given stage
> that obviously weakens your position.

In the short term, this policy created an element of stability in workplace
industrial relations, but in the long term it also had extremely damaging
consequences for shop-floor union organization.

Apart from the fear of job loss, Jack Boyle was able to justify his intense
aversion to shop-floor militancy by pointing to a variety of management concessions he was able to obtain through an alternative 'strong
bargaining relations' approach. Having invested £10 million in new
machinery and assembly lines Birds Eye had launched a number of new
products in the Kirkby plant, and, with production levels rising substantially, the factory operated at nearly full capacity. In these circumstances,
management were willing to make some concessions to the stewards whilst
still retaining a distinct advantage in the bargaining relationship. Yet such
gains were strictly limited. Certainly, manning levels were significantly
increased in Unit 2 and Jack Boyle broke completely new ground by
getting management finally to concede a bereavement leave agreement
(for close family relations) and a medical leave agreement (for hospital
and dental appointments) with paid time off work; he also negotiated a
plant-level reduction in the working week from 40 hours to 39 hours.
As Terry acknowledged:

> The company agreed to things Martin Roberts could never get off them.
> Jack got them just like that. He'd get up at a meeting with the members
> and say: 'Roberts couldn't get *this*, look how I've got *that*.'

On the face of it, such negotiated concessions seemed impressive; they certainly boosted Jack Boyle's esteem and authority amongst many shop-floor workers.

The underlying reality was rather less convincing. To begin with, the increase in manning levels in Unit 2, particularly the three-shift area, was won almost exclusively through the efforts of the sectional stewards, rather than the convenor. Meanwhile, the other gains did not cost the company very much, and nothing of substance – in terms of any real improvement in working conditions – was actually conceded. In fact, in relation to the reduction in the working week, the contrary was the case. Thus, Jack Boyle presented the company with an offer it could not refuse: the production of 40 hours' work within 39 hours. In effect, management's limited concessions were readily traded off in return for the convenor's compliance with wide-ranging flexibility aimed at boosting production output, which in the long term only served to impair workers' hard-won shop-floor conditions.

Nonetheless, the substantial material pressures and incentives towards more conciliatory bargaining relations and a less militant perspective should not be underestimated. At least for a large section of workers these gains, however limited in nature, were real enough and appeared to confirm the merits of a strategy of accommodation rather than confrontation. It meant fewer strikes, less disruption to production and the apparent security of employment amidst a hostile environment; in the circumstances an alternative militant approach to management appeared as merely self-destructive. In this sense, Jack Boyle's routinized bargaining relations were located within and made possible by actual material conditions and their reflection in shop-floor workers' consciousness. Even so, the pursuit of plant-level 'strong bargaining relations' continued to meet some resistance from various sections of workers and stewards. They appeared to make a distinction between 'having to compromise', in circumstances that were not favourable to shop-floor union organization, and the active 'celebration of compromise', which embraced managerial logic and contributed significantly to the demobilization of collective shop-floor activity and the disarming of union strength that followed.

The unevenness in stewards' bargaining leverage between the different sections of the plant which had been evident in the 1970s became even more marked in the 1980s, especially between the relatively much better organized all-male departments, such as the three-shift area, the butchery department and the cold store, compared with the much less well organized all-women chicken-stripping department and the mixed male and female assembly area of Unit 2. In part, this was a consequence of workers' varying strategic relationship to production, of the different organization of work, of the type of supervisory and managerial approach adopted, and of the nature of sectional shop stewards' leadership provided.

Many groups of both male and female workers in most departments managed to carve out some control over their jobs (independently of their shop stewards) by operating what was colloquially referred to as the 'welt system', an unofficial system of covering for absent colleagues on a tea break. It was evidence of the manner in which workers' own collective organization was used to relieve the grinding monotony of the job and undermine management's control mechanisms. But the practice also had its weaknesses, which is probably why management for the most part came to tolerate the practice. Not only did it sometimes mean a group of workers worked even more intensively than they might otherwise have done, but it also had the effect of backfiring against other sections of workers. Carole described how the ingenious use of the practice by some men created antagonisms amongst some women on the lines:

> What happened was they didn't just work the 'welt', they worked the 'welt on the welt'. Say two people started work at six o'clock in the morning. Well, someone might take the first break until half-past six and then come in – and the other person then went off until seven o'clock. But what actually happened was that one would go off at twenty-five past six and his relief wouldn't come in until twenty-five to seven. Then one would go off again at five to and the other wouldn't take over until five past. So they weren't ever putting half an hour in. But that left the women on the line shouting: 'Where's the work he's supposed to be supplying us with?' And we'd be left stuck on the line for nearly two hours because our relief was only one in five.

Thus, the informal organization of the men in relation to unofficial changeovers adversely affected the women workers whilst advantaging the male workers.

Instead of fighting for the women to be granted a better relief system, to level the organization upwards, the stewards were more concerned not to do anything that might jeopardize the men's relatively favourable position. Even though the introduction of new technology provided new possibilities there was very little breakdown of the strict demarcation between male and female jobs in the factory during the 1980s. Carole recalled: 'The convenor was even known to have said: "A woman will get on a fork-lift truck over my dead body."' Meanwhile, the earnings of the women compared with the men continued to be vastly inferior, partly as a result of the new 'balanced pay structure' imposed on the stewards after the lock-out, but also because most male workers tended to work high rates of overtime and were granted better holiday pay than most women workers.

Nonetheless, there were occasions when the stewards were able to construct unity between the men and women workers, despite the debilitation of different work practices. Steve, the deputy convenor, who worked very closely with Jack Boyle and was very much a 'moderate' member of the negotiating committee, related an example of the type of unity that was still possible between men and women when they were engaged in dispute with management:

> There was a young girl the company wanted to dismiss one Friday night. I was called in and told the manager: 'Don't you realize, if you sack her you'll have a stoppage on your hands?' – because I knew the strength of feeling there was. But they took no notice. And all the shift stopped work, there was about 200 men and women, although it was about two to one women to men. I got everyone together for a meeting and told them to stay in work and I said: 'If that girl doesn't start work first thing on Monday morning then we'll all walk out.' And the manager withdrew the sacking. So we got the unity between men and women then.

Whilst such unity between male and female workers was undoubtedly possible it was not facilitated by the virtual collapse of sectional disputes that occurred in the factory during the 1980s, in part a consequence of the 'don't rock the boat' philosophy of the senior stewards themselves.

Paradoxically, despite the marked decline in *sectional* stoppages of work, the Birds Eye shop stewards organized a number of all-out *plant*-wide demonstration strikes. At first glance, this paradox may appear incongruous, but appearances can often be deceptive. The actual nature of the disputes provides some measure of their overall significance. Thus, in May 1980 the stewards organized a one-day stoppage of the plant in support of the TUC's Day of Action against the Conservative government's anti-union legislation (Branch minutes, 13 April 1980); in June and September 1982 they organized two one-day stoppages, in pursuance of the Birds Eye national wage claim and as part of the TUC Day of Action in support of National Health Service workers (Branch minutes, 13 June 1982, 12 September 1982); in March and July of 1984 there were two one-day plant-wide strikes, in support of Liverpool city council's defiance of local government ratecapping and against the redundancy terms being offered for closure of the Birds Eye Yarmouth plant (Branch minutes, 17 March 1984, 8 July 1984); and in September 1985, the plant was brought to a halt for three days when stewards persuaded their members not to cross a picket line set up by strikers from the Gloucester Birds Eye plant (Branch minutes, 27 September 1985).

On the one hand, the Kirkby stewards' ability to organize such action showed they had by no means been completely co-opted by management and illustrated the potential industrial muscle that could still be wielded. The willingness of shop-floor union members to follow their stewards' lead revealed a strong commitment to basic trade union principles of unity and solidarity and was a testimony to the continuing resilience of workplace union organization in the plant despite the set-back inflicted during the 1977–78 lock-out and the series of workers' defeats inside the British labour movement generally. On the other hand, it would be a mistake to ignore the actual limitations that were simultaneously built into these stoppages. Firstly, every single one of them – except the dispute in support of the Gloucester strikers – was initiated not by the Kirkby shop stewards themselves but by full-time trade union officials. Secondly, strictly speaking, only one of the stoppages, the pay claim in 1982, directly affected the concrete day-to-day struggle on the shop-floor between workers and management in the Birds Eye Kirkby plant itself, and even that was something that could only be negotiated above factory level. By contrast, virtually every one of the other disputes was a solidarity strike, taken not so much to extract concessions from Kirkby management, but rather to demonstrate support for other sections of the working class – whether within the Birds Eye group (as in the case of the disputes backing the Yarmouth and Gloucester plants) or outside it (as in the case of those backing hospital workers and Liverpool city council).

The key point here is that such solidarity action for *external* reasons was not paralleled by and translated into workplace bargaining activity *internally* within the Kirkby plant itself. This is not to counterpose one to the other: winning solidarity for other sections of workers could have been used as an important mechanism for restoring shop-floor morale and rebuilding an organized core of opposition to management at local level, the one feeding into the other. Instead, what happened was that the one effectively became a substitute for the other. Ray believed that although there was the potential to revitalize union organization across the plant the senior stewards did not seek to exploit the situation to their advantage:

> We specialized in the MenuMaster range on the multi-vacs lines. Well, I think it took the company by surprise. It took off better than their wildest dreams, it was one of our best sellers, we actually couldn't make enough for the market. So the factory was booming. After 1983 some stewards felt more confident that with investment still going into the place, the time to sit back was finished. We should now progress the aspirations of our members and push the company a little further every time. But that didn't materialize because as far as Jack Boyle was concerned, the factory was always in a tenuous state. He wouldn't recognize there was a strength of feeling building up from amongst the stewards and from the members as to their terms and conditions. We were always told: 'No, it's not the right time to strike.' But it was never the right time to strike. We kept being told we shouldn't go for this, we shouldn't go for that, we shouldn't go for the other. Jack Boyle would say: 'We've got to keep our powder dry.'

But in many respects 'keeping the powder dry' over a prolonged period of time was a self-defeating exercise. Despite the willingness of the Kirkby senior stewards to organize the occasional one-day plant-wide stoppage of work in support of other workers, they were usually explicitly opposed to the encouragement of similar activity against their own management. Not only did this strategy weaken their potential bargaining position on the shop-floor (and their relationship to rank-and-file members) but also it meant that when their organization was put to the decisive test in the late 1980s it proved unable to deliver.

1985–89: The Downward Slope

The closure of the butchery department without any effective shop-floor resistance during 1985 further undermined the strength of the stewards' organization. A similar process occurred with the closure of the chicken-stripping department in 1986. Although the chicken-stripping department stewards appealed to the stewards' committee for plant-wide strike action to resist the closure, a tactical blunder combined with the years of damage to shop-floor union organization threw away the chance of a potential victory. Ray explained what happened:

> There was an argument on the stewards' committee over the timing of a call for a stoppage. The chicken-room stewards wanted to take the issue immediately to a mass meeting of the members in the November. Jack Boyle and some stewards argued against this, that the time would not be right until after Christmas. But the stewards' committee voted to call a meeting that Saturday and recommend a stoppage. It was a highly charged atmosphere because it was such an integral part of the site and had been for many years. A lot of stewards were really angry and felt we had to stand up and fight. But the membership overturned us. All we could do was go back to the company with our tail between our legs and negotiate the closure.

Almost inevitably the 'don't rock the boat' policy had begun to catch up with the stewards' committee; having previously stamped on shop-floor militancy their hesitant and divided stance over mounting opposition to the closure merely served to feed the doubts and lack of confidence felt by many of their members. The closure of the butchery and chicken-stripping departments left only the Unit 2 area of the plant functioning. Although there were no compulsory redundancies involved there was a steady decline in the numbers employed in the plant between 1985 and 1989, with the loss of about 270 jobs. This was achieved through voluntary redundancy, natural wastage and redeployment.

Meanwhile, during 1985 Birds Eye corporate management had embarked on a long-term plan – termed 'Workstyle' – aimed at introducing radical new working practices into its plants across the country. This provoked a strike at Gloucester which subsequently spread to Kirkby. Initially, the Kirkby stewards' negotiating committee resisted Workstyle because of the perceived threat it posed to working conditions and job security. But by 1987 they approached management and asked to have Workstyle implemented, partly because, with its £7.50 weekly supplement, workers at the Gloucester and Lowestoft plants were earning more money than at Kirkby, and partly because the extensive new investment made at the two plants to accompany Workstyle was desperately sought in Kirkby as a demonstration of the company's long-term commitment to the plant. Yet as Ritchie acknowledged, some of the stewards had somewhat myopic expectations:

What the factory general manager did at first was pull the wool over our eyes. He told us the introduction of Workstyle would not lead to redundancies. It would be phased in and a continuation of the levels of natural wastage we had over the last five years would take care of the reduction of labour. Its introduction would be subject to agreement from a monitoring group set up in the factory with the negotiating committee being represented. So we thought, 'OK, we'll accept that.' We'll go in and negotiate what for us was a lifeline to better pay and conditions. And a number of stewards including myself went and visited the other factories to see Workstyle in operation.

In fact, it soon became patently obvious there would be no real consultation or negotiation over Workstyle whatsoever.

At the end of 1987 a new personnel manager and factory general manager were drafted into Kirkby and immediately confronted the stewards with draconian terms for the introduction of Workstyle. As Ritchie explained:

We knew Workstyle would mean losing jobs, we thought we would lose about 60 people. But the company's view was that we'd lose 380 jobs, a third of the workforce. That was unpalatable to us. My department in the three-shift area was going to be ravaged. Where we had 29 to a shift we would have 11. We argued the department couldn't work on that, the whole thing was a farce. The reaction from the stewards' body was: 'There's no way you're going to get away with it.'

Whilst the stewards were prepared, in principle, to accept some redundancies, the financial terms offered by Birds Eye were rejected, and whilst they were prepared, in principle, to accept radical new working practices, the company's insistence on imposing them with no negotiation was also unacceptable. But the real sticking point for the stewards was the company's refusal to give a firm commitment to future investment in the Kirkby plant to secure its long-term future. The stewards' resistance took the form of boycotting all formal negotiations with plant-level management with an insistence on a company investment plan as a precondition of its introduction. At the end of 1988 a ballot of the workforce overwhelmingly backed the stewards' stance.

However, in March 1989 Birds Eye announced that the plant would be shut down with the loss of almost 1000 jobs, blaming the decision on the workforce's failure to agree to changes in working practices, to increased productivity and to acceptance of 380 redundancies. It seems more likely that the real reason for closure was the cut-throat battle with competitors that challenged Birds Eye's former supremacy within the frozen food industry. During the preceding ten years the company had seen the loss of a third of its market share and was obviously determined to cut costs to protect profits, if necessary by making workers pay the cost. Birds Eye had already cut 5000 production jobs in other plants in pursuit of 'maximum efficiency' over the previous few years, and the Kirkby plant became merely the latest casualty. At the same time, in the run-up to the removal of trade barriers in 1992, Unilever, Birds Eye's parent company, was anxious to undertake a massive reorganization and rationalization of its entire food operations across Europe. The need to integrate its European food business meant reducing costs even further, with production confined to a limited number of strategically positioned factories located nearer to the centre of the European market (*Financial Times*, 18 April 1989). The result was investment of £30 million in its Grimsby factory – where the company ultimately planned to transfer Kirkby's production.

It seems reasonable to assume a company like Unilever makes tactical decisions on a weekly basis, such as whether to raise or lower output and how to deal with strikes, whereas strategic decisions, such as which products to make, where the main production units will be sited and how these plants are to be integrated, are usually decided years in advance. Thus, it would seem that Birds Eye, operating under the direction of Unilever, had no intention of introducing Workstyle into the Kirkby plant, given that its closure was imminent. This explains why management, after stewards had themselves requested Workstyle, presented them with conditions which they knew would prove unacceptable. Birds Eye was then able to use their rejection as the pretext for the closure decision. No doubt the two new adversarial plant managers appointed to the Kirkby plant in 1987 were placed there with the preconceived purpose of over-seeing the closure.

Between the announcement in March and the plant's anticipated closure in September the shop stewards' committee launched a public campaign aimed at trying to convince the company to reverse its decision. They launched a community-based Birds Eye Support Group, which held weekly meetings of up to 40 supporters and organized visits to other Birds Eye plants to win blacking of the MenuMaster range of products. A 3000-

strong solidarity demonstration was held in Kirkby, with delegations from the Gloucester, Lowestoft and Hull factories (Birds Eye Support Group minutes, 9 May 1989). But in many respects the stewards' strategy of resistance to the closure was fatally compromised.

To begin with, the stewards' approach was undermined by the 'moderate' ideological stance around which they chose to base their campaign. Concerned above all to play down exaggerated national media reports of the plant's industrial militancy being the key factor behind the closure, the stewards' public campaign literature carried the following 'balance sheet':

> COMPANY CLAIM: That the Kirkby workforce has continually resisted Workstyle, unlike all other factories.
>
> FACT: It was the unions at Kirkby that asked for discussions on Workstyle two years ago and the principles have been accepted.
>
> COMPANY CLAIM: That the Kirkby workforce is not prepared to accept job losses.
>
> FACT: The union has accepted natural wastage in which over 200 jobs have been lost in recent years and have accepted the need for 380 redundancies. All the union asked for was realistic negotiated redundancy payments.
>
> COMPANY CLAIM: That 'union bolshieness' has done enormous damage to the local economy. The Kirkby plant said 'No' to change and is to pay the inevitable penalty.
>
> FACT: The Kirkby Birds Eye factory is a moderate reasonable workforce. In fact the last major strike took place 11 years ago (Birds Eye Support Group/TGWU leaflet, May 1989).

The problem with this 'we are very responsible' approach was that underlying it was a rather misplaced hope that Birds Eye might be pressurized to change its mind through sheer force of logical and reasoned argument. Also, trying to marry a policy of opposition to the closure with such a defensive strategy inevitably became shipwrecked on its own internal contradictions. For example, accepting in principle that there would have to be a number of redundancies considerably undermined the stewards' assertion that the workforce was 'efficient' and the plant 'viable' and should be kept open. If the factory was 'overmanned' where should the line be drawn as to the number of jobs to be lost: the 380 originally sought, all those wanting voluntary redundancy, or the entire workforce, as the company demanded?

Following a warning from the TGWU district full-time official Kevin Dobson, against what he called 'stunts which would provoke management', the stewards' committee chose not to call for a plant-wide all-out strike or an occupation immediately the closure decision was announced, Ray related:

> There was a stewards' meeting held on the Friday afternoon. What we considered was what line we should take with our members at a mass meeting the following day. Obviously there was a lot of panic, some people were dumbstruck. It was decided to get a commitment from the members to oppose the closure in every way, shape or form. But it was felt at the time by both the convenor and Kevin Dobson that we weren't in a strong enough position to call a strike. The idea was considered and rejected.

Steve, the deputy convenor, justified the decision not to call an immediate strike:

> We knew the company had stockpiled beforehand and could keep going for four to six weeks even if we had gone on strike. In fact, they had anticipated that we *would* go on strike and couldn't believe it when we didn't. So the stewards decided we would continue working and wait for the stocks to go down . . . And we wanted to show the rest of the Birds Eye factories that we weren't wildcats, that we went through procedure.

Yet despite the stockpiling it is likely such action at Kirkby would have had a cumulative impact on the company that would have hit it hard financially; production at the other frozen food plants was particularly vulnerable to stoppages, as it was the height of the green season. Such action could have been a most effective way of harnessing the latent anger of many union members and mobilizing them for the task of appealing for solidarity action at the other three Birds Eye plants across the country. The divisions within the stewards' committee on whether to call for strike action are vividly illustrated by Ray's comments:

> I felt if a strong recommendation to take strike action had been given from day one the outcome could have been different. I always argued

that there was only one way to save the factory – that was to have a go
ourselves. If that lead had been given it might have changed things. We
would have been in a position where we could have made sure nothing
moved out of the site and we could have gone round the other sites. But
the policy of the stewards' committee was to take the fight so far and
not take it over the hill. What was said at the time was that our
members' redundancy pay was at stake . . . The formation of links
between the stewards' committee and the community was perfectly
correct. But I think we let a lot of people down in the way the fight was
actually waged. At the end of the day there was no real will to save the
factory.

Whether such strike action could have succeeded in reversing Birds Eye's
closure decision is, of course, debatable, since it was likely to have involved
a bitter, hard-fought battle with the company. Nonetheless, it would seem
that the stewards' initial response of not recommending any form of
industrial action quickly had the effect of dissipating the mood of
resistance, which was initially quite widespread on the shop-floor, and
reinforcing the passivity of those who tended to view the closure as
inevitable.

Another problem was the way the stewards' committee, again following
the advice of the local TGWU full-time official, relied on support from the
other Birds Eye plants to win the fight for them. After it became apparent
that 'responsible' appeals to Birds Eye to withdraw the closure decision
were falling on deaf ears, the stewards eventually began to threaten all-out
strike action. But in practice they were not prepared to take such action
without simultaneous strikes occurring at the other Birds Eye plants.
Finally, three months after the closure announcement had been made and
only after official TGWU approval had been granted, a jointly organized
strike ballot was held in all three plants. Kirkby voted six to one for strike
action – although the apparent high vote concealed the fact that many
workers who wanted to take voluntary redundancy agreed to vote in
favour of a strike in exchange for the stewards' agreement to open up
negotiations with management over improved severance terms. The
Gloucester and Lowestoft plants voted against strike action, by majorities
of 200 and 30 respectively. From that moment on the campaign against
the closure of the Kirkby factory was formally abandoned.

Of course, there was a logic to the stewards' strategy. They were
acutely aware that unless solidarity action was taken at the other Birds

Eye plants it was unlikely that an isolated all-out strike in Kirkby would force management's hand over the closure decision. They feared jeopardizing workers' redundancy payments in a doomed adventurist set-piece battle. But the question arises: unless Kirkby had taken the initiative in organizing strike action themselves, how realistic was it to expect the other plants to act on their behalf? As Terry commented:

> My reaction as an individual was that I was prepared to have a go. If we couldn't stand up and defend ourselves no one was going to come along to defend us. So I felt the cart was put before the horse to a certain extent. 'Let's have the ballot first, and then we'll all walk at the same time' – that was utopian. We should have gone on strike and then gone to the other plants for their support. We would have been in a much stronger position to make an appeal if we had done it that way round.

No doubt it was Kirkby's excellent past record of solidarity for other Birds Eye workers which raised false expectations amongst the stewards that they could rely on support from the other plants, as if the Fifth Cavalry would come charging to their defence. Thus, at the end of the day, the factory was closed without any effective form of action whatsoever being taken against the company.

Stewards' Relationship to Members: The 1970s/1980s

The 1970s: Forging the Links

During the 1960s, plant-level negotiations with management were conducted virtually exclusively by the convenor, with shop stewards playing a subordinate role. Only the establishment of a negotiating committee, shortly after Martin Roberts's election, ensured there was a more collectivist leadership style during the 1970s. Even so, the convenor's position remained central in the plant. This was partly because although the senior stewards were involved in important bargaining issues affecting the plant, it was left to the convenor to conduct most day-to-day negotiations with management; as the only steward on 100 per cent time off work the convenor was regularly called upon by stewards to deal with shop-floor grievances. In addition, Martin Roberts himself was a charismatic and influential figure. His socialist politics and militant style of leadership ensured a distinctive set of workplace union relations.

Despite his authoritative position within the factory, he appears to have lacked the ability or the will to concentrate power systematically into his hands, and his dramatic resignation from the convenor's position in late 1975 was an illustration of the severe constraints he felt imposed on him by the stewards' committee in general and the negotiating committee in particular. Nonetheless, Martin Roberts occupied a central position within the plant during the 1970s and in order to illuminate some of the dilemmas involved in the relationship between the stewards' body as a whole and their members it is particularly interesting to focus attention, initially at least, on the role played by the convenor.

Perhaps one of the most intriguing aspects of the relationship between Martin Roberts and shop-floor union members was his attitude towards stoppages of work. On the one hand, he was favourably disposed towards calling for *plant-wide* strike action on a number of occasions, for example over the 'guaranteed working week', annual wage negotiations, bonus payments and fixed-term contracts. Usually, it was the anger of rank-and-file members at management's heavy-handed approach that helped create the conditions for such action. But sometimes it was Martin Roberts who took the initiative in recommending a stoppage, on a number of occasions winning overwhelming backing for his appeals. The dramatic solidarity shown for the engineers' strike in 1978, which subsequently led to management's lock-out, highlighted in sharp relief the significance of Martin Roberts's socialist and militant commitment to 'trade union principles'. Ray related how the convenor's intervention was critical in galvanizing support for the engineers:

> The company thought there would be little sympathy amongst TGWU members when the engineers walked out. We immediately called a stewards' meeting to discuss what we were going to do about the threat of lay-offs. We met in the training hut – which was right by the main gate. It had big windows in it and people walking past could see the stewards inside. Some of our members started shouting, 'We're not going out on strike.' So we were under a little bit of pressure from some of our members because they didn't want to become embroiled in another dispute having just been out on the tiles themselves. And some stewards said we shouldn't bother supporting the engineers, as they'd walked past our picket lines when we were out. The meeting went on for about four hours. But at the end of the day it was Martin Roberts's very persuasive arguments about the branch's policy of not crossing picket lines that won

the day. So what we told the company was that although we would not withdraw our labour in support of the engineers, if they mounted a picket on the gates then no T and G member would cross it.

This was an extremely difficult decision to take. There was not the time available for the stewards to organize a mass meeting to put the arguments and convince the members through open debate. Instead, having agreed to adopt a principled stand, they joined the engineers' picket line the following morning so as to turn their members away. Martin Roberts's authority amongst the mass of union members was indisputably a critical factor in winning their initial support and then retaining it throughout the 18-week lock-out.

On the other hand, although he was often very sympathetic to members and stewards involved in *departmental* disputes he also sought to develop rules governing the rights and duties of shop stewards and their sections, particularly where sectional activity threatened the bargaining cohesiveness of plant-wide union organization. The real dilemma arose whenever sectional strikes threatened lay-offs across the whole plant, creating tensions between sectional concerns and the unity of the whole workforce. The difficulties facing convenors and stewards can be discerned by considering two incidents that occurred at different periods of time. Firstly, according to shop steward committee minutes for 1977, there was a stoppage of work by 'knock-out' men in the freeze-and-case department over demands for an increase in job rate, which took place against the advice of their shop steward. The minutes report:

[Martin Roberts] felt the men had a reasonable claim . . . He had invited them to meet with the shop stewards' committee to resolve the issue. The men complained they had repeatedly approached their steward for action of some description but none had been forthcoming so they had decided to act by themselves. The men agreed to return to work after the stewards' committee agreed to look into their grievance and report back in a few days' time. [Martin Roberts] warned the stewards about unauthorized stoppages of work and the repercussions it could bring . . . He said it appeared the freeze-and-case workers lacked faith in their steward and stewards should report back to members as much as possible thereby giving satisfaction that their problem was being looked into. They should encourage members to bring their problems to light to light to discourage wildcat action and they should have the confidence of their members, otherwise the stewards' ability to negotiate was impaired (Stewards' committee minutes, 4 February 1977).

On this occasion not only was Martin Roberts highly sensitive to workers' sectional grievances but he was also acutely aware of the need for the close accountability of shop stewards to their rank-and-file members. He managed to overcome the danger of lay-offs by promising to get the issue resolved in favour of the minority on strike whilst convincing them to call off their action. In many respects the incident provides a vivid example of how Martin Roberts, as the convenor of the plant, had to balance the immediate day-to-day grievances of union members with the desire to provide a long-term strategy to protect the interests of the majority of workers across the plant. It is clear that his main preoccupation throughout was to find a solution that not only was satisfactory to most concerned, but also would lead to a strengthening of workplace union organization at management's expense.

This freeze-and-case department dispute stands in stark contrast with the attitude adopted by Martin Roberts towards workers' militancy in the cold store department at an earlier period in 1972. Shop steward minute books reveal that during one dispute:

[Martin Roberts] acknowledged cold store departmental managers were being deliberately provocative but warned that walk-outs threatened lay-offs and advised the shop stewards' committee to dissociate themselves from the action. (Branch minutes, 26 March 1972)

Ironically, when Birds Eye set up an inquiry into the cold store department it was with Martin Roberts's willing approval and participation, despite the vigorous protests from the stewards on the section. Why did Martin Roberts take this negative attitude towards sectional militancy in the cold store? Ray offered an explanation:

I think Martin recognized that the cold store lads took things a bit further than they ought to on some occasions. So much so that when Martin said to them: 'Let's try and negotiate our way out of this one rather than just walk out' – even *he* had a job to convince them. There was always a built-in animosity towards that. There was always a gulf between the cold store and the rest of the factory and to a certain extent there was an élitist element amongst some of the cold store workers who didn't

think about factory organization. They only thought about their own
parochial aims and once the cold store stopped everything else
shuddered to a halt with people losing their bonus and screaming, 'It's
those bolshie bastards in the cold store again.' Martin felt it wasn't good
for the future of the factory to have a massive operation disrupting the
factory practically on a weekly basis.

Yet paradoxically it was the strength of the cold store department that
helped to give the stewards' committee in the plant its overall authority
vis-à-vis management.

Indeed, arguably sectional strength is the bedrock of any strong
stewards' organization and its success depends upon stewards in each
section of a workplace building union organization through successfully
taking up immediate issues and involving the members. This is precisely
what appears to have occurred in the cold store department, where
workers' strategic relationship to production greatly assisted their negotiating power. Of course, although sectional strength is vital, *sectionalism*,
simply being concerned with sectional pay and conditions and ignoring
everybody else, is a recipe for disaster. Again, this tendency towards
parochialism appears to have been evident in the cold store department.
Material conditions, in the form of a division of labour, reinforced such
sectional divisions and was reflected in the problematic nature of aspects
of workers' self-activity. But the network of social relations that existed
also provided the basis for a more collectivist response.

One important way of attempting to deal with the problem would
have been for Martin Roberts and other stewards, including those in the
cold store department, to have made a conscious effort to encourage a
generalization of the self-confidence and organizational strength of the
cold store workers across the rest of the factory. That would have meant
arguing with the cold store workers to take a lead not just on the immediate
issues affecting them in their own department but on the wider issues
confronting the whole workforce as well. If this had been done it is possible
the cold store shop stewards could have set the benchmark for those less
confident and less well organized in a way that strengthened the power of
the stewards' organization generally.

Certainly, such an approach would have been difficult and by no means
straightforward. The argument for militant action across the plant was
something Martin Roberts already sometimes had difficulties in convincing the senior stewards to support. But at least such an approach

would have had the merit of attempting to accentuate the *positive* and overcome the *negative*; strengthening the level of shop stewards' organization in the factory at management's expense. The alternative stance adopted by Martin Roberts (and the senior stewards) proved to be self-defeating. Agreeing to participate in the company's inquiry into the cold store conceded that the problem lay with the level of shop-floor militancy and workers' organization rather than with the nature of work itself and management's intransigence. The break-up of the best-organized section in the factory only served to weaken the stewards' organization overall. It may have also served to encourage the senior stewards' reluctance to back Martin Roberts's subsequent calls for action, which in turn eventually led to his first resignation as convenor.

Martin Roberts's contrasting attitude to the problem of sectional disputes in these two examples, in 1977 and 1972, had their origins in a multitude of factors, including the differences in the regularity of disputes in the two departments (much more frequent in the cold store than in the freeze-and-case department) and changes in Martin Roberts's own authority within the stewards' committee (much weaker in the early 1970s compared with the period after his re-election in 1977). Yet there also appears to have been an underlying equivocation in his approach towards sectional disputes, influenced by his Labour left politics; whilst he saw an important role for workers' struggles from below it was essentially only as an adjunct to his negotiating abilities as a convenor from above, as well as his relations with the stewards' committee.

The relationship between the shop stewards and their members was also marked by a number of interesting features. Although there was significant variation between departments, there appears to have been a relatively democratic and accountable relationship between the stewards and their members during the 1970s, at least until after the lock-out in 1978. At the heart of this dynamic interaction was the way in which shop-floor workers and their stewards were able to develop a relatively confident view of their collective struggles as well as a willingness to engage in collective action in pursuit of their concerns. Stewards negotiated over job evaluation, bonus payments and condition rates, which helped them build up the strength of their section and enhance their prestige in the eyes of their constituents. As well as responding to disputes within their own departments, the stewards' committee took the initiative in recommending plant-wide strike action on nine separate occasions during the 1970s, each time receiving the overwhelming backing of the members.

Holding together the union organization throughout the period of the 1977–78 lock-out and maintaining the support of the members was a testimony to the leadership abilities not only of the convenor but of the stewards' body in the plant as a whole. Peter related:

> We had mass meetings with our members every fortnight during the lock-out. There was good contact there and it was part of the reason why we kept together for so long. Some of the T and G stewards even used to go to the engineers' mass meetings and boost their morale by speaking in support of the dispute.

Throughout the 1970s every steward continued to work on the job and therefore maintained day-to-day contact with their constituents. As compared with the 1960s, management allowed the stewards more leeway in taking time off work to deal with their members' grievances, although it often depended on the type of job a steward was engaged on and the availability of reliefs. Whilst the senior stewards on the negotiating committee had much greater facility time available to them, particularly for meetings with management, they did not appear to take much time away from their shop-floor job.

Formally, stewards were elected every two years in each department; the minute books for the 1970s reveal that although a small core of about 10–12 stewards remained in office for a number of years there was a consistent turnover of the other 15–20 steward positions. Lack of a detailed breakdown makes it difficult to assess how much variation there was between departments, although one of the cold store stewards remained in office for over 15 years. Ray remembered there was a clear difference between the 1970s and the 1980s:

> We had more stewards' positions contested in the '70s than we had in the '80s. And more positions were contested in the middle '70s compared with the late '70s. We used to sometimes have two or three candidates for one job. That's because with the factory booming there was a lot more people in the place. So it was quite a healthy situation.

Nonetheless, there is little doubt that the contesting of stewards' positions at election time was a regular feature, an indication of the general interest in union affairs. There was not a strong tradition of sectional or departmental meetings in the factory; such meetings were only organized by stewards on specific occasions, such as a walk-out of the members. Equally, mass meetings on site were far from common.

The main formal channel of democratic accountability between shop stewards and rank-and-file members was the TGWU branch meeting, held monthly on a Sunday morning, to which the convenor gave a report back on failures to agree, national pay negotiations, and so on. But in the early 1970s the branch was in a pretty moribund state. It was only after an influx of some younger and more political stewards that it turned into a more lively forum for debate and argument about both industrial and political issues, as Ray explained:

> When I started in the factory there was no politics discussed at all in the branch. Only about 20–30 people went to meetings. But by 1974–75 time some of the older stewards started to drift away and relatively new stewards, like myself, came in. With Martin Roberts, we gradually introduced an element of politics into the branch. For example, we supported the Right to Work Campaign, the Anti-Nazi League and that. And those were the days when there were two or three trade union conferences going on every month and we always tried to send delegates to them. The branch started to play a much higher political profile.

Guest speakers were periodically invited to address the branch meetings; there was the adoption of some basic trade union principles, such as respect for picket lines; and solidarity donations were given to workers in struggle, such as local strikers at Plessey, Roneo Vickers and Ford Halewood (Branch minutes, 20 March 1977, 24 February 1979; Stewards' committee minutes, 10 November 1978). General resolutions adopted by the branch included opposition to the late 1970s Corrie anti-abortion bill and the Official Secrets Act (Branch minutes, 11 November 1979; 14 May 1978).

According to Harry, who worked as a fitter's mate in the engineering department at Birds Eye for 33 years and was a member of the TGWU branch committee throughout the 1970s and 1980s, by 1977 there were between 50 and 60 members regularly attending branch meetings, with up to 200 if there was a dispute in the factory. Quite a few women became actively involved in the branch, including women shop stewards. Branch minute books also reveal that the number of stewards active increased from an average of nine in 1973 to 15 in 1977 (Branch minutes,

30 September 1973, 8 May 1977). Yet whilst the transformation of the TGWU branch helped to involve more shop stewards and members in union affairs and allowed for some political debate, there was a tendency for the left-wing activists, who provided much of its initiative and driving force, to overemphasize the branch's importance compared with union organization on the shop-floor inside the factory. As a result, the branch on occasion adopted some rather bureaucratic decisions, for example decreeing that stewards absent from two consecutive union branch meetings had to forfeit their steward's card. In addition, there was little attempt made to try to connect the political and socialist arguments that were held within the branch with the day-to-day interests and concerns of shop-floor union members back inside the factory.

A noticeable feature was the generally low involvement of women in union activities compared with men in the factory. Of course, there were specific reasons for this disparity. Unmarried women traditionally did not expect to be working in the job for more than a few years, and therefore did not normally show a great deal of interest in union activities. The older married women, who returned to work as their children reached school age, were often impeded from playing a central organizing role in the workplace because the continued responsibility for childcare forced many of them into part-time work, which limited their ability to go to union branch meetings.

Nonetheless, it appears that women workers at Birds Eye came to the fore when the workforce as a whole was moving forward in struggle. During the 1970s it seems their double oppression, as women and workers, acted as a spur driving a number of women to quite high levels of activism and commitment. Union records reveal that in 1968 the deputy convenor was a woman (Branch minutes, 25 August 1968). When the negotiating committee was set up in 1971 one of its five members was a woman (Branch minutes, 10 October 1971). In 1972 the shop stewards' committee had 30 members of whom 14 were women (Company list of stewards, April 1972). But when the workforce as a whole was in retreat in the period following the lock-out it appears to have had the reverse effect, of being a fetter which prevented them playing a full and effective role in sustaining the union organization. Marion compared the period of the early 1970s with the period after the lock-out:

> I can remember a time when the chicken-stripping department and the freeze-and-case department had some good, strong women stewards

who wouldn't take any hassle from the company. They'd stand up and be counted . . . The factory was larger in the '70s and the ratio of women stewards was higher. But for a number of reasons we lost our good women stewards: some retired, others stayed on but their departments closed down and they didn't become stewards in the new departments they were transferred to . . . Obviously the lock-out and redundancies cut the workforce and after that there were fewer women prepared to come forward as stewards.

Union records reveal that by 1978 there were only five women shop stewards out of about 30 (Stewards' committee minutes, 16 June 1978) ; by 1979 there were only two women on a branch committee of about 15 (Branch committee minutes, 6 September 1979) and none on the negotiating committee of five senior stewards (Stewards' committee minutes, 29 October 1979).

The sexual division of labour in the factory and the male dominance of the stewards' committee impeded the relationship between stewards and members. Nonetheless, the stewards' committee was prepared to take up issues directly affecting women workers, such as a day nursery (Branch minutes, 23 December 1969), equal pay (Branch minutes, 27 September 1970) and maternity leave (Branch minutes, 1 December 1974), as well as such general issues affecting women as bonus payments on the 'racque' pie line. Moreover, the active involvement of some women in union affairs and the participation of most women in the relatively high level of disputes in the factory helped ensure that the divisions did not become an insurmountable handicap, although the lock-out clearly arrested the process.

Arguably, a key limitation of the shop stewards' organization in the Birds Eye plant during the 1970s, although not sharply exposed at the time, was the lack of an organized and coherent alternative to the politics of 'Labourism' within its ranks. Of course, Martin Roberts and the handful of younger shop stewards not only were industrial militants but also held political ideas which were to varying degrees distinct from and more radical than those of traditional Labourism. Martin Roberts was a left-wing member of the Labour Party, whilst the others had a basic socialist, class commitment without any fixed political affiliation, although one or two (including Ray and Terry) had been influenced by revolutionary socialist organizations in the past. Paradoxically, although these individual trade union activists raised political issues, it was usually in the abstract or outside the workplace in the union branch. There was a separation between their political ideas and their industrial/union practice on the shop-floor. They took this attitude because they believed that overtly political issues went beyond the shop steward committee's bounds inside the factory and that they should limit themselves to issues of wages and conditions which could unite all workers.

If one term had to be used to describe the politics of these stewards and union activists it would be 'syndicalist', except that this implies they had arrived at a finished ideological position, which was far from being the case. But they combined a form of quasi-syndicalism with a sharp division between economics and politics, concentrating exclusively on industrial struggle to the detriment of political organization. This did not prevent them from offering a lead to shop-floor struggles and building up the strength of union organization in the plant during the 1970s. On the contrary, it was often their initiative that pulled the other, less militant stewards into action. Nonetheless, the lack of a wider layer of left militants who attempted to link broad socialist arguments with a practical day-to-day shop-floor strategy within the plant meant they found it increasingly difficult to challenge the policy of co-operation with management that was adopted by the stewards' body during the recession years of the 1980s.

The 1980s: Loosening of the Links

Overall there was a very different relationship between shop stewards and members in the Birds Eye plant during the 1980s as compared with the 1970s, with the pendulum swinging towards a relatively much more bureaucratic linkage. Firstly, there was the role of the new convenor. Jack Boyle's 'strong bargaining relationship' with management resulted in a concentration of decision making in the convenor's hands and ultimately served to weaken the close interaction previously established with shop-floor members. Terry recalled:

> Martin Roberts very regularly walked round the factory, visited each department and had a talk with people on the shop-floor to see if there were any problems. Jack Boyle tended to stick very closely to the union office . . . Martin was more prepared to back disputes that started. Whereas one of the things that Jack Boyle was most proud of as convenor was that there'd never been a major stoppage during his tenure of office. That is not a boast you'd have heard Martin Roberts making.

Carole described the perception of the new convenor held by many union members:

> Jack was like a ghost. You knew he was there, you knew his name, but you hardly ever saw him. He'd be stuck in the union office for days unless the stewards went looking for him. But the ordinary member didn't have that access to him.

The approach by the convenor was complemented by an increasing passivity by the negotiating committee, effectively rubber-stamping decisions taken by the convenor and his deputy. Only in the mid-1980s did sections of the stewards' committee become so unhappy with their behaviour that they felt compelled to make a rather belated and tentative move towards exercising some control over the co-operative relationship with management that had been systematically cultivated. Ritchie related what happened:

> There was pressure in 1986 from some stewards, including myself, about the role of the negotiating committee. It was felt that the Jack–Steve partnership had to be broken up. There was a feeling that it was an unhealthy alliance because they were so alike, they thought and spoke alike. It was felt there had to be a change and new blood injected so that Jack Boyle would have a deputy who was prepared to criticize him and push him further, to make him stronger. Shop stewards were going to Jack Boyle and felt they weren't getting the full representation . . . It wasn't a left–right challenge, it was aimed at breaking up the complacency, a mutual appreciation society.

With three new senior stewards elected, including Ritchie himself, the negotiating committee's composition altered substantially. This meant that in future whenever management wanted to introduce a change of any significance, the full negotiating committee became involved. However, the approach by the convenor and deputy convenor remained intact and there was no serious change to the policy of co-operation with management, until the company's insistence on introducing 'Workstyle' at the beginning of 1988 finally led to the suspension of plant-level negotiations.

Throughout the 1980s, Jack Boyle consistently and systematically enforced procedural mechanisms against those departments, like the three-shift area, that wanted to take action, by using the weekly stewards' committee meetings to insist on sectional stewards' obligations to the wider interests of plant-wide union organization. Steve justified the convenors approach thus:

> Martin Roberts would let people run and lose money. Jack tried to do it differently. He would always say: 'Don't walk out, give me the opportunity to negotiate. I'll do the talking.' Under Martin the cold store was the powerhouse of the factory but with Jack Boyle it was the three-shift area. Sometimes Jack had a terrible time with the stewards. He didn't want any wildcats. He always wanted things to go through procedure, he would play things through the book.

Of course, underpinning Jack Boyle's hostile attitude towards departmental stoppages was the general lack of shop-floor confidence to engage in militant struggle in most of the less well organized departments. A substantial section of the workforce backed his co-operative stance. But this 'keep your head down' mood of much of the workforce was by no means an automatic or static phenomenon; on occasions it could be transformed depending upon whether workers were *themselves* directly at the receiving end of management attacks.

On a number of occasions the anger and willingness of some sections of workers to fight was dissipated by the convenors active intervention. Ray related an example of a dispute in the two-shift area of Unit 2:

> I was on the negotiating committee myself when we had a number of disputes. OK, sometimes you'd say: 'I'll control the situation.' Other times you'd say: 'No, I'm not going to control it even if I could. I'm going to let people go home.' Usually I'd stay behind to inform Jack of what had happened. We had some right ding-dongs in the office. He'd say to me: 'What did you let them walk out for?' I remember once when the whole of the 2–10 shift walked out. It was mainly a women's dispute, led by the women themselves. Jack Boyle wasn't around and I was rung up at home by the boss. He told me the steward was in a state of panic because the women had walked off the lines and he couldn't get them back to work even though he'd made an agreement. So I went in to get them back to work. Carole was one of them. I promised them faithfully the matter would be dealt with by the convenor the next day. The next day Jack had a meeting with the women in the snack bar and

said: 'All right, I'll go and see the boss tomorrow.' One of the women shouted out: 'Why can't you go this afternoon?' And he said: 'I've got another meeting this afternoon.' Well, the women always looked at that episode as the union cocking a snook at them. I don't think the issue ever got dealt with actually. And I felt I'd let the women down.

In other words, such co-operation with management backfired on the stewards' body at times, as workers lost confidence in their ability to obtain substantive shop-floor improvements: As Peter explained:

By and large, the rest of the stewards' committee went along with Jack Boyle's philosophy. To my way of thinking they had the mistaken idea that every problem could be solved by negotiation. But a lot of the bargaining we did with the company we came out with the wrong end of it. A lot of people lost faith in the shop stewards' committee because of that.

The 'don't rock the boat' philosophy was successfully implemented for a combination of reasons. Amidst the generally hostile economic and political environment it appeared to be the only realistic option and most workers and stewards were resigned to it most of the time; disputes tended not to blow up across the plant but were isolated pockets of resistance. The limited, but real, concessions granted by management appeared to vindicate the co-operative policy and the few militant left-wing stewards in the three-shift area were marginalized and failed to provide a coherent political challenge to the prevailing orthodoxy. Yet the convenor's and senior stewards' hostile attitude towards departmental stoppages and their 'pragmatic' bargaining relationship with management helped in the long term to loosen the close links that had been forged between stewards and rank-and-file members in the 1970s.

Throughout the 1980s, all shop stewards, apart from the convenor, worked on the job. Freedom of access to members was rather more restricted for stewards who worked on the assembly lines in Unit 2, where the nature of the production system and the tight discipline imposed by management meant stewards were unable to take time off work unless they could get somebody to cover for them, compared with the three-shift area, a 'free working' environment. The pressure on stewards varied from department to department. Peter recalled:

> The most active stewards were in the three-shift area. That was a male-dominated area where there were a number of stoppages and a steward had to get his finger out and get cracking, so they were more active in that sense. They had regular contact with the members and they kept them informed of developments.

Significantly, the tenure of office of stewards was much longer in the 1980s than in the 1970s, with a majority of stewards remaining in office for over 10 years. Peter reported:

> Compared with the '70s there was less change-over and less contesting of positions because the automation at Birds Eye, the anti-union legislation and that in the early '80s meant a lot of stewards were reluctant to get involved, because it was a bloody headache. In the '70s you used to have two or three people contesting for the stewards' position. People felt more positive about being able to get somewhere. But in the '80s although there was a lot of disgruntlement no one wanted the steward's job. Instead, there was apathy. In fact, at one time we had to force a competition by introducing a policy into the branch whereby no steward automatically stood for re-election, because some of the stewards thought they were in a sacrosanct position, they'd been in that long.

Carole recalled the problem with the women shop stewards in the two-shift area of Unit 2:

> The women stewards on my shift were all terribly weak, they really were. They tended to see management's point of view more than male shop stewards' and take management's side in a dispute, even with regards to the women. [One steward] was mouth almighty but she was a creep. She put the talk on when the boss was around, it was so obvious. [Another steward] did try to take the bull by the horns a bit and give a little bit of leadership. But she didn't stick out the steward's job long. None of them were shop stewards for long: 12 months to three years at the most.

In other words, if there was a lengthy tenure of office amongst male stewards the opposite problem arose amongst the female stewards.

Despite the efforts of one of the left-wing militants in the plant, it proved very difficult to get women to stand and only about five out of the 30 stewards' committee positions were held by women at any one time during the 1980s. Ray explained:

> There were a few women who when you spoke to them seemed genuinely interested in changing things and fighting the status quo. But you couldn't cajole them to coming forward at the right time, they wouldn't take it as far as getting a steward's card. That was a problem we had all during the '80s . . . The women stewards were very passive at the stewards' committee, they very rarely got involved in the discussions and debates that went on – compared with the '70s when women were leading some of the debates. Basically, there was a lack of commitment from the women stewards. Even if you talk about issues you would expect women shop stewards and trade unionists to raise themselves – cancer screening, things of that nature – they were never raised by the women, they were raised by the men, the likes of myself, who saw it as an important element of collective bargaining. But we found it very hard to motivate our women stewards to go on courses even and the attendance of women at branch meetings, even the female stewards, was pretty poor.

Carole explained her own unwillingness to become a steward:

> I played a role on the shop-floor with my mouth. I would be one of the first to stand up and say: 'That's not right – something should be done about it' and oppose an injustice. But I didn't want to be a steward. It's difficult for a woman. That's because while you're doing the job you're thinking: 'What have I got in for tea tonight, who's picking the kids up after school, is it dry weather – can I put my washing out, blah, blah, blah. Men don't think of anything like that, but *women* do. They've constantly got things on their mind. I didn't take the shop steward's job because one in the family was enough, it was too much hassle.'

But the shop stewards' organization was handicapped by the lack of active participation of women during the 1980s. It meant that women workers' specific and immediate work-related grievances often remained at the level of individual and group discontent rather than being channelled into structures of plant-wide collective union representation. It also meant that the degree of satisfaction felt towards the stewards' committee from a large proportion of the workforce was rather less than it might have been.

Meanwhile, the role of the TGWU branch in shop-floor union organization also became less significant during the 1980s. Although resolutions were regularly passed at branch meetings in support of workers' disputes, including Massey-Ferguson in 1980, Liverpool council typists in 1981, the miners in 1984 and Moat House Hotel in 1987 (Branch minutes, 9 March 1980; 14 June 1981; 10 June 1984; 14 June 1987), the number of stewards and members (including women members) attending declined. As Harry, a branch committee member for over 20 years, recalled:

> The branch only got about 15 people to meetings in the 1980s. About half of them were shop stewards. But it was much less important than it had been. The branch committee went down to 15 and then 12. The company knew we were struggling to get branch meetings off the ground. They knew there was a change of attitude in the steward organization in general. They sensed the trade union side was beginning to buckle, to get weaker.

Branch meetings effectively became a talking shop where the committed activists could exchange information and debate about union policy but with little direct connection with union members on the shop-floor.

Despite its limitations, the strength of workplace union organization inside the Birds Eye plant during the 1970s came from what workers were prepared to do collectively themselves combined with active leadership from the shop stewards. Struggles over job evaluation, flexibility and so on, including strikes, both on a departmental and factory-wide basis, were crucial to building the power of the stewards' body *vis-à-vis* management. By contrast, during the 1980s, few stewards had experience of organizing strikes at departmental level; negotiating skills fostered through 'strong bargaining relations' with management seemed much more important. As a result, in many departments the stewards found it difficult to mobilize their members into activity on those occasions when they *did* think it necessary – for example in opposition to the closure of the chicken-stripping department in 1986.

Above all, the overwhelming majority of shop stewards lacked the socialist politics and self-confidence to reject the arguments of management that only increased efficiency and profitability could save jobs. They became trapped into accepting the overall trend of managerial policy (albeit whilst arguing over the small print) and were browbeaten into abandoning or restraining militant struggle. Of course, such arguments had been accepted in the 1970s although that had not prevented stewards from being prepared, on occasion, to engage in confrontation with management to win shop-floor gains. The chief difference in the 1980s was that the economic crisis, rising level of unemployment and overhanging threat to close the Birds Eye plant helped reinforce the power of such arguments. As a consequence the close links between stewards and members evident during the 1970s, based upon day-to-day struggle, gradually became loosened during the 1980s.

Nonetheless, it was still possible for Jack Boyle and the stewards' committee periodically to make successful recommendations for one-day plant-wide strikes, albeit only with the backing of full-time union officials and mostly in solidarity with other sections of workers rather than directly for themselves. The most emphatic illustration of this occurred in 1985 when the Kirkby plant was brought to a standstill in support of the strike-bound Birds Eye plant in Gloucester. The Gloucester strikers (in dispute over the implementation of Workstyle) informed the Kirkby stewards that four pickets would be sent to seek support. Terry recalled the Merseyside response:

> The reaction of the stewards' committee at first was outright panic. The decision we had to make was basically, do we uphold the branch's policy of not crossing picket lines or do we tear it up into little pieces? Really the stewards' committee was bounced into the decision, because from a purely self-respecting point of view, to retain any credibility within themselves, they had no option but to inform the members that when the picket arrived they'd expect them to observe the policy of the branch. Although there was rumblings against it when it was put to a recommendation it carried the day. They sent four pickets up but they could've sent a dog with a placard round its neck if they'd wanted. No one would have crossed that picket line.

This was an impressive display of solidarity. Significantly, it also showed that when the stewards took the initiative and provided a lead, on this occasion independently of full-time union officials, then the members were willing to engage in industrial action.

Ray described the dynamic interaction between the members' collectivist traditions and shop stewards' leadership:

> One thing about Kirkby people, and Liverpool people in general, is that
> although they get whacked about the head by various companies and the
> media – one of the things you've got to take your hat off to is that they
> do have a sense of trade union tradition that I would say is unequalled
> anywhere in this country. When you appeal to their sense of tradition
> then you get their support. But it was also down to the leadership in the
> factory, the way the stewards' committee actually got it together and
> said, 'This is the line we're taking in support of Gloucester', and by
> arguing that a strike wouldn't last long before the company backtracked.

Production at the Kirkby plant was brought to a complete halt for two
days before the Gloucester dispute was settled. Birds Eye was forced
to agree to negotiate rather than unilaterally impose new working
practices.

Yet, as has already been commented upon, the willingness of rank-and-
file members to take such action in support of other workers was never
encouraged as a way of forcing concessions from management inside the
Kirkby plant. Instead, the closure of two major departments in the
factory without effective resistance and the deadlocked negotiations over
the implementation of Workstyle gradually had the effect of sapping
the morale and confidence of many shop-floor workers. The stewards'
acceptance of 350 redundancies in 1988 as part of Workstyle meant that
when the closure of the plant was announced, a large proportion of
workers had already become resigned to accepting job losses. Although
there was still a substantial section of workers who were genuinely
interested in fighting to keep the factory open, the stewards' equivocal
strategy, which was championed by TGWU officialdom, was in many
respects doomed to failure. As Tommy, a union member in Unit 2,
complained:

> The problem with the stewards was that first and foremost they did
> nothing. They said plenty and they got messages of solidarity to take
> secondary action if necessary. But what use is that if you're not prepared
> to take primary action? That's where they lost out. I remember the
> convenor coming out with the absurd argument that it would suit
> management if we downed tools and walked out. At very best all they
> did was shadow box. They never seriously mounted a campaign of
> action against the closure – it was purely verbal. Had we taken action
> and then called for support you might have had a very different result. It

might not have kept the place open, but it could have done. Instead, they basically asked other people to do the battle for us.

Accepting redundancies at the same time as mounting opposition to the factory's closure effectively cut the ground from underneath the stewards' entire strategy. By playing to the lowest common denominator the stewards reinforced the hesitations and doubts of the less confident elements of the workforce and in turn sapped the spirit of those willing to fight.

Ultimately, as Ritchie acknowledged, the stewards' weakness was political:

> The shop stewards changed from the hard-nosed trade union style of the '70s to a less involved, less political, less committed body of the '80s – obviously, because the environment had changed and people's attitudes had changed.

Even the left-wing stewards, isolated in the three-shift area, failed to mount a challenge or pose a coherent political alternative to the stewards' committee strategy, further weakening the possibilities for mobilizing the type of militant action that might possibly have been more successful in forcing Birds Eye to keep the plant open.

Shop Stewards' Relationship to Full-Time Union Officials: The 1970s/1980s

The 1970s: Tied to the Lowest Common Denominator

During the 1970s there was a relatively independent relationship between the Kirkby shop stewards and Birds Eye full-time union officials. The large size of the workplace meant there was a well-established and reasonably 'sophisticated' stewards' organization that was able to deal with its own affairs in many respects. As Ray explained:

> If we had a major falling-out with the company, and we had a failure to agree at local level, then we'd call in the local district officer. But we weren't one of those factories that as soon as we had a problem we shouted out for him. Most of the time we looked after ourselves. They used to say it was the easiest plant a district officer could get because

we very rarely wanted him in. It wasn't really a question of not trusting the officials, it's just that we felt we could do better without having them in.

Significantly, most of the plant-wide strikes during the 1970s were initiated by the stewards themselves, on occasions irrespective of the wishes of union officials. At the same time, the nature of the bargaining system meant there was an important element of *plant-based* wage determination – over job evaluation, bonus schemes and condition rates – in which stewards were able to increase substantially the take-home pay of their members independently of officials.

Annual wage negotiations were conducted by top-level corporate Birds Eye managers and national and local full-time TGWU officials through a JNC on behalf of the four Birds Eye plants in Kirkby, Yarmouth, Lowestoft and Eastbourne, and later on in Gloucester. (The Birds Eye plants in Hull and Grimsby had entirely separate national bargaining arrangements with the General and Municipal Workers' Union.) Only from 1973, after some pressure from the steward committees, a pragmatic devolving of power within the TGWU and Birds Eye's own reform plans, were the convenors from each of the four Birds Eye plants allowed to attend JNC meetings; and only in 1984 did the plant deputy convenors also become part of the negotiating forum.

A problem that confronted the Kirkby stewards was that, despite being the best union-organized plant in the Birds Eye combine, their bargaining strength over basic rates of pay tended to be tied to the lowest common denominator of the other, weaker plants. Steve, Kirkby deputy convenor and representative on the JNC during the late 1980s, explained the predicament they faced:

We used to do quite well locally in job evaluation and that, but when it came to national level we didn't. We were always sold out by the other sites. Every year we rejected the wage offer but to a certain extent the national officers' hands were tied because Lowestoft and Yarmouth would accept less than we were prepared to accept and would defeat us if it went to a ballot. Because the other sites were not prepared to take any action we had to accept it in the end. All the other plants were badly organized. They had a lot of seasonal and part-time labour, without good union organization.

Only on one occasion in 1974 did the Kirkby stewards organize plant-wide industrial action over national wage rates. It was limited to a one-hour demonstration stoppage which was tied to a local protest over canteen price increases (Branch minutes, 24 April 1974). Even though annual pay increases were consistently poor and sometimes below the rate of inflation, the stewards tended to concentrate their attention on trying to bolster pay packets independently of the officials through the element of local pay bargaining that was available to them. By negotiating local productivity deals they were able to skirt around the problem of wage restraint under the period of the Labour government's 'Social Contract' of the mid- to late 1970s.

The stewards' independent stance was also reinforced by the quite high level of disputes inside the Kirkby plant, which encouraged a reliance on local strength, and by the fact that from the mid-1970s the Merseyside region of the TGWU became one of the most left-wing in the country, with Phil Donovan, a former militant convenor from the Ford Halewood plant, as the local full-time official from 1974. Not only was there a very friendly personal link between Martin Roberts and Phil Donovan, but the latter also seemed quite prepared to allow the stewards to act autonomously in many respects. As Ray related:

> Phil was very much looked upon as one of us, as one of the Left. Phil's role was basically to get involved in wage negotiations. We very rarely had him into the factory unless we had a failure to agree over someone getting sacked or something. But he didn't take part in any local negotiations in the plant really.

Of course, the stewards' body was by no means completely autonomous from official trade union structures. For example, Ray became the TGWU branch delegate to the union's Merseyside district committee and the union's national trade group committee for the food, drink and tobacco sector; and, following the election of the Labour government in 1974, most stewards in the plant were able to attend both TUC and TGWU day release educational courses. It was through such involvement that the stewards' committee was kept informed of general industrial and corporate developments and union policies, as well as providing channels through which they could express their own demands. It reinforced their identification with the union on a more official basis than the *ad hoc* manner than had previously existed.

The formalization of relations between the plant and the official union structure also meant the stewards' committee increasingly came under varying levels of pressure from regional and national union officials to keep all shop-floor grievances within procedure and to avoid plant-wide disputes, particularly of an unofficial nature. Thus, in some respects the top-level support provided by the TGWU national leadership for the Labour government's 'Social Contract' appears to have underlain some of the senior stewards' opposition to what was perceived to be Martin Roberts's style of militant leadership. On occasions, national union officials were able to exercise a decisively negative role, as for example in 1976 (in the wake of the resignation of the convenor and negotiating committee) when a redundancy agreement for all of the Birds Eye plants, which had previously not existed, was signed unilaterally over the heads of the Kirkby stewards' body.

It was a foretaste of the type of bureaucratic approach the stewards increasingly had to endure, even after Martin Roberts's return as convenor. For example in 1977, following the announcement of Birds Eye's Five Year Plan aimed at centralizing products and moving various kits from one site to another across the country, the Kirkby plant was faced with the transfer of its steaklet and beefburger range of products with little being exchanged in return. Ray described the stewards' strategy:

> We fought very hard against the Five Year Plan because we felt that some of the products they wanted to take from Kirkby were the mainstay of the factory. What the company was doing was getting a bone and throwing it in the middle and saying 'Go on dogs, fight over it' . . . We tried to get meetings with stewards at the other Birds Eye factories to discuss centralization. We wanted them to adopt a very broad policy which said, 'We don't accept your work being transferred and you don't accept ours.' In other words, what we've got, we hold. As part of our strategy we tried to form a national stewards' combine committee.

Yet the combine committee never really got off the ground, in part because of the unwillingness of the TGWU nationally to fund the Kirkby stewards' initiative:

> There'd been attempts in the past to get the stewards together across the sites to form a national combine but the other stewards' committees weren't as highly organized as we were at the time and we just couldn't

get the commitment from the other sites. So we appealed to the T and G
to help us set up a combine committee and fund it on a quarterly basis.
But the national officer said no, the union couldn't afford it. We were left
trying to fund it ourselves, but when it came down to it the other
branches weren't prepared to help set it up.

Without a national combine committee the Kirkby stewards' campaign to
win the other sites to a strategy of resistance to Birds Eye's product
transfers was considerably hamstrung and, ultimately, unsuccessful.

The lack of financial support from the national union did not prevent
the stewards from mounting a four-week unofficial plant-wide strike in
1977 over bonus payments which involved secondary picketing of the
Lowestoft plant, or organizing the impressive gesture of solidarity with
striking engineers by convincing their members not to cross AUEW picket
lines. However, a separate but related set of problems confronted the
stewards' committee, namely the opposition by national officials to seemingly independent steward action. After management's lock-out of the
workforce, the national officials were eventually able to steamroller a
return to work on the company's draconian terms and conditions, even
though the local TGWU official was completely solid behind the stewards'
defiant stance, as Ray related:

> Phil Donovan used to attend every meeting of the Joint Liaison
> committee [the TGWU and AUEW stewards' body set up to coordinate
> the strike]. He was under a hell of a lot of pressure that was bearing
> down on him from London, from the national officers and the general
> secretary of the union, to get the dispute settled. But what he told them
> was: 'Look, every time we try to settle it they move the goalposts again.'
> He played a leading role with us in that dispute. There is one thing I
> would never fault about Phil and that was his commitment to the joint
> shop stewards' committee throughout that eighteen-week dispute.

According to Peter, the same could not be said about the TGWU regional
and national officials:

> Once the company threatened the closure of the site the T and G
> panicked nationally. You were talking about a booming factory losing
> 1000 jobs. What started to happen was that control of the dispute
> started to drift away from the joint liaison committee to the national

full-time officials of both the T and G and the AUEW, who started to get
more and more involved in the dispute. They had clandestine meetings
with the company in London with no lay representation allowed. Then
the T and G regional organizer was ordered by the national official and
the general secretary of the T and G to attend the next meeting of the
joint liaison committee and spell out to the AUEW that if they didn't
terminate the dispute forthwith then he would be ordering our members
to go back to work. Give him his due; he actually told us what he had
been told to say. But he was told in no uncertain terms by the T and G
stewards that we would be sticking to our policies and that no union
official would order us back to work. We told him we would go back only
when the dispute was properly concluded.

Nonetheless, the Kirkby stewards were not able to hold out indefinitely
against the pressure bearing down on them from the officials. Ray
remembered:

The national officers in the eighteen-week dispute never once came to
Kirkby. There was a lot of criticism of them for not actively participating.
They wouldn't even come up to talk to us. The major input they had into
the dispute was bringing it to a close. The company demanded total and
unconditional surrender before they'd agree to reopen the site. And that
was the agreement the national officers of all unions reached with the
company. It was put to the members with no options whatsoever: 'If you
don't go back to work then the place will remain shut.' So people felt
they had no alternative but to terminate the dispute and return to work.
The stewards recommended rejection but we were overturned because
people were worried about their jobs.

Thus, the stewards' organization suffered a severe set-back in the aftermath of the lock-out, although it had recovered sufficient strength by 1979
to defy national officials and threaten a plant-wide overtime ban, which
successfully forced management to discontinue employment of workers on
short fixed-term contracts.

The 1980s: Looking Upwards
If, during the 1970s, the stewards' organization enjoyed quite a high
degree of self-reliance and initiative *vis-à-vis* full-time union officials, the
pendulum tilted towards a much more dependent relationship during the

1980s. To begin with, the introduction of measured day work in 1978 ended the element of local pay determination that existed inside the Kirkby plant and obliged the stewards to become much more reliant on pay rates negotiated at national level by TGWU officials. Even though stewards continued to feel aggrieved at the level of national settlements, they did not feel strong enough to take action to bolster their hand at the negotiating table, at least independently of a lead from the officials themselves. Ironically, whilst the national officials preferred to secure a 'satisfactory' settlement through negotiation from above rather than encouraging militant action from below, they were led on some occasions during the early 1980s, to threaten, and even organize, industrial action across the plants (particularly when they sensed their bargaining role being utterly undermined by Birds Eye corporate managers).

For example, in 1981, when Birds Eye adopted a belligerent attitude in top-level pay talks by refusing to improve its 9 per cent offer and referring to TGWU national officials as 'messenger boys', it provoked a walk-out by the union's negotiators and the collapse of all negotiations with the company (Stewards' committee minutes, 14 July 1981). National officials responded by calling for a one-day strike at their four Birds Eye factories, unless the company improved its offer. The Kirkby stewards' committee voted their support, but the Day of Action was eventually called off after the company made a minor concession in the pay package, sufficient for the national officials to recommend acceptance of the offer to the membership. Whilst the Kirkby steward minutes book reports that there 'was a great deal of criticism' of the company–union deal, it was approved by a slim majority. Again in 1982, when Birds Eye refused point-blank to improve its 7 per cent wage offer, TGWU national officials felt unable to accept such a deal without at least a show of disapproval, even though they preferred only limited token action. They called for another 24-hour strike across all the Birds Eye plants, to be followed at a later date by an indefinite strike, unless the company agreed to improve its offer. On this occasion, the strike actually took place and the Kirkby plant actively participated.

Nonetheless, the TGWU officials' apparent change of approach was short-lived. They used the equivocation of General and Municipal Workers' Union officials – who insisted on a two-thirds majority ballot vote in favour of strike action within the Humberside plants – to call off the strike, even though an individual head count of all the factories had recorded a two to one majority against the company's offer (Branch minutes, 11 July 1982). TGWU officials subsequently put the company's unchanged pay offer to another vote of the membership without recommending acceptance or rejection. Although both the Kirkby plant stewards' committee and their rank-and-file membership voted against the deal it was accepted by a majority across the other plants. Once more in 1984, the national officials were spurred into calling a 24-hour strike, following Birds Eye's closure of the Yarmouth plant and the transfer of some labour to its Lowestoft site without an adequate redundancy agreement (Branch minutes, 8 July 1984). Again, Kirkby joined the stoppage. Otherwise the TUC's 'new realism' pervaded national negotiations and whilst the Kirkby stewards often voted against pay settlements they applied no direct pressure themselves and took no independent initiatives.

Meanwhile, even though the stewards' body organized a number of one-day plant-wide solidarity stoppages during the 1980s, it is important to note that such action was, almost exclusively, taken only after having been initiated, sanctioned and even formally proposed at mass meetings by full-time union officials in line with official TUC or TGWU policy. The only exception was the two-day unofficial strike in support of the Birds Eye Gloucester plant in 1985, when the Kirkby stewards recommended that their members respect workers' pickets lines. However, whilst consenting to such solidarity action at the time, the convenor, Jack Boyle, immediately set about afterwards to ensure the Kirkby plant would not be placed in the same situation again (Branch minutes, 27 September 1985). Thus, a national meeting of convenors from all Birds Eye factories later agreed to his proposed policy statement that in future: 'Before any pickets can be placed on the gates of another plant, the action has to be sanctioned by the national officers or by a full recall of the national negotiating committee' (Branch minutes, 19 January 1986).

The full extent of the stewards' reliance on the union officials became evident during the subsequent campaigns against Workstyle and closure announcement of the Kirkby plant. In 1987 a newly appointed left-wing Merseyside TGWU district official, Kevin Dobson, became instrumental in the process of finally establishing a Birds Eye national shop stewards' combine committee that linked the union-organized Kirkby, Hull, Gloucester and Lowestoft plants. Peter related:

> The impetus for that to be set up was obviously the change in the company's strategy for the '90s. They had decided that Workstyle was coming in across the country. But the real driving force behind the

combine committee, it's got to be said, was Kevin Dobson. Martin Roberts had tried to get a committee off the ground but didn't get the backing. Dobson provided us with the extra impetus. He was the architect of the committee. He phoned round the officers and got it off the ground.

The Birds Eye stewards' combine committee held a number of joint meetings and adopted a formal declaration that each site would take solidarity action if any plant was faced with enforced redundancies as a result of Workstyle. However, it is of crucial significance that Kevin Dobson's influence on the Kirkby stewards' resistance to Workstyle tended to be of an all-pervasive nature. Thus, it was on his explicit advice that the stewards agreed to the company's demand for 380 redundancies, albeit only on a voluntary basis and if the severance terms were improved. On the one hand, Dobson's own militant shop steward history and left-wing credentials ensured a strong element of trust amongst those workers looking for a fighting lead. On the other hand, his attempt to carry *all* sections of the workforce, including those who wanted to take redundancy, meant he also retained the allegiance of Jack Boyle and others on the stewards' committee. This was a strategy he developed following experience of negotiating increased redundancy payments at other Merseyside plants facing closure. Yet however understandable such a defensive strategy might have been, it had the effect of subverting the possibilities for mounting an effective fight-back when the factory's closure was subsequently announced. Terry explained how the district official attempted to forge a united front between those who wanted to retain their jobs and those who wanted to take the redundancy money:

> It was all Kevin Dobson's strategy. His argument at mass meetings was to say: 'We've always accepted there'd have to be redundancies but if you do want to go – the only way to get better money and help yourself is to get behind those who are fighting for their jobs.' What he did was always hammer home that he was capable of a getting a good few bob for redundancy payments. He'd say: 'Those of you who want out – I can get you a good deal.' He'd quote figures and of course the pound signs would be flashing in front of their eyes, you know. All right, at the end of the day, certainly if people have to go I agree they shouldn't be sent out of the gate with nothing, but he shouldn't have been stressing *that* at the expense of the people who wanted to keep their jobs.

After weeks of procrastination the stewards finally called for all-out strike action against the closure. But their decision to tie any possible action taken in Kirkby to simultaneous action in the two other Birds Eye plants was also very much the brainchild of Kevin Dobson, with official backing from TGWU national officials. In the event, the strategy ultimately backfired when a large section of the members in Kirkby successfully pressurized the stewards' committee to open up negotiations with the company over improved severance terms *at the same time* as they organized the strike ballot against closure.

Although *formally* Kirkby voted in favour of strike action, the vast majority of the workforce, including many who had initially wanted to resist the closure, had, by then, accepted redundancy as a *fait accompli*. Ironically, it was the votes against supporting Kirkby taken by the Gloucester and Lowestoft plants which provided Kevin Dobson and national TGWU officials with a convenient excuse for the collapse of the campaign. Certainly, Terry was highly critical of the influential role played by the local union official:

> When Workstyle was first mentioned it was negotiable and should have been dealt with by the negotiating committee. All right, involve the full-time official in an advisory capacity, certainly keep him informed of what's going on, invite him to meetings. But keep control of it, because *we're* part of the factory, *he* isn't. He's not involved to the same extent as we are and it's our property. What ultimately happened is that it was Dobson who was basically running it at the end of the day. The negotiating committee became more or less a cipher. There is a lesson to be learnt there, it was an over-involvement of the full-time official.

Ray echoed these sentiments:

> We had a position with Kevin Dobson where we would be kept waiting to have a stewards' meeting and he would be with the negotiating committee and they would always keep us waiting. That's where the real decisions were made in the last 12 months – within that particular body. So much so they used to use the stewards' committee as just a rubber stamp for their ideas. There was a lot of opposition in the last three months to that. We even had the embarrassing position once, when half the stewards' committee decided to go and picket the union office inside the factory where the negotiating committee was meeting, because they should have been with us an hour before.

Even though a few individual left-wing members of the stewards' committee raised the argument for immediate strike action when the factory's closure was announced, there was no serious attempt to challenge or campaign against the dominant strategy adopted by Kevin Dobson and the negotiating committee. In effect, at the same time as the Kirkby workforce were encouraged to look outwards to the other Birds Eye plants, the negotiating committee tended to look upwards to the local full-time official to pull some magic trick out of the bag. Arguably, their dependence on Kevin Dobson (and national TGWU officials) resulted in a fatally flawed campaign of opposition to the factory's closure.

Some Issues and Themes

The experience of the shop stewards' organization in Birds Eye during the 1970s and 1980s raises a variety of interesting questions about the dynamics of workplace unionism which relate to some of the wider debates mentioned earlier and specifically to the critique of Batstone's work.

It sheds some light on the difference between a relatively militant shop stewards' strategy *vis-à-vis* management (exemplified by Martin Roberts) compared with a more 'strong bargaining relations' type of approach (exemplified by Jack Boyle). During the 1970s, it was shop-floor activity from below that succeeded in improving workers' material conditions and provided the basis upon which a strong workplace union organization could be built. By contrast, during the 1980s the consequence of stewards adopting 'strong bargaining relations' was the demobilization of members' self-activity, the routinization of workplace unionism and the undermining of the strength of stewards' organization, which ill-prepared them to resist the enforced closure of the plant. Of course, it was understandable that during the 1980s, within an unfavourable economic and political climate, some stewards felt it necessary to abandon the relatively militant strategy of earlier years. The real question is whether the stewards' 'pragmatic' strategy was the *only* feasible or 'cost-effective' response that could have been adopted, and whether the frontier of resistance could not have been pushed much more than occurred. Arguably, despite the immense obstacles to the success of a more militant stance there was no fatalistic inevitability about the success of corporate restructuring.

Another interesting theme to emerge was the fallacy of Batstone's notion that 'nothing much has changed', that stewards' organization was basically as hierarchical, centralized and bureaucratic in the 1980s as it ever was in the 1970s. In Birds Eye it is clear that the relationship between stewards and their members did undergo a qualitative shift. Despite aspects of both 'representative' and 'participatory' democracy (or 'leader' and 'populist' to use Batstone's terms) the pendulum was pushed much more towards the latter during the 1970s, partly as a result of the pressure from rank-and-file workers in response to management policies and partly as a result of the active intervention of the stewards. In other words, there was a direct connection between the level of shop-floor confidence, activity and militancy *vis-à-vis* management and the relatively democratic relationship that existed between stewards and members. This was in sharp contrast to the 1980s when, in the context of a more conciliatory relationship with management, the pendulum swung towards a more bureaucratic relationship between stewards and members. The implications of this, in terms of a vibrant form of workplace unionism, cut against the grain of Batstone's 'top-down' view of 'sophisticated' stewards' organization.

Also important were the various factors creating fragmentation and disunity between different groups of workers which served to undermine the strength of stewards' organization and make collective action more difficult: for example, the sexual division of labour and 'welt working'. Clearly, although rank-and-file workers sometimes present a challenge to management which can be suppressed by stewards, it is also necessary to be sensitive to the problematical features of workers' self-activity. Shop-floor workers, like stewards, are not pristine pure, but also experience the dilemmas of workplace unionism. On occasions, there can be a tension between rank-and-file workers' sectional activity and the steward committees' plant-wide strategic perpectives. Nonetheless, the case study suggests there is no Chinese wall between sectionalism and generalization, and that often it depends upon the effectiveness of the stewards' leadership to which rank-and-file workers are exposed.

The relationship between workers' activity and union collectivism on the one hand, and the role of political leadership of shop stewards on the other, was also important. The key role of certain left-wing stewards in building up the strength of shop-floor union organization was one feature of this, although their political limitations in the face of the challenges of the 1980s was another. This raises the question, although purely speculative, of whether a sizeable group of revolutionary socialists inside the plant could have made any fundamental difference to the 1980s restructuring process.

Finally, the central role played by full-time union officials, although sometimes a feature of workplace relations ignored by commentators, became more than apparent in Birds Eye. Despite some differentiation between local and national officials, their responsibility for the failed campaign against closure was of major significance.

All of the above themes are reconsidered within different contexts in the Bemrose and Ford case studies which follow, and a comparative assessment is provided in Chapter 7.

5 BEMROSE

Introduction

The Eric Bemrose printing plant was established on its single Liverpool site in 1939 as an independent family company, with control passing to the News of the World organization in the late 1960s, which in turn was itself taken over by the British arm of Rupert Murdoch's global media empire, News International. Murdoch's British interests include national newspapers (*The Sun*, *News of the World*, *The Times*, *Sunday Times*, *Financial Times* and *Today*); magazines (*New Woman*); provincial papers (eight dailies and 69 weeklies); books (HarperCollins); and television (British Sky Broadcasting). Murdoch's News Corporation also has extensive worldwide interests in media corporations, particularly in Australia and the United States (including 20th Century Fox and national television networks) and reported profits of £101.7 million in 1991 (*Guardian*, 4 September 1989).

Situated close to the famous Grand National racecourse in Aintree, Eric Bemrose was, until its closure in 1991, one of the three major photogravure colour printing plants in Britain, specializing in long-run, high-speed and high-quality printing. During the 1950s and 1960s it printed mainly children's comics such as *Eagle*, *Swift*, *Robin* and *Girl*, plus other periodicals such as *Arcade*, *Autocar* and *Practical Motorist*. In the 1970s the main print run involved all 13 editions of the *TV Times* magazine. By the 1980s Bemrose printed mainly colour supplements for the *Sunday Express*, *Sunday Telegraph* and *News of the World*, as well as the 'rewinds' (preprinted colour pages) for many national newspapers, including the *Daily Mail* and *Daily Express*.

The chief characteristic of photogravure work is that the printing surface is a copper cylinder treated in such a way that the printing areas are lower than their surroundings. Ink flows into these areas and is drawn on to the paper as it passes over the revolving cylinder on a printing machine. Because of the costly nature of preparing the printing cylinder, the process is generally economic only for very long runs, and is particularly suitable for the production of large-circulation periodicals. Throughout the 1970s, there were four quite separate stages of production in Bemrose, each with its own department. The number was reduced to three in the 1980s.

- The composing department, where the original text was set in lead type and made up into page form. By the early 1980s this department had been closed down and its typesetting method replaced by computerized photocomposition.
- The process department, where illustrative material such as photographs and diagrams (and from 1981 typeset artwork brought in from outside) was converted into a form suitable for printing by the production of negatives and by the production of the actual printing surface on the copper cylinders. This department was made up of ten different sections (including carbon printing, proofing and planning) until 1981 when it was reduced to five.
- The machine room, where the cylinders were fitted to the nine printing presses and where the inked printing surface and paper were brought into contact.
- The finishing department, where the edges of printed work were trimmed, separate printed sections collated into single volumes and the finished product gathered into bundles of a specified size ready for dispatch.

Developments in the highly sophisticated technology of gravure printing at Bemrose were generally in the form of small modifications or improvements, such as in the process department and in the finishing department where various forms of mechanization were introduced. Yet throughout the 1970s and 1980s, much to the dismay of the unions, there was no major new investment in plant or machinery despite the rapidly advancing technology in colour magazine and newspaper production, particularly web offset printing. For most of this period the factory employed about 1400 manual production workers, including 170 compositors, 350 process workers, 170 machine minders and 640 non-craft assistants. All but about 100 of these were male; most female workers were employed in the finishing department. The bulk of the workforce were concentrated in the process department (325), the machine room (430) and the finishing department (225). In 1981 90 compositors lost their jobs. But much more severe redundancy exercises took place in 1987 when 700 workers, over half of the workforce, were sacked (leaving 550 workers) and in 1990 when there were 413 redundancies (leaving 160 workers) before the plant was finally closed completely in 1991. The hours of work were as follows: in the process department a two-shift system, Monday–Thursday 7 am–3 pm, 3 pm–11 pm and Friday 7 am–6 pm; in the machine room and finishing department a three-shift system, 7 am–3 pm, 3 pm–11 pm and 11 pm–7 am.

The three principal production trade unions during the 1970s were the National Graphical Association (NGA), the Society of Lithographic Artists, Designers, Engravers and Process Workers (SLADE) and the Society of Graphical and Allied Trades (SOGAT). In 1982 an amalgamation at national level of SLADE and the NGA led to the formation of one trade union, known as NGA '82, leaving two production unions in Bemrose, one craft (NGA) and one non-craft (SOGAT). (The eventual merger of the NGA and SOGAT in 1991 has led to what is now known as the Graphical, Paper and Media Union.) As at most large printing plants a 'closed shop' policy operated at Bemrose for most of the 1970s and 1980s, with even departmental managers and foremen belonging to the same union as shop-floor workers. Each union organized its members into 'chapels' within the plant.

During the 1970s (and until 1982), there were separate chapels for members of SLADE and SOGAT, as well as two separate chapels for NGA members. This distribution of union members in the plant into four separate chapels was related to the four stages of production outlined above. Thus, SLADE was involved at the first stage of production (that is, with the preparation of the cylindrical gravure printing surface). The NGA was involved at two stages of production: a proportion of its members were in the composing department (setting the text material) whilst the majority were in the machine room (in charge of the printing machines). SOGAT members were to be found in many parts of the factory, for example transporting the copper cylinders between departments; but their greatest strength lay in the two departments where they acted as assistants to the skilled craft workers – the machine room and finishing department – and on the loading bay (where the finished product was dispatched).

Two important changes to these chapel arrangements occurred in the 1980s. Following the closure of the composing department in 1981, the NGA chapel in that area disappeared; and following the amalgamation of SLADE with the NGA in 1982, the old SLADE process chapel became known as the NGA '82 chapel. Thus, to recapitulate, in the 1970s there were four major separate union chapels in Bemrose: the SLADE process chapel, the NGA composing chapel, the NGA machine chapel and the SOGAT chapel. During the 1980s there were only three major chapels: the NGA '82 process chapel, the NGA machine chapel and the SOGAT chapel (although there were also small independent chapels for the EETPU and AUEW).

Each chapel elected a shop stewards' convenor, known as the 'father of the chapel' (FoC), together with a deputy FoC, a treasurer and a committee of shop stewards, known as 'committee representatives', to act on its behalf in administering the chapel's affairs and to negotiate with management. The FoC, deputy FoC and treasurer were elected annually by the chapel membership in a secret ballot. The same applied for the committee representatives (on different shifts in each department), who served for a period of two years, with half the committee up for re-election each year. The chapel committee usually met monthly, and full chapel membership meetings were held every quarter (one of which would be the Annual General Meeting). All major negotiations with management were entrusted to the FoC and deputy FoC and a chapel secretary (who was elected from within the committee).

Although reference is sometimes made to the *national* agreements between the combined printing trade unions and the British Printing Industries Federation (BPIF), Bemrose always had its own 'house agreement', usually running for one year and determined exclusively at *plant* level. During the 1960s each chapel negotiated its own separate house agreement (which specified such matters as basic rates of pay, shift premiums, holiday levels and manning arrangements). The formation of a federated house chapel in 1972 considerably reduced this fragmentation by bringing together all unions in the plant under one umbrella, except the SLADE process chapel. The federated chapel was composed of the FoC of each chapel plus one other representative, usually the deputy FoC, and although it met only infrequently it conducted all major plant-wide negotiations leading to a 'joint house agreement'. However, the SLADE process chapel continued to negotiate its own separate house agreement because it feared a joint body would jeopardize its relatively highly advantageous position. In 1981 it finally agreed to join the federated chapel.

Each Bemrose chapel was part of a wider trade union organization, namely a union branch structure that linked a number of workplace chapels throughout the local region. Thus, in the 1970s, both the NGA compositors and NGA machine chapels were represented by the Liverpool NGA branch, the SLADE process chapel by the Liverpool SLADE branch and the SOGAT chapel by the Merseyside SOGAT branch. Following the transfer of the SLADE process chapel membership into the NGA '82 branch and the disbandment of the NGA composing chapel during the early 1980s, only two union branches covered the Bemrose workforce. Throughout the 1970s and 1980s, the branches usually met quarterly, electing a branch committee by a ballot of the members throughout the region. Attendance by chapel delegates was compulsory and co-ordinated on a rota basis. Full-time union branch officials (and national officials) were involved in negotiations with Bemrose and News International management, and they were responsible for ratifying all house agreements signed by chapels to ensure they were consistent with the union's national policy.

A limited amount of time off work for union business and shop-floor negotiation was granted by management to each of the four chapels in the early 1970s, although committee representatives, including the FoC, spent most of their day working on the job. This arrangement changed in 1976–77 when management provided full-time facility status to each of the chapel FoCs and allowed much greater time off work for deputy FoCs. In addition, they provided each of the four chapels with small union offices located on the shop-floor. Only after the major redundancy exercise that occurred ten years later in 1987 did management decide to withdraw these facilities, forcing all FoCs back on to the job again.

Stewards' Relationship to Management: The 1970s

The 1970s: The Stewards' Strengths

In many respects, the 1970s represented the heyday of shop-floor union power inside the Bemrose plant. A number of objective and structural factors, combined with a conscious attempt to build strong workplace union organization, enabled the respective chapel committees to wield considerable bargaining leverage. It is possible to distinguish some of the

Chronology of Major Events

1969   Three-week SOGAT strike.

1972   Formation of Federated Chapel linking all unions except SLADE.
        Reduction of 151 different wage rates to 14.
        Bruce Matthews appointed chairman of Bemrose.

1974   Extra four editions of *TV Times* awarded, making 13 editions in total.

1977   SLADE dispute over morning shift pay.
        Four-night week granted.
        FoCs granted 100 per cent facility time off work.

1979   National TV electricians' strike halts production of *TV Times*.

1980   Joint Federated Chapel (including SLADE) established.

1981   Loss of *TV Times* magazine.
        Robert Maxwell briefly takes over Bemrose.
        Sunday magazine taken on.
        Survival Plan introduced.

1982   SLADE and NGA merge to become NGA '82.
        NGA machine chapel dispute leads to formation of Joint Working Party:
        Parity talks begin with aim of equalizing craft wage rates.

1983   NGA Warrington dispute/mass picketing.
        100 people taken on in NGA machine and SOGAT chapels.
        First year's reduction of craft differential.

1984   National miners' strike.

1985   Alan Hebden has SOGAT union card withdrawn.

1986   Final year of equalization of pay rates: two craft and two new non-craft
        rates.
        Strikers from News International's Wapping plant lobby Bemrose.

1987   Alan Hebden expelled from SOGAT.
        Loss of *Sunday Express*.
        775 redundancies reduces the workforce to 567.
        Alan Hebden forced to resign as SOGAT FoC.
        100 per cent time off work withdrawn from FoCs.

1988   House agreements temporarily terminated by company.

1990   Loss of *Sunday* magazine.
        413 redundancies reduces workforce to 160.

1991   Factory closed.

key ingredients at work. To begin with, one of the bedrocks of union organization exercised by all four chapels and their union branches (craft and non-craft) was their ability to regulate the total supply of labour. On the one hand, this was implemented through rules that governed the ratio of apprentices to time-served men (involving district-wide standards that obliged management to recruit from a list of unemployed members). On the other hand, it was implemented through the pre-entry closed shop (which ensured that only union members were hired). Such control over the supply of labour placed the Bemrose printing chapels in an exclusivist position *vis-à-vis* management.

Bill, a SLADE chapel member in the carbon printing section of the process department, the NGA '82 process chapel FoC (after the SLADE/NGA merger) and chairperson of the plant's federated chapel, described the consequences of control over the supply of labour for the SLADE process chapel in the early 1970s:

> Skilled process workers were in short supply in the North-West in the 1950s and '60s and that meant Bemrose had to pay excellent rates of pay to attract people from down south to move to Liverpool. Well, the knock-on effect was that it raised rates generally in Bemrose and in other printing establishments in the Liverpool area. In fact Bemrose became a national leader in gravure wage rates across the whole country. And it gave the unions – with a pre-entry closed shop and the apprenticeship scheme – a lot of control. They were able to say to management: 'How many do you want? Four? No, you're getting four, plus two apprentices.' By the late '60s and early '70s the number of people in the process department grew from something like 150 to 400.

Similarly, the non-craft SOGAT chapel was able to restrict and control the supply of labour through its union branch's effective role as a labour exchange. As Peter, a rank-and-file SOGAT member who had worked for 16 years in the machine room, remembered: 'People used to say: "What, get a job in Bemrose? You've got to get a letter off the Pope to get in that place."'

The state of the product market, notably Bemrose's heavy reliance upon the production of such ephemeral items as weekly periodicals, also placed the chapel committees in a strong bargaining position. During the 1960s and 1970s the factory's production output boomed as a seemingly endless variety of new magazine titles were taken on. Naturally, it was of the utmost importance to the publishers of the magazines that their periodicals were on sale on the usual day of publication. Because they wanted to be as topical as possible the original editorial material tended to be sent at the last minute, which meant that most printing was done to very tight schedules. Yet the often huge print runs made this a precarious business. Moreover, by the late 1960s the *TV Times* contract increasingly took on immense importance. At about seven million copies a week it was the largest-circulation magazine in Western Europe, and by 1974 all 13 separate regional editions were printed at Bemrose; with each individual copy being composed of two integrated sections it made a total print run of some 14 million. In these circumstances, management found themselves in an extremely vulnerable position since resistance to a union claim often appeared to make little short-term financial sense compared with the consequences of disrupted production and the loss of revenue and advertisers' confidence. As Bill observed:

> Management's strategy was to get the bloody job out, keep the thing moving, ye know. We were printing weekly publications, millions of copies, and any hiccup along the line could seriously affect production. When we printed the *TV Times* it was dated work, so if the work didn't leave the factory on a Thursday morning it wasn't going to be in the shops on time. Obviously, we took full advantage of that situation to gain some of the concessions over the years. That was the situation management had to contend with all the time. Oh yeah, Bemrose was strange, it was something else. Sometimes we'd walk out of negotiations and think, 'How the hell did we get away with that?' Basically, we had them by the bollocks in those days.

But it was not just objective factors that accounted for why the balance of workplace power was tilted in favour of union organization during the 1970s. There was also the subjective element, the high degree of conscious intervention involved in building up the strength of the chapel committees.

Each of the four chapels had highly efficient administrative arrangements and an authoritative committee structure that monitored all day-to-day working practices and drew up overtime and holiday rotas, allocating them to their members on the basis of seniority (thereby taking away from management the ability to choose people on a 'blue-eyed' system). As Peter recalled:

> If a manager had four machines running on a Saturday, he would go to his committee man and tell him he needed *so* many people. And the committee man would get the names of the individuals from the rotas to do the overtime – whether the management liked them or not. The committee determined who worked, when they worked and the number of hours they worked.

The SOGAT chapel committee also established powerful control over manning arrangements: mobility of labour both between and within departments was severely circumscribed, demarcation strictly adhered to and the manning on machines rigorously enforced.

The control exercised by the union did not materialize out of thin air; in many respects it was directly related to the left-wing political involvement of some of the principal committee activists. Alan worked at Bemrose for 30 years; elected as the SOGAT FoC in 1971, he remained in office for 16 years (serving as the Merseyside SOGAT branch president in the late 1970s) until his expulsion from the union in 1987. An active member of the Labour Party and supporter of Militant, he played a pivotal role in building the strength of chapel committee organization, particularly in relation to manning arrangements.

> After I'd become FoC I stopped the mobility of labour, people transferring from one department to another, with the primary aim of increasing the numbers employed. The agreed staffings on the machines were – for use of a better word – 'policed' by the chapel officials. In the machine room there were supposed to be ten SOGAT members and five NGA on each press. Well, from a SOGAT point of view it was obvious you were scratching around sometimes with nothing to do, but the union had the ultimate number of jobs in mind and the committee would discipline members for being absent from the press – so as to preserve jobs. That was the strength of organization on the floor.

Peter also stressed the controls over the job exercised by SOGAT chapel committee representatives:

> The movement of labour was very, very strict. If you were part of a crew on a press in the machine room you couldn't be moved to the finishing room. You could move *within* the department – they would post you from one job to another – but even then, if you worked for a certain

period of time on a machine it constituted part of the day and they
wouldn't be allowed to move you again on that day. Management
always accepted that.

Significantly, there were only a handful of strikes or stoppages of work
inside the Bemrose plant during the 1970s. Workers' strategic position
meant they felt there was little need to resort to such tactics in order to
squeeze concessions from management. Indeed, the SLADE process
chapel were never involved in a strike; the only major flashpoint occurred
in 1977 when they organized all their members to work only on the
morning shift for a week, in a bid to win shift premium for morning shift
work. The SOGAT chapel engaged in a three-week all-out strike of their
members in 1969 in a successful protest at management attempts to
increase production on the presses in the machine room from 25 000 to
30 000 copies an hour, and they were involved in a three-day all-out strike
over a similar issue in 1974, as well as a handful of other walk-outs of
two or three days' duration in the late 1970s. Generally however, major
stoppages of work were few and far between. Geoff, who worked in the
machine room from 1973 and served as a committee representative and
NGA machine chapel FoC in the late 1980s, related:

> There was only about nine major stoppages during the last 18 years and
> only about two of them involved the NGA. It was mainly SOGAT. You
> would get sanctions imposed every other year in the machine room by
> the NGA over the house agreement. It was the only way we could make
> ourselves felt because we were always chasing SLADE. We'd have
> one-hour, two-hour stoppages. Traditionally, we'd have disputes in the
> summer, because of the stinking heat in the place; it was like a biscuit
> tin. But very little disruption took place really.

Only on two occasions was an issue of the *TV Times* ever lost through
action taken by the chapels. For the vast majority of the time, despite
conflicts of interest, chapel committees and plant management were able
to find mutually acceptable arrangements and compromises with one
another through a process of 'strong bargaining relations'. Nonetheless,
as Bill pointed out, the balance was clearly tilted in favour of the unions:

> It would be 60–40 to the unions. Not over everything of course,
> management didn't lose hands down; on some issues they tried to dig

their heels in. But they didn't have it all their own way either. There
again, there wasn't any serious conflict. The unions were quite strong
and we took advantage of that.

Various forms of industrial action that fell short of a strike, such as an
overtime ban or work-to-rule, could still cause disruption and financial
damage and were used by chapel committees as a bargaining lever over
issues that were regarded as matters of principle, such as manning. Alan
described how even the threat to delay the dispatch of printed material
from the loading bay area of the finishing department was ultimately an
extremely potent weapon in the hands of the SOGAT chapel:

> It was a cat and mouse situation, guerrilla tactics rather than open
> warfare. The *TV Times* had delivery clauses, penalty clauses built into
> them. So the best negotiating tactic was to get all the magazines printed,
> get them on the loading bay, and then refuse to send them out. It would
> send the management crazy because they'd paid all the production
> costs, got it ready for delivery and the only place it could go was to pulp.
> The manager would know that and he'd cave in.

But such examples of industrial action occurred only occasionally; rarely
did any major confrontation between shop-floor workers and management
take place.

Significantly, the Bemrose company chairman from 1972 (until 1986)
was Bruce Matthews, who also played a central role at the head of
News International (the parent company), owned by Rupert Murdoch.
Murdoch's overall goals set the framework and constraints within which
Bemrose plant management in Liverpool could operate. Based at News
International headquarters in London, Matthews conducted all Bemrose's
major negotiations with the FoCs and other chapel representatives, particularly over house agreements. As Alan commented: 'Basically, the plant
was run down the end of a telephone from London.' Meanwhile, at plant
level, Bemrose management bargained separately with each of the four
workplace chapels (and their respective full-time officials from three
different unions).

The threat of redundancies or factory closure was often used by the
company, particularly when the contracts for the *TV Times* came up for
renewal, following warnings that petty restrictions by the unions were
hampering productivity and competitiveness (SLADE process chapel

committee minutes, 20 January 1972; NGA '82 process chapel committee minutes, 26 May 1981, 7 November 1983). Mark, a member of the Socialist Workers Party, who worked at Bemrose for 11 years (mainly in the machine room) and served as a SOGAT committee representative and federated chapel secretary during the 1980s, related:

> Management were always threatening redundancies. They'd say: 'If we lose a contract it will be on your head.' Obviously that was always present in people's minds but it was a bit like Peter and the Wolf. They were always wringing their hands and saying the company wasn't making money, and in fact, on the books, the company didn't make any profits from 1957 to 1987 – in accountancy terms they lost money every year. So every time they came to us with their violin stories and sob tales we simply said: 'We've heard it all before. We get the same story from you every week.'

Despite the repeated warnings the money somehow seemed to be found, the magazines continued to be printed and the plant stayed open.

Indeed, management appeared more concerned to keep production rolling smoothly with the minimum of disruption, avoiding open confrontation with the chapels. Bill provided an example of what this could mean:

> In the '70s we had three different managers who tried to make a name for themselves. They wanted to radically change things and assert their authority. They'd say: 'Why's he doing that?', because we had a lot of what they used to call 'Spanish practices' going on. But when we got a manager like that he would be told off by his own side. In fact it was quite comical for the workforce because all three of them ended up leaving the plant. Generally speaking though, they all backed the management line. They'd back off from situations rather than have a big battle over it.

Yet given that, officially at least, the plant was not profitable, it is curious to speculate as to why Bemrose and Rupert Murdoch's News International bothered to continue to keep it open for so many years. Such a question is very difficult to answer definitively, although Alan provided one extremely intriguing assessment:

> It took me quite a number of years but I eventually found out why. Obviously we were in receipt of all the balance sheets. We had access to

all the information from the company and all the information from Companies House. We employed an actuary to assist us and, when we needed them, chartered accountants to advise us. What I believe was happening is this. At the time, we were printing the largest-circulation periodical in the country. Rupert Murdoch and Bruce Matthews were presented with gold badges by the Finnish government for buying paper from them. I believe that the profit was not in the *TV Times* magazine, the profit was always in who ordered the paper. It gave Murdoch high-quality paper which gave him an advantage when it came to purchasing the paper for the *Sun* and *News of the World*, which he got at the same time probably at considerably reduced prices. Therefore, the profit went directly into the *Sun* and *News of the World* rather than going into Eric Bemrose. That is *why* I believe they ran it and *how* they ran it.

Of course, such conjecture by the SOGAT FoC is impossible to authenticate, although it might provide some explanation as to why Bemrose management appeared willing to permit the exercise of such powerful shop-floor controls by the chapel committees so long as production was maintained at consistently high rates throughout the 1970s.

The 1970s: Stewards' Weaknesses

Despite the formidable strengths of the chapel committees inside the Bemrose plant there were also some inherent weaknesses which need to be considered. Whilst in many respects it was sectional muscle that provided the basis for many shop-floor union gains, there is no doubt the most debilitating handicap was the sectionalism that existed within and between the different departments, chapels and unions. Mark explained the antagonism between the craft union NGA and the non-craft union SOGAT in the machine room:

A lot of the problems between the NGA and SOGAT arose because the NGA would always stand on their laurels as being tradesmen, having served their time. I mean, I left school when I was 16 and worked in the printing industry – in Bemrose – ever since, for 17 years. But as far as the NGA are concerned you're still a labourer. They always had the attitude that you're there to brush up and clean around after them and nothing else.

There was a similar craft antagonism in the processing department between SLADE and SOGAT chapel members, as Bill acknowledged:

Some of the SLADE members were very élitist, ye know, very right-wing. They looked down on others, at this riff-raff if you like, the unskilled people in SOGAT. I mean OK, I carried a briefcase into work – but it was full of union stuff. But you would get some SLADE members coming into work with a briefcase with their bloody pyjamas or something in it, anything to look the businessman type . . . The pecking order in terms of élitism and craftism was SLADE at the top, the two NGA chapels underneath them and all them looking down on SOGAT.

Craft and union demarcations, rooted in a jealous guarding of control over aspects of the production process, were a perennial source of friction between the chapels, as Alan related:

The hatred on the shop-floor was on a daily basis. When you placed a cylinder in a machine it was two NGA and two SOGAT. The two NGA could only hold the bar – if they put the end on, SOGAT just walked away. You couldn't hold a *bar*, they couldn't hold the *cup*, that's how strict it was. Then in the finishing department if you were webbing a machine up you had to have your correct number up, because if your number wasn't there the NGA would snitch on you and vice versa. Every job was fought for, every job was determined. Hence the mistrust, the conflict came to a head. People could be standing around for a couple of hours arguing whose job it was.

These craft tensions were exacerbated by changes in work organization, such as modifications to machinery, which made some of the traditional operations open to replacement by simpler and quicker processes. Ironically, some of the most serious disputes in the factory occurred between the chapels themselves rather than with management, particularly between SOGAT and the SLADE or NGA chapels (SLADE process chapel committee minutes, 31 August 1971). Such inter-union rivalry was very damaging to shop-floor union organization.

At one level the problem of sectionalism can be seen on the issue of pay. Up until 1972 each chapel negotiated its own separate house agreement (which did not necessarily run for concurrent periods). This fragmented negotiating structure ensured a jungle of competing wage rates and conditions with each chapel grabbing what it could depending on the strength of its bargaining position or abilities of its negotiators. No fewer than 151 different pay grades operated across the factory; not only were there different rates for craft and non-craft, but some were also based on the different types of machinery a person operated, for example working with colour as opposed to monochrome. Many workers, even members of the same union, did not know what wages others in the plant received. When the SOGAT chapel took strike action in 1969 over pay, management conceded an increase of £2.86 for their members in the machine room, but the dispute dragged on for three weeks because both the NGA and SLADE chapels refused to work with SOGAT until management agreed to maintain a 12.5 per cent differential between them. Alan remembered:

> Because of the 1969 SOGAT dispute it was obvious nobody could go it alone. So I set about to organize the other unions collectively rather than going in individually and sniping at one another. I tried to organize a united front, but it was extremely difficult because of the historical factor of the print unions and their distrust of one another. You had to try to rise above that and convince them that as trade unionists the concept, the principle, was the most important thing, not individuals. Obviously, at chapel meetings it was easy to stand up and say, 'Fuck the NGA.' But I used to have to convince my own that whether we liked it or not we had to reconcile the position that they were always going to be there. And we *did* get a federated chapel.

Only in 1972, after intense lobbying (mainly by the SOGAT FoC) and delicate negotiations was agreement finally reached to form a federated house chapel in Bemrose (effectively a joint shop stewards' committee), which subsequently succeeded in reducing the number of different pay rates to 14.

Nonetheless, whilst most of the workplace chapels (namely the SOGAT, NGA machine and NGA composing chapels, as well as the smaller maintenance union chapels) became party to a joint house agreement between Bemrose and a new federated chapel organization, the SLADE process members (later known as the NGA '82 chapel) proceeded to negotiate their own *separate* house agreement right up until the mid-1980s. The highly specialized skills of SLADE process members encouraged them to guard their highly advantageous position, which in 1976 enabled SLADE members to earn on average £72 a week compared with £63 for NGA members and £42 for SOGAT members. In fact, following a dispute involving SLADE in 1977, the differential widened even further and by 1980 they earned an average of £26 a week over and above the NGA (Bill's working notes). Bill recalled why the SLADE chapel insisted on maintaining a separate bargaining forum:

> Management did try to get a joint negotiating forum but the blockage point was the SLADE chapel because we said: 'Hang on, no, we've got an exclusive position here, we want to retain it, ye know. We don't want to get involved in the zoo, in the in-fighting.' The other chapels were in a joint negotiating forum, but they spent a lot of their time arguing amongst themselves, holding on to their own autonomies, whereas SLADE's only adversary was the company.

Rob worked for 28 years in the finishing department, serving as a SOGAT committee rep between 1973 and 1987 and federated chapel secretary between 1984 and 1987. A left-wing member of the Labour Party, he emphasized how the 'unwritten law' of differentials between craft and non-craft workers ensured, even under the new federated chapel umbrella, an enduring sectionalism:

> The NGA machine chapel had loads of different rates but they used to keep three of their members – the mono hands in the blade shop – on their lowest rate to make sure they kept the differential with SOGAT. We used to encourage the NGA to go in for as much as they could get on the basis that everybody would benefit; if they got more then so would we because we got 87.5 per cent of it. But we couldn't get that home to them. To a certain extent they didn't want to know. They were that busy looking over their shoulder to see what SOGAT were doing they never bothered looking in front of them to see what SLADE were doing. The NGA fella would be on about £12 000 and the SLADE fella would be on about £16 000, but the NGA fella was happy because he was earning more than the SOGAT fella. Those bigots would sooner keep *your* wages down than see you fighting management.

The autonomy of each union and of individual chapels became a deeply rooted part of print workers' attitudes in Bemrose. It coloured the outlook of even the most socialist of chapel committee representatives. As Alan acknowledged: 'We fell in with the macho image of "our union is better than yours" from time to to time without a doubt.' Not surprisingly, management were able to exploit such divisions, sometimes setting one chapel up against the other and avoiding a situation where all the chapels could present an effective united challenge.

A second factor weakening the strength of the chapel committees' organization was the retention of low-level management as members of the craft unions SLADE and NGA. Unlike in many manufacturing plants where shop-floor workers belong to one trade union and supervisors and management to another, in Bemrose, as with other printing plants, the situation was much less clear cut. In SLADE, there were 'deputy managers', who provided low-level supervision within the process department and received 10 per cent better wages. But the NGA had the more ambiguous arrangement, particularly in the machine room, with not only chargehands (known as 'number ones') and shift foremen (known as 'whitecoats') but also departmental shift managers allowed to be members of the union and attend union meetings. Almost inevitably, they tended to act as a buffer between workers and management. Bob Henderson outlined the ambiguous role of the 'number ones':

> The problem with the number ones from a trade union point of view was getting to grips with them. They were left in an island. If the chapel wanted to kick somebody they kicked the number one. But the number ones didn't want the hassle of slowing down production because they'd have to answer for it. So they'd report the problem to the whitecoat and in turn it'd go to the shift manager. But it went the other way as well. The machine room management would kick the whitecoat, the whitecoat would kick the number one and the number one would kick the rest of the workforce. Very often they'd know they couldn't win. If they sided with the chapel committee, management was against them, and if they sided with management they created a friction on the shop-floor. It's because of that friction we were always kicking our own union. At least SOGAT have a different union to kick when it comes to management.

In many respects, this contradiction was the NGA machine chapel's Achilles' heel. Mark explained:

> In the NGA the well-worn route was to do your apprenticeship, do a couple of years on the chapel committee, get elected as a chapel officer, become a whitecoat supervisor and then become a manager and reach the other side. The vast majority of chargehands had been NGA committee men and one of their longer-serving FoCs was a number one

and went on to be the shift manager in the machine room. In fact, at the same time as he put his name forward to be branch secretary of the NGA branch he put in his application to be a whitecoat.

Many shop-floor NGA members, who felt forever indebted to number ones for protecting their particular job niche in the past, continued to display their loyalty and gratitude even after the latter had advanced into the ranks of management. As a consequence, plant managers were able to utilize a network of contacts within the NGA chapel to be kept informed of confidential committee deliberations and decisions. As Alan related:

> It meant there was no trust between the chapels. We couldn't quite confidently make suggestions of what we were going to do in an open forum because within minutes management were well aware of what we were going to do.

The existence of a transmission belt from the shop-floor upwards to management inside the NGA undermined the strength of the SOGAT chapel committee.

The third weakness of chapel organization was the contradictory nature of the FoCs' position *vis-à-vis* management, in particular the tendencies towards a semi-managerial role. The house agreements were relatively highly formalized and meticulously codified documents covering many aspects of working arrangements, including the machine running speeds and the output anticipated both on a daily and weekly basis. Alan explained the rationale behind them:

> We learnt in the early '70s that we had to draw up a detailed agreement, otherwise if it wasn't written down there was no way you could get management to agree. So we made them detailed. In fact to counteract this, what News International and Rupert Murdoch did was to appoint journalists as personnel directors or labour relations officers. They felt, because of the control the unions had with the agreements, they needed qualified people to write them up.

Obviously there were some merits to such formalized house agreements from a chapel committee's point of view: they committed management to honour jointly negotiated arrangements and made arbitrary or unilateral decision making and changes in working practices much more difficult to justify. Yet the problem was that such agreements also made it more difficult for chapel committees to evade the burden of responsibility for enforcing the terms of such agreements on their own shop-floor members, ensuring compliance with some onerous conditions. Mark recognized the dilemma:

> Rightly or wrongly there tended to be little room for interpretation because the agreement was sacrosanct, enshrined in 'tablets of stone' which both management and union had to honour. You couldn't go to a manager and say, 'We're honouring our side – you honour your side of the agreement', if he could prove that patently you weren't honouring your side. Obviously you had to enforce that with your members, you had to police them to an extent.

In effect, the FoC became a central link between the manager and workers in a department, essential to the efficient and smooth running of the plant.

A graphic illustration of the complexity of these relations was the monitoring of production figures by the FoCs. In 1976 the federated chapel won a 5 per cent pay increase and a four-night week on the night shift, changing what had been an 11 pm–5.30 am Friday night/Saturday morning shift to a 11 pm–3 am shift, which made a 32-hour working week (for the night shift). Yet against the background of the Labour government's 5 per cent wage freeze, the deal was only conceded on the basis of maintaining production output at its previous level. The deal obliged the FoCs to adopt a new role. Alan recalled what this involved within the SOGAT chapel:

> My job as FoC was to uphold our part of the agreement – which necessitated doing the production with the management. Every day I got all the production figures from management and went through them and checked to see if we were upholding our end of the deal. That was my first job each day, to check the figures for the last 24 hours.

The outcome of such a role was that not only did it spur union members to work faster but it also tended to encourage a positive attitude towards managerial production priorities and methods, something which helped to provide the basis for the logic of acquiescence in the face of subsequent product market difficulties.

The final limitation to the power of the chapel committees was evident in the way some shop-floor working practices were double-edged in their effect. For example, the so-called 'welt system' was widespread through-out the chapels, with workers operating for two hours on the job and then unofficially taking two hours off during a shift. Rob recalled:

> There was a lot of 'welt working', you could say it was rampant. Most people were able to take time off the job and get away with it because the machines were running. Management would close their eyes to a lot that went on so long as production was kept up. Some people on nights were virtually never there and the job was done by somebody else, and the next week the other bloke would be off, it was the 'week about'.

The question naturally arises, why did management tolerate such workers' job controls – even if they disputed their application in particular cases? Partly, it was because the chapels had the power to impose various practices willy-nilly, but it was also because turning a blind eye to certain shop-floor practices kept the chapels relatively satisfied and encouraged them not to make 'excessive' demands. Moreover, despite the 'welt working', production figures in the plant were actually kept at consistently quite high rates. Ironically, it also meant that in some departments a work-to-rule, adopted as a sanction against management by the chapel committees, effectively backfired because it ended up with workers being even more 'productive' than previously.

The problem of overtime encapsulated the contradiction in sharp relief. Throughout the 1970s there was a massive amount of regular overtime working in the plant. Bill emphasized the obvious material gain for many shop-floor workers:

> The overtime rates were absolutely phenomenal. You could work four hours a day mid-week and maybe a day at the weekend. We used to call that a 'Chinese weekend'. All overtime was at double time, something like £14 an hour, so some people were taking out three or four weeks' wages.

High rates of overtime working resulted partly from the inherent problems of printing 13 separate regional editions of the *TV Times* every week, with many millions of copies, and from the fluctuating and seasonal nature of magazine production, with its peaks and troughs during the week and at different times of the year. Formally, the chapels and union branches placed limits on the overtime they were prepared to allow their members to work – in SOGAT there was a limit of four hours a week – after which they were only offered further hours after everyone else in the factory had had the opportunity to do a stint. In practice, much more overtime became available than the chapel committees would have preferred, providing management with a useful carrot to dangle in front of workers to buy shop-floor peace. Rob reflected:

> As a trade unionist and socialist, I and others felt that what we should really have been doing is not relying on overtime for a decent wage. Unfortunately, in those times of high overtime we saw people thinking pure and simply for themselves. People were prepared to do somebody down to get at their overtime. That was a problem and management could use that to play one off against the other, in some cases one department against another. It only needed a word in the right ear: 'I see the planning department are working Saturday.' That's all it needed. Before you knew it there was murder. It was like dogs fighting over a bone.

Such practices as high overtime working helped to create the conditions for inter-departmental and inter-union sectional rivalries.

Thus, there was an extremely contradictory relationship between the chapel committees and management in the Bemrose plant during the 1970s. On the one hand, the degree of power exercised by the unions through a 'strong bargaining relationship' with management was much higher than in many manufacturing plants. On the other hand, their sectional divisions and peculiar working arrangements tended to handicap shop-floor unity much deeper than elsewhere. It was a curious mixture. But if the balance of workplace power lay to the advantage of the chapel committees during the 1970s the product market crisis of the 1980s changed the situation dramatically.

Stewards' Relationship to Management: The 1980s

The Early 1980s: 'Coming Unstuck'

During the early 1980s the British printing industry, under increasing competitive pressure from European companies, began urgently to embark on the task of replacing ageing machinery with new computer technology. At the same time, economic recession put the squeeze on profitability; shop-floor peace could no longer be bought at any price and many national and provincial printing companies raced to use the new technology to break the closed shop, transform working practices and slash the number of jobs. For example, in 1978 *The Times* newspaper management locked out its workforce for 11 months in a bid to force changes in working practices and wrest control from chapel union organization. Similarly, the other two of the 'Big Three' gravure factories in the country, the Odhams and Sun plant in Watford and the Purnell plant in Bristol, suffered massive job cuts.

Bemrose was not immune from such competitive pressures. Suffering from a chronic lack of new investment, the plant was under constant threat of closure. The crisis in the product market led to a sudden abandonment of Bemrose management's 'strong bargaining relations' with the chapel committees in favour of a more confrontational stance. Evidence of such a shift began to become apparent after the 1979 all-out national strike by electricians on Independent Television blacked out scheduled ITV programmes throughout the country and brought an abrupt halt to production of the *TV Times* magazine in the Bemrose plant for 10 weeks. Although shop-floor workers were paid their full wages during this time there was a great deal of uncertainty as to the long-term future of the Merseyside site. It was the threat posed to jobs (as well as the impending merger of SLADE and the NGA) which provided the spur for the formation of a joint federated chapel committee embracing all the chapels on site (including, for the first time, the SLADE process chapel).

The loss of the *TV Times* magazine, albeit for a temporary period, was to be only a foretaste of what would happen a year later at the beginning of 1981, when Bemrose's single most important contract was lost completely. As Mark described, the shock was devastating:

> Most of the people who had just been taken on at Bemrose, like me, had been taken on on the understanding that Bemrose was printing the *TV Times*. There was a seven-year contract up for grabs and Bemrose was the only individual gravure house in the country that had the capacity to print the whole thing in one go. We'd been fairly confident we would retain it because we were doing the whole job under one roof, everything from artwork origination through finishing to dispatch. So when we heard we hadn't won the renewed contract it was like a bolt from the blue. We were confronted, yet again, with a period of about 10–12 weeks where

we had no work. We were still going into work and being paid, but we just sat there doing nothing. For me, that was the beginning of the slippery slope, that was when things started to come unstuck.

Officially, the loss of the *TV Times* contract resulted from the undercutting of Bemrose's bid to continue its production by its arch-rival the British Printing and Communications Corporation (BPCC) owned by Robert Maxwell, who subsequently organized for the printing of the magazine in six different plants across the country, and its dispatch from a seventh. It is questionable whether production costs became any cheaper as a result of such a dispersed printing arrangement. Certainly, there was intense speculation amongst the leading chapel activists that rather than 'losing' the *TV Times* contract Murdoch actually handed it over to Maxwell. They believed this could have occurred possibly because of the constant problems of printing an allegedly unprofitable magazine or because the Finnish government connection was no longer central to Murdoch's global operations. Again, such speculation is impossible to confirm, but it is of major significance that the chapel activists became convinced that tremendous intrigue surrounded the intense behind-the-scenes competition between media magnates Rupert Murdoch and Robert Maxwell.

Not surprisingly, losing the *TV Times* contract, this time permanently, threw the chapel committees in Bemrose into some disarray as the prospect of large-scale redundancies loomed over the horizon. The company quickly took the opportunity to present a 'Survival Plan' document, aimed at involving the unions in a collaborative effort to make the plant more efficient through wide-ranging changes in working practices and manning arrangements. They produced a barrage of figures to demonstrate their poor financial performance and bad labour productivity. As Bill emphasized, negotiations over the Survival Plan opened up against the background of great uncertainty as to the long-term future of the plant:

Management said they were going to negotiate the Survival Plan with us. It contained things like changed job practices, more mobility and interchangeability. It was a dramatic announcement. They told us we were under threat of the whole factory collapsing, we were losing so much money. They said they had to make maximum use of the workforce available. They'd used threats of job loss in the past but this was much more serious.

The chapels stood firm, initially at least, in resisting the Survival Plan. But their resolve was severely put to the test when simultaneous house agreement negotiations (which had become deadlocked over a dispute with the NGA machine chapel) were abruptly suspended following the direct intervention of Rupert Murdoch. Murdoch threatened the plant would be closed within two weeks unless a 7.5 per cent pay offer was accepted, and warned that any dispute in the interim would also precipitate closure (NGA '82 process chapel committee minutes, 26 May 1981). Such unexpected belligerency was enough to force the federated chapel's hand, and the house agreement was signed on the company's terms within the deadline stipulated.

Soon afterwards, in June 1981, there were even more unprecedented developments, when all FoCs, local branch secretaries and full-time national union officials were summoned to a 'Future of Bemrose' crisis meeting held at the prestigious Adelphi Hotel located in Liverpool's city centre. Much to everyone's amazement they were informed of the complete takeover of Bemrose by Robert Maxwell's BPCC (NGA '82 process chapel committee minutes, 25 June 1981). Maxwell, owner of the Mirror Group Newspapers (including the *Daily Mirror*, *Sunday Mirror*, *People* and *Sporting Life*) and with extensive interests in publishing (including Macmillan and Pergamon) and television (including Central TV), had been engaged in cut-throat competition with Murdoch for a number of years in the scramble to control Britain's press. Nonetheless, it seemed to union activists that he was being offered Bemrose on a plate by his foremost adversary. Mark takes up the story:

> Suddenly the ownership of the company changed hands. Murdoch gave the company lock, stock and barrel to Robert Maxwell. He gave him the factory, the contracts, the machinery, the management, the workforce, the whole lot. All he wanted him to give him in return was the pension fund, in cash.

The chapel committees viewed Maxwell's sudden and immediate takeover of the Bemrose plant with deep foreboding, as Bill related:

> People were terrified of Maxwell, because they thought, 'Here's the wheeler dealer, he's only bought it to flog it off.' Although the funny thing is, he wasn't buying it, he was being given it by Murdoch. The way we looked at it Maxwell was picking it up so he could dispose of it, a

classic asset-stripping operation. We were pretty certain he would have
closed us down as a way of getting rid of the competition to his BPCC
plants. Maxwell owned two of the four gravure houses in the country. He
made massive redundancies a day or two after taking over Sun and
Odhams in Watford and we could see exactly the same kind of scenario
in Liverpool. We knew the only reason he would want Bemrose would be
to close it down and transfer the work to his other two plants so they
could be run at full capacity. Bemrose was expendable.

On the surface, at least for a period of ten weeks, the Murdoch–Maxwell
deal apparently began to take effect. Robert Maxwell actually visited the
Merseyside plant, addressed a meeting of the workforce declaring, 'I now
own Bemrose', and moved his appointed managers on to the site to take
over day-to-day operational control. But behind the official veneer, the
exchange deal had not been conclusively signed and eventually fell apart
just as spectacularly as it had been cobbled together, after Maxwell was
apparently unable to raise the pension fund cash.

The machinations that lay behind the on/off deal are quite complex and
have proved impossible to fathom out entirely, even though Alan provided
a plausible explanation:

> I'm convinced from what we have found out since, that Rupert Murdoch
> was attempting to take full control of Collins, the publishers. He only had
> 40 per cent of the shares and Maxwell had X amount of shares. What he
> attempted to do was give him Bemrose, which was worth nothing – at
> the time we estimated the factory was worth about £5 million over the
> ten years Maxwell was going to pay him back. But for that, Maxwell
> would get rid of a major competitor in Eric Bemrose. In return, he would
> sell the shares in Collins to Murdoch. They definitely did a deal. But
> basically the main reason Maxwell dropped it in the end was because he
> couldn't stump up the cash for the pension fund and the deal didn't go
> through.

Whatever the stratagem that lay behind the takeover deal, the whole thing
had been cancelled by October 1981, when Rupert Murdoch resumed
ownership of the Bemrose plant. The immediate practical outcome was an
acceleration in the implementation of the Survival Plan, placed on the
table for negotiation earlier in the year.

The takeover débâcle deepened the chapel committees' fears of future job prospects and induced a greater willingness to make substantial concessions to improve the plant's efficiency. Rob noted:

> They put the Survival Plan on the table and said if we were going to survive in the long term this is what we were going to have to come to some agreement on. A lot of people put their head in their hands and said, 'Thank Christ I've still got a job': that was the response to it.

This 'new realism' was further deepened when the company confirmed speculation that it would be going ahead and launching a new, large-circulation magazine, the *News of the World* colour supplement *Sunday*, to be printed at Bemrose to replace the *TV Times*, which at six million copies per week would became the second biggest gravure job in Western Europe. Although it held out the immediate prospect of job security the company was able skilfully to exploit the vulnerability of chapel organization by making acceptance of the terms and conditions of its original Survival Plan a precondition of the Bemrose plant receiving the new contract. The chapel committees, seeing their counterparts in other printing plants across the country (who were endangered by new technology and the breakdown of occupational demarcations) acquiescing to massive changes, felt they could do little to defend their own formerly highly advantageous bargaining position and reluctantly accepted the company terms. In the circumstances, it would seem the chapel committees had little option but to accept that compromise and retreat were necessary. The threat of redundancies or even plant closure proved decisive.

But with the benefit of hindsight, it later became apparent to some committee representatives that the chapels' submission was probably far from necessary. Once Bemrose had announced it intended to take on the new *Sunday* contract it became clear that News International (the owner of the *News of the World*) had known for some months beforehand that it would be launching a new in-house magazine, even if there was uncertainty about where it would be printed. But once Rupert Murdoch had resumed ownership of Bemrose, the Merseyside site became the obvious choice, particularly as, by now, the *TV Times* contract no longer existed. In other words, it seems highly likely Bemrose had no real intention of closing the plant down. If it had wanted to do so it had thrown away three perfect opportunities, firstly, during the 10-week TV electricians' strike; secondly, following the loss of the *TV Times* magazine contract; or thirdly, immediately after the collapse of the Maxwell takeover. Instead, preparing to take on the *Sunday* magazine was a clear signal that Bemrose intended to continue production at its Merseyside plant, at least for the immediate future.

What this suggests is that, notwithstanding their real concern about job losses, it might have been possible for the federated chapel to have maintained some limited shop-floor resistance to the Survival Plan. Such action might have forced the company to backtrack, at least on some of its more draconian measures. But tremendous weight was also being placed on the SOGAT chapel committee from another quarter, as Alan related:

> The main aim of the Survival Plan from the company's point of view was to make the place more efficient. But there was also pressure coming from the national union. So we were getting kicked from both ends, from the company and the national union. We had to be seen to be doing something. What we didn't want was to have the union officials coming in, because they would have agreed to anything.

National full-time officials claimed the Survival Plan was essential for the survival of Bemrose and that resistance would not only be futile but akin to a modern form of Luddism. Thus, a pincer movement between News International and national union officials effectively forced the Bemrose chapels to submit to the bulk of the changes in working practices stipulated in the Survival Plan.

Even though the federated chapel were subsequently able to bargain over the details of its actual implementation, the Plan was severe in its overall effect. To start with, the old 'hot-metal' composing department became a victim of the new computerized technology which was sweeping the printing industry. It was completely closed down with the loss of 93 jobs; this led to the disbandment of the NGA composing chapel and left only three major union chapels on the site. Enforced retirement at the age of 65 further reduced the workforce by another 61 people, mainly from the process department. But by far the most serious development involved the introduction of wide-ranging flexibility in working practices throughout the plant. The Survival Plan document stated:

> The following measures have been agreed between the management and chapels in a determined effort to try to restore the company to a viable operating condition, to improve the company's ability to compete for

work, both at home and abroad . . . the principle is accepted that, in departments where there is insufficient work, there will be no manning up to predetermined numbers . . . in SOGAT departments full interchangeability will apply within each department . . . there will be no overtime, either mid-week or at weekends, to make up shift numbers and all overtime will relate to production requirements . . . there will be no restrictions whatsoever on outputs . . . the officers of the various chapels undertake to discourage any activity which appears detrimental to the efficiency and/or economic performance of the company.

(Eric Bemrose Survival Plan, 1981)

Despite the apparent adverse circumstances in which the Survival Plan had been introduced the federated chapel were subsequently able to convince management to make a *quid pro quo* agreement to reduce the number of different wage rates in the factory from 14 to four (although this still excluded the SLADE chapel, which remained independent). This in turn helped to overcome some of the traditional rivalries between the different unions in the plant.

An indication of the continuing resilience of workplace chapel organization was the campaign for parity of craft rates that ensued in 1982. The driving force behind the demand for parity was the NGA machine chapel, who had seen the differential between their pay rates and the NGA '82 process chapel (formerly SLADE) widen considerably. The recent merger of the two craft unions, even though separate chapels remained in Bemrose, provided a further incentive for the machine chapel to seek a levelling of the craft rates within the plant. The consequential adjustment to the rates that would be paid to non-craft SOGAT members helped to ensure a much broader layer of support for parity generally. After an overtime ban and work-to-rule had been imposed without success, the NGA machine chapel walked out on unofficial strike for a week before management finally agreed to open up immediate preparations for a phased equalization of craft rates of pay. A joint working party was set up between the federated chapel and management, and by 1986, after a prolonged and arduous four-year phasing-in exercise, only two craft and two non-craft rates of pay remained within the factory.

Given that, traditionally, differentials are sacrosanct within the printing industry, agreeing to *uniform* rates heralded a unique achievement. For the vast majority of the workforce in Bemrose it meant a substantial pay increase. At the same time, despite persistent internal rifts, the federated chapel were gradually able to steer a course that united all workplace union representatives towards a common objective. Nonetheless, parity was achieved at a tremendous price. The final terms of the deal were accepted only after management threatened to cancel a new contract to print the *Sunday Express* colour magazine and after national full-time trade union officials had made an agreement over the heads of the chapel committees. Moreover, the key principle underlining the deal, on which there was unanimity from chapel committees and union officials alike, stipulated:

> The cost of equalizing craft rates and the proportional adjustment to on-craft rates will be funded through the productivity savings generated through changes in working practices and manning arrangements aimed at improving efficiency and maximizing output in all departments of the factory. (Joint Working Party Agreement, August 1983)

In other words, management only agreed to parity on the basis that it as a *self-financing* arrangement; the £1.75 million necessary to fund it was actually raised by shop-floor workers themselves. Thus, each year for four years, the productivity savings made by workers in each department were put into a 'common pool' on a pro rata basis, and a proportion of it was distributed to the workforce. For example, in the first year 80 per cent of the savings went to the unions and 20 per cent to management. Parity was achieved in four stages, 20 per cent, 40 per cent, 20 per cent and 20 per cent. Any small additional savings which exceeded the cost of parity were shared out equally amongst all the chapels.

Having previously enjoyed disproportionately high rates of pay the NGA '82 process chapel were placed in the extremely invidious position of having to agree to make productivity savings which would contribute towards achieving parity for the *other* chapels. Apart from receiving the national printing industry minimum award the process chapel pay levels were kept at a relatively static level. Yet with the introduction of new technology (particularly laser scanners and a litho conversion unit) the process department also faced a severe cutback in jobs. However, it was the SOGAT chapel, by virtue of being half the workforce, that had to make the most severe sacrifices to fund the parity exercise. Mark acknowledged:

> Management agreed to parity because on a long-term basis it was in
> their interest. It was a way of whittling down staff because the major
> savings from it came from the non-replacement of labour. If they could
> make the workforce more efficient they could bring more work in and
> thus generate more profit . . . We did several things, we gave up the
> right to overtime cover on holidays, we de-manned on the presses,
> speeds went up wherever possible, there were faster change-overs.

In the absence of any substantial investment by the company, new
working methods were accepted that led to what Alan referred to as
'MFI' – mobility, flexibility and interchangeability; traditional lines of
demarcation between departments were cut out (particularly in the process department where a new negative assembly area was set up combining
the retouching, planning and camera sections) (Joint Working Party
Agreement, August 1983); a programme of natural wastage which had
begun earlier continued, resulting in an overall reduction of the workforce
from 1400-plus to 1338; and overtime levels were virtually eradicated
throughout the plant, reducing the company's bill by £1.5 million. By
1986 Bemrose's apparent loss-making position had been turned around
into a profit of £4.7 million (Federated Chapel campaign brochure, 1987).

Whilst the chapel committees' acceptance of self-financing wage
increases (like their acquiescence to improved efficiency and productivity)
followed managerial rationality, there were some important countervailing tendencies to those working to undermine shop-floor bargaining
leverage. Ironically, despite the reduction in labour achieved through
natural wastage, management soon discovered that the sheer volume of
production meant they had to employ an extra 100 NGA printers and
SOGAT assistants in the machine room and other departments; this
brought the overall numbers employed in the plant by 1986 back to
previous levels; and even the amount of overtime was increased slightly in
some departments. This meant that for many Bemrose workers the plant
appeared to have been cushioned from the full rigours of the recession and
wave of redundancies occurring elsewhere across Merseyside. Moreover,
although management had encroached on hitherto 'excessive' shop-floor
working practices and 'overmanning' of machines, the chapel committees
still retained control over many aspects of their immediate work situation.
As Mark recalled:

> Management did try to reassert their authority. We went through a phase
> where the company tried to sack us on a regular basis and then reinstate

us all the next day. They did it regularly in the machine room just to test
how far they could go over flexibility. We used to call it the '15-minute
warning'. We were forever doing deals over the mobility of labour and of
course they would come to us and say they wanted to move somebody
to another department. We'd say: 'Fine, but he's got to be trained and
be paid for it.' Once the manager in the machine room gave me and
another committee man the 15-minute warning to comply with an
instruction – otherwise we would be sacked. Well, we'd already had a
chapel meeting and agreed that if they sent one of us home the whole
section walked. So everyone just clocked off. I'd say we had people
sacked five or six times over a period in 1986 . . . We finally came to an
agreement that there would be a list of volunteers ready to be moved,
but they would be paid on a higher band worth about £17 a week, and
they could only be moved once a week.

Thus, even if management felt much more confident in confronting the
power of the chapels they were by no means able to get their own way on
every issue.

On the other hand, the relatively much more conciliatory relationship
with management established during the 1980s reflected a significant
shift in the balance of workplace power to the disadvantage of chapel union
organization. Apart from the product market crisis, two other factors,
both internal and external, reinforced this trend. Firstly, there was the
removal of Alan (Hebden) as SOGAT chapel FoC and his expulsion
from the union by full-time officials, which had the effect of dissipating
the energies of the SOGAT chapel committee and impairing its bargaining
effectiveness *vis-à-vis* management (explored in more detail below).
Secondly, there was the impact of the defeats of workers' struggles within
the trade union movement generally and the print industry in particular.
Thus, in November 1983 ranks of riot police repeatedly baton-charged
NGA '82 pickets outside the printworks of the *Stockport Messenger* newspaper in Warrington, where (with the help of Conservative government
anti-union legislation) Eddie Shah had set up a non-union factory
equipped with computer technology (Dickenson, 1984). The effect on
Bemrose workers, especially those groups who attended the nearby picket
line, was devastating, as Bill described:

When people saw what was going on they said, 'Good God, is this
Britain?' They were very shocked by it, when they saw that militia

coming out smacking people over their heads with truncheons. The
effect it had was the opposite of what we had wanted. It was clearly
shown to the people who went, what was to come if you tried to beat
Thatcherism, if you ever really tried anything on. If anything it fed the
feeling you can't win . . . The NGA had a hut there and it just got turned
over, smashed to bits. I mean, it's like someone knocking your house
down, ye know. That's our little castle, it was a psychological blow. The
effect was to terrify many people.

The defeat of the national miners' strike of 1984–85 was another
psychological blow; having regularly made financial contributions to
miners' pickets from local pits in Lancashire, Bemrose workers felt its
impact quite deeply. Even more devastating was Rupert Murdoch's defeat
of the bitter, long-drawn-out strike by 5000 sacked print workers at
News International's Wapping plant in 1986–87, which signalled the
scale of the transformation taking place in Britain's newspaper and
printing industry.

1987–1991: Redundancies and Closure
The decisive blow to chapel strength was delivered in April 1987 when
management announced 775 redundancies, a 60 per cent reduction of the
workforce from 1342 to 567, involving the total closure of certain areas
of the factory including the 'front end' of the process department. In
addition, Bemrose sought the replacement of the in-house transport
department by News International's own TNT distribution network,
and the sub-contracting of catering, cleaning and security operations.
The justification offered for such a massive restructuring of production
was the loss of the *Sunday Express* colour magazine contract to Robert
Maxwell's BPCC organization – a loss of revenue of £10 million. Bemrose
insisted there was no room for negotiation either on the level of the job
losses decreed or on the company's arbitrary selection of individuals. In
response, the federated chapel launched an immediate public campaign
of opposition to the redundancies, publishing a 12-page glossy information brochure and winning support from local Labour MPs. But their
campaign was handicapped by a number of problems.

Firstly, there was the continuing dispute between the SOGAT FoC
and full-time local and national union officials, which considerably
emasculated the authority of the SOGAT chapel committee and resulted
in the union's refusal to provide assistance whilst Alan Hebden remained

in office. Secondly, the redundancies announcement came shortly after the company had outlined plans to build a completely new newspaper printing plant on a 'greenfield site' in the neighbouring borough of Knowsley. Because many workers who were *not* chosen for redundancy believed that, despite a reduction in manning levels in Aintree, they would be able to get jobs in the new Knowsley plant, their opposition to the job cuts was somewhat neutered. Thirdly, the high average age of the sizeable proportion of those who *were* chosen for redundancy encouraged many of the older workers, who stood to gain large redundancy payments, to accept the decision as a *fait accompli*. Fourthly, previous acceptance of management's ideological justification for increased labour productivity (to hold down costs in face of external competition and to fund pay parity) had itself encouraged a sense of resignation to the logic of job losses. Mark explained the union approach was to merely minimize job loss:

> The argument was about having some control over redundancies, not about the principle of redundancies; that was accepted virtually from the word go. All along, the negotiations were aimed at minimizing the redundancies. There was never a fightback as such. We just tried to keep as many people as possible. We suggested a 'last in, first out' and management categorically rejected that. We asked if they would accept volunteers first, they said 'No'. Every proposal and every step on the road they said 'No'.

Despite these obstacles, there was still a tremendous sense of bitterness amongst quite a wide layer of shop-floor workers. With a decisive lead from full-time national union officials and the chapel committees it is possible that these members could have been galvanized into taking some form of industrial action. It is true that given the lack of investment and ultimately outmoded nature of the plant's machinery, the long-term future of the Aintree site looked uncertain. But stopping mass production of the *Sunday* colour magazine could possibly have put tremendous pressure on Rupert Murdoch to have backed off, at least to some degree. The fact is that for all its sophistication and corporate power News International was still dependent upon the goodwill of the Bemrose workforce, whose collective strength could have given them an important leverage. Mark believed one important potential focus for such action during the campaign against redundancies was thrown away:

The company told us the transport was being contracted out to TNT. TNT weren't thought of very highly in the light of the Wapping dispute. Well, when we went into work one day there was a TNT trailer parked outside. Our members approached the committee men on site, including myself, [saying] that he shouldn't be loaded in view of what had gone on at Wapping and in view of the fact that management were clearly not negotiating with us at all. We went to the loading bay and the lads said they didn't want him on the premises. So we told the driver to fuck off out of it. At the end of the day though we had a site meeting of committee men and fellas off the loading bay. We were advised by Alan it would be in our best interests to load the fella up and what a difficult situation the company were in. That would have been a focus for a fight with the company, not necessarily a full-scale dispute but at least it would have said to the company, you haven't smashed us, we still find certain issues disagreeable and this is what we're going to do about it . . . But the company never budged on any issue right throughout the 90 days and we never forced them to do anything, and that is a criticism.

Instead, the chapel committees' campaign of opposition was kept essentially at the level of moral protest. Alas, to no avail. Management rode roughshod over the federated chapel's muted protests and what had been once an extremely powerful shop-floor chapel organization effectively collapsed without so much as a whisper of a fightback.

The redundancy exercise effectively broke the back of shop-floor union organization in the Bemrose plant. The NGA '82 process chapel saw a reduction in labour of 75 per cent from 208 to 52; the SOGAT chapel was cut by more than half from 706 to 338; and the NGA '82 machine chapel from 174 to 86. At the same time, each of the chapel committees suffered a deep haemorrhage within their ranks: every member of the NGA '82 process chapel committee was made redundant, except for the FoC (and federated chapel chairperson), Bill; many of the key SOGAT committee activists were also sacked, except for Alan Hebden who, having been forced to resign as FoC and facing expulsion from the union, was no longer seen as posing any serious threat to the company; there was a similar loss of union activists in the NGA '82 machine chapel, although the FoC actually took voluntary redundancy.

Management continued to press home their advantage with the remaining workforce. A number of union facilities were immediately withdrawn, including 100 per cent time off work for each of the three chapel FoCs, and the facility to hold both chapel committee and full chapel meetings within the factory. The balance of workplace power was wrenched decisively in favour of management. Peter remembered:

> Management's attitude totally altered from the Monday morning after the
> redundancies when they came in wielding the big stick: 'You will do this,
> you will do that.' No negotiation. 'If you don't like it, get your coat on
> and get out.' At every opportunity management tried to ridicule the
> unions. It was: 'Now I've got you down I'm going to keep you that way.'

To all intents and purposes, management ignored previously negotiated house agreements and treated the federated chapel with utter disdain.

In 1988 the company announced the termination of all existing agreements and issued draft proposals for a completely new package that included: pay rises that took no account of the BPIF national minimum awards; an agreement that would last for 15 months instead of 12; no strikes and no involvement of local full-time union officials in chapel affairs (NGA '82 process chapel committee minutes, 24 November 1988). In 1989 they even threatened to introduce individual contracts and withdraw recognition from the unions for negotiation purposes unless the federated chapel accepted a 7.5 per cent pay offer (NGA '82 process chapel committee minutes, 4 April 1989). Management eventually withdrew most of these original demands but only because such draconian threats enabled them to successfully force compliance over many other significant changes. Bill explained:

> The last two or three years' house agreements were almost a
> non-negotiation in real terms; there wasn't any free collective bargaining
> by any stretch of the imagination. It was a matter of what you could
> persuade them to keep – never mind improve things. It was looked on
> almost as a victory if we held on to something, if we stopped them
> taking something away from us.

The transformation of working practices proceeded apace.

> In the process chapel the changes in production methods and changed
> work practices accounted for something like a 40 per cent increase in
> output per man after the redundancies. For instance, in my own
> department [the carbon printing department] I had to develop a cylinder

in a tank and prepare my next job at the same time whereas I would only have done one job at a time before. Managers involved themselves in the job where they never did before. There was a lot more flexibility. SOGAT members were moved from the finishing department to the machine room and back again if they were wanted later on in the shift.

The massive cutback in jobs and changes to working practices were justified on the grounds of low productivity that provided international rivals with a competitive advantage. Yet even after such alleged barriers had been removed and the company had been returned to profitability the long-term threat of plant closure remained. It was an illustration of how the 'efficiency' and 'viability' of the plant had little to do with the productivity of the workers involved. Much more significant were the rapid advances in printing technology that enabled colour pages to be printed directly into many daily newspapers and made the preprinted colour rewinds that Bemrose specialized in increasingly outmoded, as new printing methods such as web offset superseded the factory's photogravure operation. Yet despite repeated shop-floor union requests, Bemrose consistently refused to embark on a substantial plant investment programme to secure the site's future. In fact, despite a profit of £9 million in 1989, Bemrose provocatively declared its intention to repay News International's 'accumulated losses' from previous years, of £12 million (NGA '82 process chapel minutes, 21 April 1989).

Finally, in May 1990, News International effectively declared the death knell of the factory after confirming transfer of the contract for the *Sunday* magazine to the West German publishing and printing group Burda GmbH. The £220 million deal (the largest in the European magazine market) was part of Rupert Murdoch's strategy to prepare for the removal of European trade barriers in 1992 (*Liverpool Echo*, 8 June 1990). The loss of the *Sunday* (which accounted for 85 per cent of the Bemrose workload at that time) led to a further 413 redundancies. There was no resistance to the job losses and about 160 workers were kept on for another 12 months to complete various contractual obligations before the factory was finally closed at the end of 1991. Only about 90 ex-Bemrose workers were employed at News International's high-tech newspaper plant in Knowsley.

Stewards' Relationship to Members: The 1970s/1980s

The 1970s: Benevolent Control from Above

In many respects the Bemrose chapel committees had a relatively close and accountable relationship with their rank-and-file members during the early 1970s. This was particularly evident within the SOGAT chapel. The SOGAT chapel committee was composed of about 15 shop-floor representatives elected from production areas such as the machine room and finishing department (on the basis of one committee member per shift) and non-production areas such as the warehouse and ink mill (on the basis of one committee member per department). Each individual committee representative was elected by a ballot of the entire chapel membership for a two-year term of office, with half the committee up for re-election every year. Monthly committee meetings were held inside the factory, although usually outside working hours. A small executive committee composed of the Father of the Chapel (FoC), deputy FoC, secretary, chairperson and treasurer administered the chapel's day-to-day affairs. All committee representatives (including the FoC until 1976) held full-time jobs on the shop-floor but were able to obtain a limited amount of time off to attend to grievances and union business at management's discretion.

At the centre of the committee's shop-floor strength was the day-to-day control exercised by union representatives over the manning of jobs, movement of labour and overtime rotas, reflected through the operation of a strict seniority system. According to Peter, the job experience and bargaining ability of the SOGAT committee representatives was viewed with some respect by rank-and-file members:

> When I started in Bemrose I was shown round the factory by the committee man who told me the do's and don'ts. Well, you couldn't really sneeze without consulting the committee man then – they'd boxed everything, the overtime, they sorted the holidays out. At that time management accepted quite readily the unions were in charge.

Contesting of committee positions varied between the different chapels. Within the SLADE process chapel committee, there was not a great deal of competition for positions other than FoC. In this case, that did not necessarily reflect a lack of participation. On the contrary, in many areas of the process department chapel members took it in turns to hold a committee position with the incumbent stepping down after a short period in office, thereby nullifying the need for a formal election contest. By contrast, within the NGA machine chapel there was a much more obvious level of involvement. According to Geoff:

> All through the '70s everyone wanted to be on the committee, well let's say 10 per cent of the chapel wanted to be on the committee. There'd be a regular contest, you'd get a couple of candidates for the position . . . Once we had a vote of no confidence in the FoC because of a shabby deal he'd made and all the committee resigned. About half of them were re-elected, but there was about 19 candidates for the ten positions.

There was a similar level of active participation in the SOGAT chapel. Mark related:

> It was very rare for someone to be elected unopposed. You would generally have someone young and up and coming, and the sitting tenant. Once you ousted the sitting tenant you could guarantee that at the next election he would be nominated to oppose you. So you would always have two people vying for positions. Sometimes there was three or four.

The tenure of office also varied. Within the SLADE process chapel the turnover of many of the committee positions was generally quite frequent, about every two years. In contrast, within the NGA machine chapel there tended to be a larger core of longer-serving committee representatives, whilst in the SOGAT chapel only a handful of committee representatives were permanent fixtures, namely the FoC, deputy FoC, treasurer and a few other individuals.

Mass meetings of the *whole* workforce, embracing members of all chapels, were rarely held. Sectional meetings, of members within particular departments, were occasionally organized. But the chief forum for the direct accountability of committee representatives to members was chapel meetings, held at local union branch offices three, four or six times a year in the NGA machine, SOGAT and SLADE process chapels respectively. The procedure at these membership meetings was usually extremely formal, complementing the highly efficient administrative arrangements of the chapel committees and their meticulous minute book keeping. Strict union rules enforced by the committee, such as fines or disciplinary action for non-attendance at meetings, reinforced the cohesiveness of the chapel and its collective interests.

About 90 women (SOGAT members) were employed in the plant prior to 1987, concentrated in the finishing department where they worked alongside male workers. The SOGAT chapel committee successfully negotiated an equal-pay agreement in 1972, the first SOGAT chapel on Merseyside to do so; holidays and general working conditions in Bemrose were also the same for both men and women. Partly, this was a direct result of the influence of the two women representatives on the chapel committee, including a Mother of the Chapel (MoC), and the pressure of shop-floor women members themselves. Partly, it was because of the role played by the left-wing SOGAT chapel FoC. As Alan related:

> By and large there were always two women on the committee. They weren't that trade union or politically orientated, they were just women looking after women's issues and quite rightly making sure they weren't being given inferior conditions. You had to pressurize them to take on the positions, on the basis that if you didn't have a woman representative on the committee they wouldn't get a fair crack of the whip. You had to force them into the position. It depended on the characteristics of some of the committee men: if they were anti-women you always got a woman on, because there were people who did take advantage of the women in terms of doing their job on overtime.

Val, a rank-and-file SOGAT member in the finishing department throughout the 1970s and 1980s, described some of the problems the women faced on the shop-floor:

> There was an argument when I first started in the area where the girls worked, where we sorted out the *TV Times*. The committee man wanted his men to work overtime on the job the girls were doing and there was murder between the committee man and the MoC. There was fighting and arguing and everything on the floor. He was working downstairs but he wanted the men to come up and take the job off those girls and get the money for it. It was the same when the girls were working the 3–11 shift: they were working at night but they weren't allowed to work overtime until the morning, it had to go to the men. It was a bit bad really. But Alan sorted it out and the women went on to a night shift and the overtime went to the women on whose job it was, and it was fair.

Yet the prejudices of some male committee representatives did not prevent the women from seeking representation from others whenever necessary:

> You always had committee men you could go to. If the MoC was off – say on her holidays or something – the women would go to a man who was on the committee, depending on who he was. A lot of times you would be wasting your time talking to the committee man we had upstairs, so you would go downstairs and find another one or take it straight to the FoC.

It is significant that committee representatives generally, from across all four different chapels, did not play as prominent a role in shaping the outcome of most of the main issues facing workers as the FoCs. Of course, it is true that committee representatives were involved in dealing with shop-floor grievances and in the formulation of chapel policy. Monthly chapel committee meetings were also an important forum for debate, as Mark pointed out:

> If there was a situation that occurred outside of an agreement that wasn't of major consequence, then we would debate a policy. The committee discussed everything that went on in the factory, the fair and equal distribution of the overtime, the production requirements and production outputs. The committee decided a policy that would be uniform throughout the factory.

On the other hand, committee representatives were viewed purely as an auxiliary to the key bargaining role carried out on behalf of the chapel by the FoC (and deputy FoC and secretary), who, for example, travelled down to London for house agreement negotiations with Bruce Matthews of News International. The pivotal role of the FoC was considerably enhanced in 1977 after management provided office facilities for each of the separate chapels within the plant and encouraged each of the FoCs to take 100 per cent time off work to represent their members. Alan outlined the essential factor underlining management's new strategy and his misgivings about his new-found full-time status as SOGAT chapel FoC:

> Management offered it in my opinion because of the thread they were kept on. You've got to picture it. When you went in on a Monday morning, it was a powder keg, that only went *phsssshh* every week, but

nevertheless it was ready to explode. They were obviously aware of the
tactics being adopted by the union. Hence they thought we might as well
have him here so we don't have to send out for him, so he can deal with
the problems as they arise every day. But it was certainly not my wish to
be a full-time FoC because I firmly believe, and I did then, that one of the
fundamental mistakes in the trade union movement was isolating people.
Because as has been proved right, you *do* become isolated from the
feeling on the floor.

Yet Alan was undoubtedly regarded with tremendous respect by SOGAT
chapel committee and shop-floor union members alike. Representing a
wide range of members scattered across every department in the factory
he was uniquely placed to keep abreast of day-to-day developments and
offer a strategic form of leadership. Mark commented:

I can't remember anyone ever being put up against him. As an FoC, as
far as I was concerned, he was superb. He was the most complete FoC
you'll ever come across. His facts, figures, his contacts – pensions,
wages, anything you wanted to discuss. He was a shrewd organizer, a
negotiator, he was the type of guy who could put a price on anything.

Pat, a SOGAT chapel committee representative for a number of years in
the finishing department, spoke for many others when he paid tribute to
Alan's role within the plant:

The first thing he would do when he went into work was to visit every
department. He went through all the transport information, so he knew
what was going in and going out. He would go into every office, look at
what was on the board, and see what was getting produced, how many,
where for. Every aspect Alan knew and management let him, because
they knew he was competent in his job. He knew everything about the
place, he was an oracle. People wanted to tell him everything, so he had
that ability. Alan's committee was such that whoever was on the shift
that touched him – earlies or afternoons – he took them into meetings
with management, they were his men. They didn't speak around the
table independently, everything went through Alan, but he made sure
they were well aware of the agreements, the history of the place.

Certainly, the substantive gains achieved by the SOGAT chapel committee with Alan Hebden at the helm during the 1970s, including high

wage rates, substantial control over manning and strong union organization, are testimony to the FoC's influential leadership abilities. His lengthy tenure of office, which lasted for 16 years from 1971 to 1987, was further evidence of the confidence consistently expressed by shop-floor members. (By comparison, during the same period there were five different FoCs in both the SLADE process and NGA machine chapels.)

Nonetheless, the nature of the bargaining system (with its formal house agreements) and the structure of workplace union organization (with its highly autonomous collection of separate chapels and full-time FoCs) facilitated the development of a highly centralized form of leadership within all four chapel committees. This was a process that was accentuated even further within the SOGAT chapel by the long-standing intervention of the highly influential FoC. As Mark reflected:

> The general was on the pinnacle of the pyramid, there was no sort of intermediate structure, there was no heir apparent. One of the things I used to say is that it would be a disastrous day if Alan ever walked out on to Long Lane and got knocked over by a bus. A lot of us on the committee wouldn't have known what was going on. Alan kept a lot of things to himself. Obviously he had confidants, but two of his deputies – although they held office – certainly never did the job, and that suited Alan. He could go and do his own thing and he had them in tow. Alan could run rings round them and get virtually everything he wanted.

Alan himself recognized the problem of a chapel committee whose role was strictly circumscribed:

> That's right. Regrettably on looking back, that was one of the mistakes we made. The responsibility was left more with the FoC and deputy, and the committee men. Other than for holidays and overtime, the committee men didn't play much of a role. They just reported an issue to the FoC.

Contact between the FoC and departmental managers and supervisors was frequent and concerned not only issues of terms and conditions of employment but also production difficulties, work allocations and output levels. Rob explained:

> He met with management on a regular basis to discuss productivity, which was monitored by both parties. Agreed levels of productivity were

arrived at, so that could be used for negotiating purposes. He was always constantly made aware of exactly where we were on production schedules at any given time of the day. If there was a problem on any particular job, where we were likely to be behind the schedule, he was always made aware of that and he always kept his eye on it.

Having previously negotiated house agreements stipulating production targets the FoC was obliged, on occasion, to encourage shop-floor members to increase their pace of work. Peter remarked:

Say we were coming round to pay negotiations. He would say: 'I've told management that we'll produce X amount of copies per week. Now you've got to be seen to be making it work – if you want the extra £10 a week pay rise.' If people were sluggish, with some people trying to create overtime, he'd have a say so.

Despite the fact that this involved Alan Hebden in a semi-managerial role, the FoC's advice was complied with, if sometimes reluctantly, essentially because in general terms his bargaining approach appeared to 'deliver the goods' in terms of high pay awards and advantageous working conditions. As Pat noted:

There was always that much more to gain in respect to overtime and working conditions that whenever the FoC said, 'Management are within their rights, it's within the agreement', it was generally accepted. People might voice their disagreement and it would be taken on board and dealt with. In the main, it didn't occur, because they were all doing so well.

At the heart of the relationship between the chapel committees and rank-and-file members was the nature of sectional organization inside the Bemrose plant. As was noted earlier, the sectional strength of the various chapels was dependent not simply on their strength against management, but also on their ability to exclude other workers who were not members of the same chapel from certain aspects of the production process. This was maintained by job demarcation. Such sectional organization was traditionally very successful. For many years workers could improve their wages and conditions without engaging in widespread or militant activity. The number of actual strikes was quite small and they usually involved few workers and ended very quickly.

But this had an inevitable impact on the organization and consciousness of Bemrose workers, breeding among the great majority a tradition of moderation and of only being interested in what happened in the particular section of the particular union which they belonged to. It also meant they tended to rely on the chapel officials to do things for them, to act *on their behalf*. The strength and loyalty to the chapel arising from this sort of organization meant that when the chapel committees called for action they usually got it. But it also meant there was no opposition when the, often token, action was called off, and there was little independent initiative outside of established chapel procedures, as few members were prepared to challenge the official chapel leadership.

In SOGAT, even though sanctions aimed at hitting production were often collectively agreed at chapel meetings they were usually initiated, tightly organized and strictly controlled from above by the FoC and committee representatives. Rob related:

> If we were coming up to the yearly house agreements and management were sticking on particular points that we felt we had an excellent case on, we might threaten to use a tactic such as working to rule, or an overtime ban if necessary. We would pick on a department with the least amount of people but who could cause the maximum amount of chaos to take action on behalf of the chapel to put pressure on management.

SOGAT members in the loading bay, a small department of 27 members on three shifts, often formed the shock troops for this strategy, as Alan pointed out:

> While they were only small in number they were very much a united section and under the influence of a committee man who was an exceptionally honest individual and the members had a great deal of trust in him. If they were ever called upon by the chapel to restrict production it would be done without having to run round pleading with them. It usually had excellent results because you could produce as much work as you like, but if you couldn't get it into the wagons, it just built up.

Spontaneous shop-floor disputes were few and far between and on the rare occasion a 'wildcat' stoppage of work did occur, it was invariably quickly brought under chapel committee control. Peter remembered:

> If there was a major problem in the machine room Alan Hebden would say, 'Hang on, we'll confine it to that press, keep all the other presses going', and then try to sort it out. Because there'd be lads from the machine opposite saying, 'Hey, you've got a problem there', and they would stop working. But the FoC would try to keep it isolated to people on that machine or that crew, without letting it spread throughout the factory.

For the FoC, such shop-floor discipline helped bolster a 'strong bargaining relationship' with management. As Alan remarked:

> Once the management saw that you'd evaluated the situation and done your homework and you were quite as strong with your own members as you were with the management, that you wouldn't take arbitrary stoppages on the shop-floor willy-nilly, that everything had to be conducted through the meetings, and there was a person of authority, whilst they didn't like you, at least they came to respect you, because you meant what you said.

Chapels felt able to stop or threaten production without the need to ask other chapels for solidarity. The idea grew up not only that solidarity action was not necessary but that it was better for workers to go to work and take the money than to stop work in support. With strong demarcation no workers would do the work of the few striking workers. Not only was this attitude adopted towards members of *different* chapels in dispute, but it also meant members of the *same* chapel would usually continue working normally. Yet the isolation of action to the particular section of a chapel had the general effect of demobilizing the self-activity of workers and reinforcing inter-departmental sectionalism. It threw away the valuable opportunity of forging shop-floor links across individual chapels and building up a united approach to management across the plant.

Whilst material conditions created the basis for the sectional divisions, the existence of a layer of politically committed union activists and socialists across the chapels provided the potential basis for the organization of a more collectivist response. Yet despite persistent efforts by some individuals, the organizational mechanisms that could facilitate this process were very weak. Thus, there was no equivalent of the joint shop stewards' committee that predominates in many manufacturing plants. The federated chapel was merely an umbrella body that came together for formal house agreement negotiations. Not only did it exclude the SLADE process chapel (until 1986) but it also played only a minimal role in terms of formulating claims, day-to-day negotiation and the monitoring of agreements, which instead was undertaken by the respective chapel committees.

The 1980s: Political Limitations

Throughout the 1980s the influence of left-wing political activists within the chapel committees inside the Bemrose plant was an important factor to be taken into consideration. As has already been noted, Alan Hebden, the SOGAT chapel FoC, was a leading supporter of the Militant Tendency and actively involved in the Liverpool Labour Party. A number of other individual SOGAT members, some of them committee representatives, were also left-wing Labour activists. At first glance, this socialist influence may seem a paradox. After all, print workers have traditionally been regarded as rather conservative politically. Ostensibly, within the NGA machine chapel this picture appeared to have been the case, at least amongst a section of the membership. According to Geoff:

> I would say that about 40 per cent of the chapel voted Tory. You see, the more money they have the more they change, they move in better circles, their spots *do* fade. You couldn't really talk about Labour Party politics in the golf club or yachting club where some of our members went.

Despite this apparent conservatism, the NGA machine chapel also had within its ranks a handful of Labour left activists, and the deputy FoC of the NGA composing room chapel during the early 1980s, Tony Mulhearn, was an extremely prominent Militant supporter, president of the Liverpool Labour Party and one of the 47 city councillors surcharged and disqualified from office in 1987 after being in the forefront of a bruising battle against the Conservative government's rate-capping. As Geoff acknowledged, they were elected to office because:

> They were the best of those who put up irrespective of politics. The average person voted for them to represent them on the shop-floor because a person who was not going to open their mouth was no good.

Even in the highly craft conscious SLADE process chapel, the role of certain left-wing individuals was important. Bill explained:

A handful of individuals were instrumental in building up the chapel besides myself. We all thought the same politically as far as socialism was concerned. We were all socialist minded, but not active in terms of the Labour Party. All our activities were centred on Bemrose, we weren't involved in anything outside the factory.

Undoubtedly, Militant had the most political influence in Bemrose, particularly within the SOGAT chapel. Mark observed:

Right up until the redundancies in 1987, Militant had a lot of supporters in the factory, about a dozen at least. Tony Mulhearn was the star man, he was a leading light in Militant. He was the deputy FoC for the NGA comps – but that was more an honorary position given his other responsibilities on the City Council. On the SOGAT committee there was two fellas. There was another fella who was a Labour councillor on the Wirral. And there was Alan Hebden.

They also had supporters in the NGA machine chapel. Geoff recalled:

Within the chapel we had a lot of people in the Labour Party and there was a hard core of Militant. We had quite a section of those people. And there were some on the committee.

Significantly, the supporters of Militant in Bemrose did not openly organize politically on the shop-floor during the 1980s. This was partly because of their particular brand of politics, which was necessarily ambiguous given the constraints of the wider social democratic organization to which they attached themselves. Thus they combined an amorphous amalgam of revolutionary and reformist political traditions. It was also partly because of the Labour leadership's political and disciplinary assault, which led to the expulsion from the party of five members of *The Militant* newspaper editorial board in 1983 and the subsequent expulsion of many of its grassroots adherents in Liverpool from 1986 onwards, including Tony Mulhearn from Bemrose. As Mark explained:

They stood for committee men but they never operated as a political faction in the factory. When we had a meeting, you could tell they'd caucused beforehand, but they didn't have a real workplace base to their politics. They saw their role as being active in the Labour Party.

Whilst they were good trade unionists they saw the way forward as moving resolutions in the Labour Party. Organizing on the shop-floor was secondary to that. They were more concerned with achieving positions within the chapel and using that as a springboard to get positions within the Labour Party. They saw the Labour Party as a panacea for all ills and all their energies went into trying to transform it.

The other side of the same political coin was an emphasis on attempting to replace right-wing full-time union officials with left-wingers through 'Broad Left' groupings. Militant supporters in the SOGAT chapel viewed their primary task as backing up the bargaining activities of the FoC and his attempt to capture control of the lower echelons of the union machine for the left. With Alan Hebden in a pre-eminent position in both the chapel and union branch, they did not consider their main priority to be the strengthening of independent shop-floor union organization through the advocacy of workplace struggle that built workers' confidence, organization and political consciousness. But their 'control from above' strategy merely served to nurture a reliance on Alan Hebden which discouraged chapel members' own activity and disarmed them from preparing for the kind of all-out fight that might, potentially at least, have more successfully resisted management's offensive (and in the process made the removal of Alan Hebden as FoC and his expulsion from the union more difficult).

All the inherent shortcomings in the relationship between the chapel committees and their members in the Bemrose plant, particularly in terms of the political leadership provided, were exposed in bold relief during the product market crises of the early 1980s. The Maxwell take-over débâcle and subsequent Murdoch reacquisition proved a severe test of the chapels' capacity to defend shop-floor organization. But the chapel committees lacked the ideological and political resources to resist the terms and conditions of the Survival Plan, subsequently introduced by Murdoch. Even the Militant supporters, despite general expressions of opposition, did not put forward a concrete plan of action around which resistance could be generated. Thus, many union members, at least partly because of the lack of an alternative approach, accepted the arguments put by management and full-time union officials, that their highly advantageous shop-floor position of the 1970s could no longer be maintained in the 1980s. Wide-ranging changes in working practices were the necessary price for long-term job security. As Bill emphasized:

To some extent a lot of us accepted there had to be changes, that eventually change had to come: you had to be realistic about it. With government legislation against the unions and everything going on around you, of course you had to accept there was going to be some changes.

But reluctantly accepting change in working practices as part of an organized retreat was one thing, actively co-operating in its application as part of a joint effort to improve 'efficiency' was something else entirely.

In many respects, the semi-managerial role adopted by chapel FoCs in the 1970s had not helped prepare the ground for an independent shop-floor response to the product market difficulties of the 1980s. Even more significantly, the newly formed all-embracing federated chapel transformed itself into a joint working party, by bringing together up to 20 chapel committee representatives (excluding union branch and national officials) in regular meetings with management. Over 50 meetings of the joint working party were held over a four-year period to negotiate the equalization of craft rates (Rob Baker, 'Industrial Relations as a Social Comment: Eric Bemrose Ltd Joint Working Party', essay for Diploma in Trade Union Studies, Liverpool Royal Institute, 1985). Underlining the whole process was a belief that changes in working practices were necessary to achieve parity and to help make the company profitable. Yet by accepting shop-floor responsibility for the 'viability' of the Bemrose plant, the chapel committees effectively hamstrung any real challenge to the restructuring of production that ensued. It was an illustration of how far the shop-floor leadership accepted a managerial logic and lacked the political resources to pose any alternative approach. Not that the chapel committees lacked such resources any more than they had in the 1970s. But in the 1980s there was a disproportion between this deficiency and its practical consequences. It was precisely in this disproportion that the ebb of chapel power in Bemrose was expressed during this period.

Despite the disciplinary action taken against him by the national union leadership, the SOGAT chapel membership in Bemrose provided loyal backing for Alan Hebden, spurning demands that he resign from the FoC position. Yet in general terms the chapel committees' more co-operative relationship with management inevitably had an effect on their relationship with their members. There is no evidence of a dramatic reduction in attendance at chapel meetings or of a change in the contesting of committee positions or tenure of office. But with virtually all key decisions affecting the life of the plant being taken at top-level joint working party meetings, the chapel committees' role became much diminished. Union members became even more passive spectators of decisions taken from *above* rather than being actively encouraged to shape the outcome of events themselves from *below*.

The redundancy exercise of 1987 exposed the weaknesses of chapel organization in graphic relief. Rather than campaigning for industrial action to defend jobs the chapel committees basically adopted a public relations exercise. Yet whilst some of the older shop-floor union members were prepared to take the redundancy money there was a sizeable section of the workforce who were not. Pat noted:

> When we heard about the redundancies there was a buzz on the shop-floor. The people I worked with were all new. We got together and were amazed the machines were still running. But stopping the machines would have created a problem on the shop-floor which Alan Hebden would have had to go down and address. People were aware of that and that's why it didn't happen. People said: 'No, keep it going, wait for Alan Hebden to come down and administer the bread, there's no way Alan is going to let 775 people go out of this plant, he's never lost a job before and he never will.'

The tradition of relying on the FoC's bargaining abilities meant that instead of acting for themselves most SOGAT members continued to look upwards for something to be pulled out of the hat. Mark pointed out:

> Alan Hebden was looked upon with a great amount of awe because he had delivered the goods. Every year he delivered a better deal than the national union. I think our members thought – and you always got the impression from Alan – 'He's got something up his sleeve'; and 95 per cent of the time he had. But on this occasion he hadn't.

The tradition of 'strong bargaining relations' with management, in which the chapel committees had felt little need to call on their members to take action, meant they became paralysed by Bemrose's intransigence over the redundancies. The refusal of SOGAT full-time officials to provide any defence for the victimized Alan Hebden further disarmed the campaign of resistance.

In the aftermath of the 1987 job losses the relationship between the chapel committees and their members was completely transformed. Each chapel committee suffered a loss of personnel within its ranks, including a number of left-wing activists such as Alan Hebden, who was forced to resign from the FoC position within the SOGAT chapel following pressure from national and local full-time union officials. Management withdrew 100 per cent facility time from all chapel FoCs. Pat described the severe set-back suffered by the SOGAT chapel:

> The committee structure fell apart after '87. Tom Baily never kept the flow, the continuum set by Alan Hebden. From one day it was a well-organized, forward-thinking, trade union political shop – the next it was haphazard, lacklustre, no idea. That was the immediate obvious observation. Tom Baily was deputy FoC for many years under Alan, which just goes to prove how little he learnt or wasn't allowed to by Alan.

The impotent chapel committees found themselves with little authority in the eyes of either members or management. Geoff, who took over the FoC position in the NGA '82 machine chapel, reflected:

> The FoC was tolerated by the membership but was not going to be permitted to get out of line. I felt as if my committee had been appointed for me by the management, not by the workforce. I had two chargehands on the committee – that would never have happened prior to '87. But it was to keep the FoC in check, 'Don't go off with any ideas about taking management on over anything.' They feared that any rocking the boat was going to lose them their job, their redundancy money. Really, the effect of '87 was for people to keep their head down.

Thus, it is clear there was a marked transformation in the relationship between the chapel committees and members in Bemrose during the 1980s. Against the background of product market crisis and feared job loss the federated chapel/joint working party's co-operative relationship with management had the effect of diminishing the importance of the respective chapel committees which in turn impoverished their relationship with shop-floor members.

Stewards' Relationship to Full-Time Union Officials: The 1970s/1980s

The 1970s: A Gulf between Chapel and Officials

Each of the separate chapels in Bemrose fell under the wider authority of geographically organized trade union branches (for example, linking together all the different SOGAT chapels across the Merseyside area into one umbrella structure) connected to union representation at regional and national level. With a combined membership of between 1500 and 2000 the Merseyside SOGAT branch met on a quarterly basis at its union offices in north Liverpool. It elected a branch committee through a workplace ballot of the whole membership, which consisted mainly of chapel FoCs and other lay members. The branch secretary was a full-time union official responsible for overseeing the branch's activities and assisting workplace chapel organization. The Bemrose SOGAT chapel consistently sent a number of delegates to union branch meetings and played an active part in its affairs.

Each of the union branches had two quite distinct roles to play. Firstly, they acted as labour exchanges. If Bemrose wanted to employ additional labour it notified the FoC and local branch of the union concerned, which nominated a number of workers for the jobs. In this way, the trade unions ensured that only union labour was hired and were able to control the amount of such labour offering itself for work at the plant. Secondly, the branches gave advice and support to members and their representatives. Administrative contacts took place between the branches and chapels fairly frequently on matters concerned with employment, wages, interpretations of agreements, union communications, the conduct of ballots, finance and so on.

Whenever disputes occurred or when major changes in working practices or methods were proposed, there was also contact between the chapel committees and union full-time officials, at both branch and national level. On the one hand, chapel committees at Bemrose enjoyed a considerable degree of independence from the officials. The relatively large size of each of the chapels at Bemrose (amongst the largest in their respective union branches) ensured a highly 'sophisticated' form of self-governing workplace organization, which was further enhanced with the provision of 100 per cent time off work for FoCs. Although the level of struggle was not high, the general level of confidence on the shop-floor *vis-à-vis* management reinforced this autonomy. A crucial factor was the ability of the

Bemrose chapels to achieve comparatively good wage increases and day-to-day working arrangements through their own bargaining efforts. These were superior to those negotiated elsewhere in Liverpool and across the country through the involvement of local or national full-time officials. Nowhere was this more evident than in the manning controls carved out by the SOGAT chapel committee in Bemrose during the 1970s. Rob related:

> The chapel deliberately kept everybody at arm's length because we had better agreements than anybody else. We didn't want anything to do with some of the agreements that had been made at other firms. The branch officers very rarely got involved. At one stage they only attended the place about once in two years.

Not surprisingly, the local SOGAT branch full-time official felt his traditional function and authority undermined by such independent chapel organization, as Alan explained:

> If we got to a point where we couldn't reach agreement with management we would call in not the branch, [but] the national officers. Their attitude towards the chapel was that nothing could satisfy the chapel. None of them wanted to deal with us. In the end, though, they gave a national officer, called Jimmy Pointing, the job of signing agreements with the company. It turned out that his appointment suited the chapel, because Jimmy Pointing took the attitude that if the chapel were prepared to do most of the negotiating themselves and honour the agreements, he went along with it.

This approach was vividly illustrated by the SOGAT chapel during the mid-1970s with the signing of a house agreement containing a disputed clause on pensions. Alan takes up the story:

> On two occasions when the branch secretary came in, and the company had threatened to close the place down, I refused to endorse the agreement. I refused to sign it. We didn't feel it had come up to the aspirations that we felt the company should be giving the members. While we could improve the day-to-day conditions in the factory we had great difficulty improving pension rights. They gave us *so* many hours and said if we didn't sign it they were closing the place down. The

branch secretary signed the agreement but the chairman of the
company, Bruce Matthews, said he wasn't interested in his signature, he
wanted the FoC's signature who was on the premises on a daily basis
and would make the agreement work. That sort of thing never helped the
relationship with the branch.

Thus, the SOGAT chapel exercised a powerful autonomy within the
union.

On the other hand, not all the chapels had such an autonomous
relationship with local and national full-time union officials. Certainly, the
SLADE chapel enjoyed a much closer partnership, partly owing to the
fact that the union was a comparatively small organization whose very
existence was under threat of extinction from new technology. The NGA
chapel also had a less self-governing relationship, although in Liverpool
this was partially explained by the fact that the local official, Will Fowler,
was a Militant supporter who was very sympathetic to chapel concerns.
But even in SOGAT the notion of a blanket chapel autonomy would be
misplaced. Branch and national union officials were involved in annual
house agreement negotiations, if only in an advisory capacity. Moreover,
whilst all plant-based claims were formulated and negotiated by individual
chapels, all draft agreements had to be submitted to the local branch
committees for ratification, and their vetting could lead to the amendment
or even rejection of certain items.

Chapels were also integrated into union affairs through their participation in the quarterly branch meetings and through representation on the
branch committees of their respective unions. For example, the SOGAT
chapel were entitled to send one delegate per 25 members to union branch
meetings. As one of the largest chapels in the branch (with about 750
members) that meant they were allowed about 33 delegates. The chapel
ensured its full quota was represented by means of a rota system of
volunteers, usually consisting of committee representatives, ex-committee
reps and other union activists. Not surprisingly, the chapel's power base
gave it considerable weight to influence the outcome of decision making
within the branch, both through sheer force of argument and through its
block vote. The chapel was also entitled to two representatives on the
union's branch committee. From 1978 to 1982 the branch president's
position was held by the Bemrose chapel FoC, Alan Hebden. Inevitably,
a considerable amount of his time was taken up with branch affairs, for
example attending officers' meetings (held each Monday for the whole day

at the union's Liverpool headquarters) and visiting other union members in the area – although an important distinction should be drawn between his position as a *lay* officer on the branch committee and the *full-time* union branch officials.

If the relationship between the Bemrose chapels and their union branches and local and national full-time officials was characterized by both autonomy and integration, the balance between these contradictory elements did not remain static, particularly within the SOGAT chapel. As has already been noted, there was a constant source of friction over the level of manning established in the Bemrose plant by the SOGAT chapel, which in the 1970s increased from 620 to over 700 and proved to be a source of some embarrassment to local and national union officials. Rob explained:

> In the '70s there was no way we would entertain anything such as making one person redundant or de-manning exercises. In fact we were going round the country against the wishes of the national union trying to organize to bring about a common policy in the union for national manning levels, which the union fought against.

Another contentious issue was the 32-hour week, which had been established on the night shift at Bemrose in 1977 by the chapel committees. Alan recalled:

> We assured the company that as far as we were concerned we would go out to the four corners of the country and shout it out that we had achieved the 32-hour week without loss of pay, with increased production to give them the opportunity to bring more work in. But obviously no way did the general secretary Bill Keys and the national executive council want to achieve the 32-hour week for the people of Liverpool.

The gulf between the SOGAT chapel and national full-time officials led to the formation of unofficial FoC Fellowships inside the union, both within the Liverpool branch and within the national gravure industry, operating as 'Broad Left' groupings with the aim of influencing union policy decisions and replacing right-wing officials with left-wingers. Although the Communist Party was the key political force behind it, the FoC Fellowships pulled together a much wider, albeit quite small, network of left-wing activists. The chairperson of the Merseyside FoC Fellowship was Alan:

> We used to get FoCs from different plants across Merseyside and exchange agreements. It was a sort of education for the FoCs. The branch officers wanted us to do everything through the auspices of the branch itself. Their idea was that they would exchange agreements because they were there to do a job and they would do it on behalf of the members. But quite clearly some of the terms and conditions some of the members were working under were appalling, and because of the attendance at the FoC Fellowships, we did see one or two factories get involved in disputes which got the support of the Fellowship, and we did enhance the standard of living of many of the chapels who came along to the Fellowship.

Although only about 20–30 activists attended the Merseyside FoC Fellowship, it was quite an influential force within the local union branch. But under the strain of constant attacks and threats of disciplinary action by local and national union officials alike, the Fellowship tended to disband after 18 months to two years, only to regroup again at a later date.

> We had three or four attempts to set up local or national Fellowships but every attempt was made to stop us; each time we were thwarted by national and local officers who saw it as a threat. The branch used to use the argument that it was only a platform for Bemrose, that Bemrose was only looking after themselves. Even before my time they turned the whole of the branch against Bemrose on the basis of the conditions that had been achieved. The conditions hadn't been achieved by the branch or national officers doing the negotiating, so there was always some resentment. You were subject to disciplinary action if they found you were meeting with the other gravure factories Odhams and Sun and Purnells.

Such disciplinary threats merely served to further underline the gulf between chapel activists and branch officials.

After 1978 the Bemrose SOGAT chapel became virtually completely estranged from the Merseyside union branch following the election of a new full-time branch secretary, Stuart Henderson (who defeated Alan Hebden in the ballot). Rob explained:

Relations with the branch were never very happy once Henderson
became branch secretary. Basically he wasn't happy with the control we
had over our own destiny. He wanted to be able to get in there and be
seen to be a branch secretary and we deliberately kept him at
arm's length. Only under sufferance would we have him on the
premises. The attitude of the officials was one of anti-Militant, reds under
the bed, and anybody who doesn't agree with their type of philosophy
must be in Militant. They were only really concerned with their own
positions and how to further their own interests.

Pat confirmed the antagonistic relationship that existed between the
SOGAT chapel and union branch:

Stuart Henderson had always seen Alan as a threat. The Bemrose chapel
were always a law unto themselves. They were so well protected by
each other at the chapel and through the leadership that it was like a
spinning top – the branch wouldn't go near it because they knew they
would be deflected right away. The chapel was where Alan got his
support within the branch. He used the structures within Bemrose to
perpetuate his aspirations within the branch to get policy passed.

During the early 1980s there was a constant battle for control waged within
the Merseyside SOGAT branch between Alan Hebden as lay branch
president and Stuart Henderson as full-time union branch secretary.
A sharp division arose over an attempt by the Bemrose chapel to move
a resolution at the branch meeting, to be sent to the union's biennial
delegate conference, insisting on the regular re-election of full-time
officials. Rob recalled:

We believed nobody should be in that job for life, particularly somebody
like Stuart Henderson. There was no control over him. One of the things
we learnt from the NGA was that every three years their full-time officers
stood for re-election and we endeavoured to get that in SOGAT. To say
the branch meetings were rather hostile was putting it mildly. They were
vicious because there was no way they were going to ballot. But we
reached a situation at one branch meeting where the officers' supporters
were thin on the ground and we were fractionally away from winning the
vote when Henderson threw a temper just before the vote was taken,
declared the meeting null and void and walked out. That was the type of

thing we were up against – out and out Teamster politics. But I'm convinced the national officers didn't want re-election of officials because obviously they would be next.

As a means of stamping their authority over such challenges the branch committee resorted to organizational means, such as introducing a rule change that reduced the number of delegates entitled to attend union branch meetings, to cut the Bemrose chapel's delegation to a maximum of 20.

The 1980s: 'Bringing the Union into Disrepute'

During the early 1980s, a clash of interests between all of the chapel committees and full-time national union officials, particularly within SOGAT, eventually came to a head over the advantageous terms and conditions carved out in Bemrose and the officials' view that the changed economic and political climate necessitated a change of attitude towards manning and flexible working practices to retain the long-term viability of the plant. Alan recalled:

> We realized we were coming under pressure from the national union, with attacks against the chapel. They used to say that our ideas were outdated, that we had to come to reality because of the number of people we had on the presses. We had considerable pressure on myself and the chapel. The national union used to treat the number of people we had on the machines as a joke. We used to try to explain to them that in Liverpool it was nine men to a press and we wanted nine men to a press because it was nine people employed instead of unemployed. It was difficult to get that across to the people in London and Bristol and the South-West where nobody seemed to be unemployed in the print in those areas at the time.

The turn of events during the early 1980s, namely with the loss of the *TV Times* contract, the Maxwell takeover, the Survival Plan, and the joint working party negotiations on parity, all combined to increase markedly the role of local and national full-time union officials in the Bemrose plant. Management appeared to encourage them to play a more interventionist role. Even the chapel committees, involved in constant deliberations with management aimed at making the plant more 'efficient', found themselves becoming more and more reliant on them. This was despite the fact that, in the case of SOGAT, there was a deep distrust of their ultimate intentions. Thus, in 1981 it was national full-time union officials who were instrumental in pressurizing the chapels to accept the terms and conditions of the Survival Plan as the price for long-term job security. Similarly, in 1982 it was local and national full-time officials who prevailed upon the NGA machine chapel to end their unofficial strike for parity of craft rates. As Geoff related:

> We ended up with a meeting with Tony Dubbins [general secretary] and Les Dixon [general president] from the union. It was a shouting match with them saying: 'If you don't go back to work they'll close the place.' They refused to make the strike official or get support from the national council. But it was the branch secretary, Will Fowler, who persuaded the membership to go back to work where the national officers couldn't. The terms of going back were that we would work normally, ending our overtime ban and work-to-rule. They gave us a commitment to parity with the proviso that it was self-financing, that we had to achieve the productivity.

Local full-time union officials also played a decisive role in overseeing the series of 50-plus joint working party meetings that subsequently took place between the federated chapel and Bemrose management to discuss the phased introduction of parity. In 1983, when management insisted on an immediate agreement on parity as a precondition for taking on the *Sunday Express* magazine contract, it was the local and national full-time union officials who instructed the chapel committees to accept management's terms (NGA '82 process chapel minutes, 28 August 1983). Rob later wrote up a first-hand account of what happened:

> It was disclosed by management that they had secured the contract for the printing of the *Sunday Express* magazine. The unions were told that they must accept the deal put forward on that date and had until 12 noon to do so. The SOGAT and [NGA] Process FoCs refused to sign anything, saying it was under duress. The deadline was extended, and we were further told that it could mean closure for Bemrose if this contract was not accepted. The deadline was extended more than once, with management claiming they only had 'Heads of Agreement' (meaning in essence that it was not legally binding) and that they needed signed acceptance by the unions before the contract was valid properly.

Management then repeated that it could mean closure of the plant in Liverpool. Two FoCs remained adamant that they would not sign, and eventually Messrs Parish (NGA) and Pointing (SOGAT) (national officers), and Messrs Fowler (NGA) and Henderson (SOGAT) (branch secretaries), signed this document over the heads of both FoCs. The drama, however, was not yet done. At a meeting in the plant the following week, local management then insisted that they needed the signatures of each individual FoC on the document. (This had never been deemed necessary before.) Again the two FoCs refused to sign the new document, and both branch secretaries implored them to change their minds, as it would mean massive problems for Liverpool if the factory were to close. At around 6.30 pm that night the SOGAT FoC called an on-plant emergency chapel meeting, and put his position four-square to the members. Only on their instruction did he reluctantly agree to sign the document (the Process NGA FoC having just signed also). The effect of this left a feeling of deep bitterness (Rob Baker, 'Industrial Relations as a Social Comment: Eric Bemrose Ltd Joint Working Party', Essay for Diploma in Trade Union Studies, Liverpool Royal Institute, 1985).

In other words, the external role of local and national full-time officials in constantly exhorting the Bemrose chapel activists to accept management's belligerent negotiating terms is absolutely crucial to any explanation of the changing nature of workplace relations within the plant during the early 1980s.

There was a major confrontation between the SOGAT chapel committee and the local full-time union branch secretary, Stuart Henderson, in 1984–85. It centred on Henderson's sacking of four women secretaries who worked in the Merseyside SOGAT offices, after they had made a series of complaints against him to the general secretary-elect, Brenda Dean, concerning alleged financial irregularities (*New Statesman*, 19 April 1985). Dean overruled the women's concerns and Henderson subsequently sacked them for gross misconduct. But under the leadership of Alan Hebden the Bemrose SOGAT chapel took the initiative in organizing an unofficial Merseyside branch campaign in defence of the women, refusing to cross their picket line outside the union's HQ and supporting the call for a full membership meeting to hear details of the allegations against Stuart Henderson. Future official branch meetings were boycotted and an unofficial membership meeting of 2000 members was held, with nearly half the Merseyside branch agreeing to withhold their union subscriptions in protest at the secretaries' dismissal. Rob recalled:

> The girls had a lot of respect. They picketed the building for 12 months in rain, hail and snow. There was a tremendous spirit amongst them. We began to organize not only support from the Bemrose chapel but from a number of other chapels throughout Merseyside, including from as far afield as Bebbington. It was starting to build up, the pressure was tremendous. We actually half-filled the Central Hall at one meeting and got signatures of everybody that went in, hundreds. So it wasn't just *us*, an individual chapel who had a disagreement with Henderson; there were a lot of people who felt exactly the same.

Yet the local SOGAT full-time official, with the backing of the national union, wasted no time in taking retaliatory action. More than 100 union members had their union cards withdrawn for non-payment of subscriptions and Alan Hebden, the instigator and figurehead of the campaign to have the women reinstated, was expelled from the branch committee and lost his position as president of the Merseyside branch. Eventually he was expelled from SOGAT by the national executive for 'bringing the union into disrepute' and the Bemrose chapel was ordered to elect a new FoC.

Arguably, whilst the campaign against Stuart Henderson demonstrated the tenacious and independent spirit of the Bemrose SOGAT chapel it also suffered a number of tactical mistakes. Even though support for the sacked women was gathered from many union branch members there was a strong emphasis put on looking upwards to left-wing national full-time union officials to intervene to help remove Henderson. Pat explained:

> It's worth bearing in mind it was Alan Hebden who was instrumental in getting Brenda Dean elected in 1984. So he presented this hot potato to the national office, because there was something in the society that he loved and lived for that was cancerous, Stuart Henderson. It had to be cut off. At that stage I believe Brenda Dean gave him the full authority to expose the situation, which he did.

But once Brenda Dean was firmly established as SOGAT general secretary she appeared to become determined to crush any challenge which might have reverberations on her own power base within the union. The refusal of the Merseyside branch members to pay their subs provided her with the excuse to do so. Mark was highly critical of the tactic:

> Stopping the subs was supposed to be done in concert with the other chapels. Under the rule book you could go up to 13 weeks in arrears, which we did. But then at the eleventh hour Alan Hebden paid all the subs from Bemrose. The other chapels, who were all smaller than us and looking to Bemrose for a lead – because Alan was a figure of great importance not just in Bemrose but in the branch because he was branch president – they were just left isolated. I don't know why Alan didn't inform them he was paying the subs, he didn't even inform *us* until the last minute. That was a major mistake. There were three FoCs from other chapels who were expelled from SOGAT for not paying the subs for 13 weeks. And at the end of the day Alan faced about nine or ten different charges – but they did him on a technicality of not paying subs because they were supposed to be paid in advance under union rule.

Rather than challenging Stuart Henderson's right-wing policies on more favourable issues where the chapel had its greatest strength, such as in the workplace against management's offensive, the SOGAT chapel committee's focus on defending the sacked union secretaries as the predominant weapon of counter-attack lent itself to a campaign fought virtually exclusively on the terrain of the branch, and one which ultimately left them very vulnerable to the union's disciplinary measures. Despite the fact that chapel members continued to back Alan as FoC – in an impressive gesture of loyalty – the local SOGAT branch refused to acknowledge the chapel committee or assist it in any way *vis-à-vis* negotiations with Bemrose until he agreed to step down. As a result, the chapel organization was effectively neutralized from the point of view of both management and the national union.

Meanwhile, other events served to emphasize the weaknesses of the chapel committees' relationship to full-time union officials. The set-piece strikes and picket line confrontations involving print workers at the *Stockport Messenger* in Warrington and at News International's Wapping plant in east London, as well as the long-drawn-out miners' strike, provided the political activists within Bemrose with the opportunity to organize low-level solidarity activity on the shop-floor. Mark related:

> Most of the 'politicos' were involved in Warrington. We had a constant
> shuttle laid on three times a day at the end of the shift to take people
> down to the picket by bus. It was organized and paid through the
> federated chapel. Probably something like 50–60 members went down to
> the picket at one time or another.

Again, during the year-long miners' strike the chapel committees organized shop-floor solidarity. The NGA '82 process chapel had a £1 weekly levy and contributed about £3000 to the Lancashire miners' strike fund. The SOGAT chapel also had collections and levies. Yet the defeats of both these disputes served to reinforce the 'new realism' of the trade union movement – the view that Thatcherism could not be beaten, the law had to be respected, and strikes were both 'out of date' and counter-productive.

Such attitudes became even more pronounced after Bemrose workers voted against taking sympathy action for the print strikers at News International's Wapping plant in 1986. Only after ten weeks into the dispute did Bill Freeman, a member of SOGAT's national executive committee responsible for co-ordinating support for Wapping, make a belated appeal for the blacking of all News International work, including the printing of the *Sunday* magazine at Bemrose. It was interpreted by the activists as Bemrose as a cynical manoeuvre by the officials designed to head off strikers' criticism of their handling of the dispute. Earlier attempts to stop the movement of the lorries by mounting mass pickets on the gates of the Wapping plant had been actively discouraged. Instead of calling for solidarity strike action across Fleet Street at the beginning of the dispute, the print union leaders, including Brenda Dean of SOGAT, insisted the way to fight the world's most powerful media baron was through a public relations campaign. Given the fact that, as far as Bemrose workers were concerned, the national officials had done absolutely nothing to campaign for effective solidarity action either at Bemrose or elsewhere, it was not surprising their overdue appeal was turned down by the Bemrose chapel.

Quite apart from their fear of job losses, the distrust towards national SOGAT officials, particularly for the way they were handling the dispute over Stuart Henderson within the Merseyside branch, gave the chapel committee activists little confidence to back their recommendation. Even a direct personal appeal by the Wapping strikers themselves was turned down (NGA '82 process chapel minutes, 21 April 1986). Bill related:

We had a coachload of pickets up from London on two occasions asking us to get involved by not producing for Murdoch. They said to us: 'If you don't come out you will be next.' In fact, they said: 'You'll be next anyway.' The FoCs met with them and explained we didn't have the support of the members. We really did believe that if we had got involved at that particular time Murdoch would have closed Bemrose down. They agreed that rather than picket they would lobby our members and put their case. But they were right in the end – we *were* next on the list.

Thus, fear of the consequences of solidarity action further inhibited recommendations from union leaders for active support in the dispute.

It is conceivable that if, at the very beginning of the Wapping dispute, full-time union officials had mounted a determined campaign to win sympathy action in Bemrose, they could have encouraged some token action, such as a one-day strike, that might have been a springboard for further action alongside Fleet Street. Such action could have had the effect of strengthening the chapels' resolve *vis-à-vis* Bemrose management. Instead, the refusal to take action in support of Wapping did not protect the jobs of Bemrose workers. The Wapping dispute ended in February 1987 and in April 1987 775 redundancies were announced at Bemrose. Inevitably, the SOGAT chapel committees' resistance to the redundancies was severely impeded by the stance adopted by local union and national officials. As Mark explained:

SOGAT nationally and at branch level didn't have a reaction to the redundancies. They wouldn't get involved while Alan Hebden was still the FoC. Although he had been expelled from SOGAT, the membership said: 'He's our FoC and we're sticking with him.' So basically the union refused to get involved. What they were saying was: 'The principle of one man being your FoC far outweighs those 775 going out the door; when Alan Hebden's gone we'll come in.' At the end of the day quite a large number of people, branch officers, national officers in SOGAT, were delighted with what went on at Bemrose because we had been an example to them and to a certain extent we'd held them up to ridicule because we created so many jobs. They were busy presiding over job losses while Bemrose had been recruiting people. So when the balloon burst they just sat back and said: 'We told you so.' We ended up losing

> the redundancy issue, we lost the FoC and we came out of it with a
> divided chapel. Everything that had come out of 20 years had gone.

After the redundancies, Alan Hebden finally agreed to resign from the
FoC position in order to allow the union branch to represent the chapel
membership, on the basis that further resistance would be self-defeating.
From then on until the final closure of the plant in 1991 the dependence
of the SOGAT and other chapel committees in Bemrose on the full-time
union apparatus became considerably more marked.

Some Issues and Themes

As was the case in Birds Eye, the experience of chapel committee organization in Bemrose provides some intriguing insights into the dynamics
and dilemmas of workplace unionism. Thus, there were the problems of
sectionalism and craft antagonisms between the different departments,
chapels and unions, as well as the highly ambiguous nature of some
shop-floor working practices such as 'welt working' and high overtime.
Also, the immense obstacles to a more militant and successful challenge
to managerial restructuring were apparent, although the potential for
mounting some form of rearguard action which might have changed
developments, albeit only temporarily, needs to be considered. But there
were a number of other related issues which are of particular importance
in the context of earlier comments about the nature of workplace
unionism.

Despite the 'strong bargaining relations' established with management
inside Bemrose during the 1970s the degree of power exercised by the
chapel committees was much stronger than in Birds Eye. Powerful chapel
committees developed, able to carve out a series of counter-controls to
those of management. But a significant difference between shop-floor
industrial relations in Bemrose compared with Birds Eye was the comparatively low level of workers' struggle. The chapel committees' strength
came much more from advantageous market pressures, workers' strategic
relationship to production and the institutionalized pattern of craft job
control than from the daily battles on the shop-floor which generally
characterized Birds Eye during the 1970s.

But this had all sorts of consequences for the type of workplace union
organization that emerged in Bemrose. It ensured that the committee

representatives in the respective chapels did not play as prominent a role in shop-floor relations with management as the shop stewards in Birds Eye. Instead, they were viewed as purely an auxiliary to the key bargaining role played by the FoCs. It meant there was a very highly centralized form of leadership and authority in the hands of the FoCs, which reinforced the tendency for many rank-and-file members to look to the chapel officials to act on their behalf rather than acting independently themselves. This relatively poor tradition of workers' self-activity was a debilitating feature and proved to be a major handicap to the resistance mounted against the restructuring process and the closure of the plant. The 'strong bargaining relations' of mutually acceptable arrangements and compromise also tended to reinforce the quasi-managerial role of the FoCs, who oversaw jointly negotiated agreements to ensure the smooth running of the plant.

As in Birds Eye, the activities of certain left-wing individuals in Bemrose was crucial to the nature of workplace relations. Thus, Alan Hebden, a Militant supporter, played an absolutely pivotal role in building up the strength of SOGAT chapel organization in the 1970s. But instead of focusing their energies on building up shop-floor workers' self-activity and confidence to challenge management, the left inside the plant tended to see their primary task as backing up the bargaining activities of the FoC and capturing control over the lower echelons of the union machine. This 'control from above' strategy merely served to disarm workers from preparing for the kind of all-out fight that might, potentially, have been more successful in resisting management's offensive and in defending Alan Hebden from SOGAT's disciplinary measures.

Finally, although there was little shop-floor militancy in Bemrose during the 1970s the powerful bargaining strength *vis-à-vis* management buttressed the chapel committees' relatively independent stance towards both local and national full-time union officials. By contrast, in the 1980s the product market crisis and the chapel committees' more conciliatory relationship with management resulted in a much more formalized and dependent relationship towards them. Full-time union officials were absolutely instrumental in pressurizing the chapel committees into accepting managerial demands for greater efficiency and flexible working practices, particularly within the SOGAT chapel.

Again, these recurring themes and issues will be reconsidered in more detail in Chapter 7.

6 FORD

Introduction

The Ford Halewood factory was opened in 1963 when, along with other multinational companies, Ford was attracted to Merseyside largely as a result of the government's favourable regional policy and the existence of an 'adequate pool of labour'. The Ford Motor Company, one of the largest companies in the world, manufactures, assembles and sells cars in over 100 countries (including the United States, Canada, Brazil, Australia, Mexico, Argentina, South Africa, Germany, Spain and Britain). It is the number one USA-based motor company outside North America and sells more cars in Europe than many European manufacturers. Mass production, economies of scale and internationalization of production and markets have been the key to Ford's route to economic success. Despite its spread across the world it remains very much an American company with control of the vast empire firmly held in the company's world headquarters in Dearborn, Michigan. The two decades preceding the 1990s saw continuous profits for Ford of Britain (its UK subsidary) with a record pre-tax profit of £673 million in 1988 and its second best ever profit of £483 million in 1989, although it suffered pre-tax losses of £587 million in 1991 and £353 million in 1992 (*Liverpool Echo*, 27 May 1993).

The Halewood complex covers 346 acres (equivalent to more than 30 full-sized football pitches) and is Ford's second largest manufacturing centre in Britain (after Dagenham). It comprises three plants, the Metal, Stamping and Body plant, the Paint, Trim and Assembly plant and the Transmission plant. Unlike Birds Eye and Bemrose, despite constant threats of plant closure and a substantial reduction of the workforce the site remains operational. At its peak during the late 1970s, Halewood employed nearly 14 000 workers, although for most of the 1980s the figure hovered around the 9000 level, with about 4500 workers in the Assembly plant and 3500 in the Body plant. By the early 1990s, with over 5000 hourly paid manual workers still on the payroll, Halewood remains the biggest private employer on Merseyside. The Ford Escort, produced at the Halewood plant since 1968, was Britain's top-selling car during most of the 1980s.

The study is concerned with the production workers in the Body plant and Assembly plant, both housed in one giant building on the Halewood estate. The nature of the work is rather different within the two plants. In the Body plant (employing over 2000 in the early 1990s) it is heavy manual labour; shop-floor workers operate the presses as the sheet steel is stamped to produce panels, which are then spot-welded to form sub-assemblies and finally a rigid body shape. By contrast, the Assembly plant (employing over 3000 in the early 1990s) is much more semi-skilled and labour-intensive; the welded bodies are cleaned, primed and painted and thousands of parts are installed, including the interior trim, engine, transmission and wheels. Despite computerization, welding robots and years of technical innovation, car manufacture at Halewood is still firmly dependent on the line worker, with work organized so that each operation is sub-divided into its simplest and fastest components. Within both plants there is a basic two-shift pattern with workers on a two-week turn-around, alternating between nights and days, although the press shop of the Body plant operates a three-shift system. The vast majority of production workers (87 per cent) are members of the Transport and General Workers' Union with one TGWU factory branch (6/562) spanning the two major plants.

During the early 1960s, the day-to-day life of the Halewood plant was characterized by one endless battle over the 'frontier of control'; the right of shop stewards to have freedom of access to their members and to negotiate with the supervisor over the allocation of work was established only following periods of severe conflict and stoppages of work. Only in the late 1960s did management amend their policy, granting the conveners and senior stewards full-time status and providing facilities on site, such as union offices. Throughout the 1970s and 1980s, the formal structure of shop steward organization remained constant. Huw Beynon's *Working for Ford* (1984) reported that there were 45 members of the Assembly plant shop stewards' committee in 1967; 36 were TGWU members and the remainder were members of craft unions representing the various maintenance workers in the plant, including the AUEW and EETPU. By the early 1980s, there had been a slight increase in the number of TGWU stewards to 44, despite a gradual reduction in the overall size of the workforce. This included 22 stewards on the day shift and 22 on the night shift. In addition, there were a handful of craft stewards represented on the committee. Similarly, in the Body plant, although the number of workers employed was reduced from between 5000 and 6000 workers in the 1970s to about 3000 in the 1980s, the size of the shop stewards' committee remained roughly constant at about 63 members (40 in the TGWU and the remainder in craft unions). Thus, across the two plants there were about 88 TGWU stewards during the 1970s and 1980s. However, in the mid-1990s following pressure from management, there is likely to be a significant reduction in the number of stewards represented within the Body plant.

Shop stewards are usually elected annually or bi-annually through a secret ballot. Representation is determined by geographical sections that tend to correspond to supervisory areas. For example, in the Assembly plant, each moving line in the final trim area is divided up into three sections or workgroups with about 25 people on each. A shop steward would normally represent a whole line. Although there are wide variations across the two plants, the average number of union members in a steward's constituency is about 60. Both plants have their own shop stewards' committees which function and organize semi-autonomously and meet monthly. Formally, they join together as a site-wide joint shop stewards' committee overseeing both plants only irregularly for pay negotiations or to discuss some particular local issue that affects the whole Halewood complex. However informally, senior stewards from the two plants are in regular contact with each other.

In the Assembly plant, the shop stewards' committee annually elects from its number a convenor, two deputy convenors and five other TGWU senior stewards (plus one craft steward) to serve on a joint works committee (JWC) which meets monthly with the plant and personnel manager and conducts all major negotiations. All JWC members have 100 per cent time off work. The full-time convenor remains permanently on the day-shift and has primary responsibility for negotiations with management. Along with the other JWC members (who follow the shift system of their constituents) they form a group of senior stewards who give advice to other sectional stewards and represent the central workers' leadership in the plant. Exactly the same type of JWC structure exists in the Body plant, although there are a greater number of senior stewards represented there.

Basic pay, occupational grading and major conditions of employment are negotiated at a company-wide level through a quarterly meeting of a 70-strong national joint negotiating committee (NJNC) composed of senior UK Ford managers, full-time national union officials representing the 12 different unions with members in Ford plants across the country, and the 21 plant convenors. With the rate for the job agreed at national level, day-to-day conflict on the shop-floor invariably revolves around questions of job control, such as the speed of the line, movement of labour and discipline (although pay strikes related to the national bargaining forum are also a feature of workplace relations). The tasks and responsibilities of shop stewards (and the JWCs) are carefully defined in Ford's 'Blue Book', the handbook of official rules and procedures that govern the relationship between the unions and company, which include an elaborate five-stage grievance procedure aimed at reducing the level of conflict in the plants.

Stewards' Relationship to Management: The 1970s

The 1970s: The Stewards' Strengths

The late 1960s inside the Ford Halewood plant were characterized in Beynon's account (1973) as being the years of the 'ball and chain'. Production line managers took a 'no nonsense' approach, which had been tested at Dagenham in the 1940s and 1950s and taken to the new Halewood plant when it opened in 1963. This involved an extremely abrasive management strategy aimed at preventing an effective shop-floor trade union organization from being able to bargain over conditions of work. Phil was a shop steward in the paint shop and one of the most prominent figures in the emerging stewards' organization, becoming convenor of the Assembly plant between 1968 and 1970, before leaving the factory to take up a local TGWU full-time official's position. A militant shop-floor activist, although not a member of any political party, he offered a vivid description of the plant in its early years:

> It was a hell-camp, total liberty taking. People were spoken to like dogs. You'd get Cockney supervisors coming down saying things like, 'You fucking lazy scouse bastards.' It was a totally autocratic management

Chronology of Major Events

1969 Three-week national 'penalty clause' strike. Four convenors (including two from Halewood) admitted to NJNC.

1971 Nine-week national 'parity' strike. Two-week Halewood strike over John Dillon (1st 'Riot Act').

1975 Procedure Agreement, Work Standards Agreement and Union Membership Agreement.

1976 Two-week Halewood 'trade union representation' strike (2nd 'Riot Act').

1978 NJNC reconstituted–all Ford UK plant convenors admitted. Nine-week national pay strike.

1980 Retooling of Halewood and introduction of new technology.

1981 Two-week Halewood strike over discipline code (3rd 'Riot Act').

1983 Four-week Assembly plant strike over Paul Kelly.

1985 Two-week Halewood line-workers regrading strike.

1988 Two-week national pay strike.

1990 Seven-week national craftmen's strike and lay-off of production workers.

1991 Three-day production week for long period.

1992 Three-day production week for long period.

1993 'Voluntary' compulsory redundancies withdrawn after threat of strike action.

style . . . The turnover was massive – they just walked through the place. As people poured into the factory one end you'd see them going out the other end, sacked or under their own steam.

Such a 'ball and chain' approach helped to precipitate frequent sectional and plant-wide stoppages of work, as the newly established stewards' organization only established the right to have to access to members and to negotiate with line supervisors and managers through severe bouts of conflict that sought to carve out a 'frontier of control'. John, a line worker in the Assembly plant since 1967, and now a senior steward and 'mainstream' Labour Party member, recalled:

It was an unbelievable atmosphere. You were insulted all the time and expected to kow-tow. Numerous stoppages occurred because stewards weren't made available for people – because it was at the whim of the supervisor whether they were released or not. So sometimes, the only way the steward could have a meeting with his members was to call a strike.

Halewood stewards led numerous sectional disputes over 'speed-up' on the lines, disciplinary action, work standards, manning and the 'blue-eyed system' – by which supervisors used favouritism in allocating work or in moving men from one job to another.

It was through such militant workers' resistance to managerial intransigence that a relatively powerful plant-wide collective stewards' organization was built during the late 1960s and early 1970s. Ironically, Ford's 'ball and chain' approach helped to provoke the famous 'penalty clause' national strike of 1969. Against the backcloth of the Labour-government-appointed Donovan Commission and a White Paper advocating control of the activities of shop stewards, Ford's 1969 pay package for its British workforce contained a series of penalty clauses aimed at penalizing unofficial stoppages of work. Dave, a union activist at Halewood over the past 20 years and a senior steward in the Assembly plant, remembered:

> The 1969 strike was tied into the Labour government's 'In Place Of Strife' which proposed legal fines for 'unconstitutional action'. The Ford Motor Company – anticipating things as they always do – tried to impose it before it had become a reality nationally.

Militant shop-floor opposition to the 'penalty clauses' was spearheaded by the stewards at Ford's Halewood plant. As Phil commented:

> A number of us recognized the role and significance within Ford that what they were doing today would set an industrial relations trend elsewhere tomorrow. The eyes of other car workers right across the engineering industry were going to be looking at Ford. So some of us accepted we had a wider responsibility and others outside were encouraging Ford workers to have a go.

Initiated by shop stewards at Halewood and Swansea in defiance of national union officials on the NJNC (which at that time excluded lay representation), the first ever national strike across all Ford's British plants lasted three weeks and succeeded in substantially watering down the company's conditions. The democratic reform of the union's negotiating forum followed in the wake of the 1969 strike and the victory over the company at national level boosted the confidence and willingness of rank-and-file workers and their stewards inside Ford's Halewood plant to resist managerial prerogative at local level.

In 1971 the Halewood stewards' activities reached a new height during a nine-week national 'parity' pay strike which won comparable earnings with the hitherto better paid piecework car factories of the Midlands. Again, it was the Halewood stewards' organization that provided the backbone of the strike leadership nationally. Within days of a resumption of work, following the 1971 strike, Halewood management attempted to regain the initiative by announcing that workplace industrial relations would be 'played by the Blue Book' with shop stewards being given a full 60-minute work allocation and not allowed time off the job without prior permission of the supervisor. The result of this '1st Riot Act', as it subsequently became known, was a series of disciplinary measures and suspensions against shop stewards which led to constant stoppages of work over a period of ten weeks, culminating in the sacking of John Dillon, a steward in the Assembly plant. Dave related:

> After the '71 strike the company thought they had beaten us into submission . . . We hadn't had a full week's wage packet for about 20 weeks. They thought, 'This is the time to go in and kick them, when they're down.' It was a sustained attack on the shop steward organization but we were strong enough to come through it.

The Assembly plant took all-out strike action and after two weeks forced management to reinstate the sacked steward, albeit in a different job and without recognition as a union representative. Even if not a complete victory it successfully blocked the attempt to destroy the shop stewards' authority.

In other words, by the early 1970s the balance of workplace power inside the Merseyside plant was undoubtedly weighted to the relative advantage of shop-floor workers. A similar picture existed in other Ford plants across the country, particularly at Dagenham, although possibly not quite to the same extent. In part, the shop-floor militancy in Ford's reflected the 'upturn' in workers' struggles that was taking place more generally inside the British labour movement, and, as Sander Meredeen, a Ford manager at the company's British headquarters in Warley at the time, put it: 'The company realized that it had to come to terms with this "challenge from below" ' (Friedman and Meredeen, 1980). At Halewood, management appears to have responded by gradually abandoning its 'ball and chain' approach in favour of a combination of strategies that could be characterized as the 'carrot and stick'.

This typology of management strategy during the 1970s differs slightly from Beynon's (1984). Whilst acknowledging the very real initiatives aimed at 'accommodating' to the strength of shop stewards' organization taken at senior Ford executive level, Beynon does not adequately take account of the contradictory but simultaneous policy of 'conflict' evidenced at plant level inside Halewood. Certainly, the coherence of Ford's national strategic initiatives stood in sharp contrast to Halewood management's insistence on unilateral managerial control. It was a contradiction rooted in a fundamental inability to devise a successful policy for curbing shop-floor militancy.

On the one hand, there was the 'carrot' component – which involved a policy of accommodating to, if not trying to incorporate, a layer of senior shop stewards. For the previous 20 years, Ford had operated a strongly unified and centrally controlled organizational structure within its UK plants with the power of policy making concentrated at the centre, under which closely prescribed limits were placed on the autonomy of local line management. This traditional policy and collective bargaining structure now began to change as the company took a series of initiatives, both nationally and in the plants, designed to make a significant contribution towards reducing the number of shop-floor disputes. The first fruit of this accommodation policy was the admission of four plant convenors (including two from Halewood) to Ford's National Joint Negotiating Committee (NJNC) (Friedman and Meredeen, 1980).

Ironically, the 1969 strike had revealed in sharp relief the abject failure of remote national full-time union officials to carry their members' support for new agreements. This failure persuaded senior Ford executives of the need to 'work with the newly selected leaders of the trade union side to develop a more businesslike and trusting relationship' (Friedman and Meredeen, 1980, p. 226). The preservation of the NJNC as an authoritative joint union–management bargaining forum was regarded as the company's top priority and Ford therefore welcomed the arrival of the plant convenors on the NJNC, recognizing the changed locus of power and the need to reach agreements in future with shop-floor union leaders. In stages over the next decade the NJNC was reconstituted and democratized even further, leading in 1978 to the admission of all Ford's 21 plant convenors. Thus, the two Halewood plant convenors became much more closely linked to the formal trade union machine, if not exposed to the dangers of institutionalization.

The attempt to accommodate to the presence of the shop stewards was also reflected in a new national 'Procedure Agreement' signed in 1975 which aimed at providing a more effective role for stewards by requiring that in future most problems would be settled at *plant* level without the need to constantly refer matters to the NJNC for resolution. Simultaneously, the first ever 'Work Standards Agreement' was negotiated, which provided a five-stage procedure through which grievances could be resolved; a status quo clause was conceded in return for union agreement to take no industrial action over proposed changes to 'well established working practices' during a 15-day period. This was followed in 1976 by a union membership clause which conferred exclusive bargaining rights to the NJNC unions, with provision for a 100 per cent post-entry closed shop and the collection of union dues by deduction from wages through the payroll.

Inside the Halewood plant, Ford's accommodation policy led to the convenors and senior stewards in both Body and Assembly plants (numbering about 15 individuals) being given greatly enhanced recognition and status, as well as 100 per cent time off work to conduct union business. During the 1960s, workers had struggled for the right of their shop steward to be released from the line to negotiate, but by the 1970s Halewood management adopted a generally more relaxed, if unevenly applied, policy. A new layer of senior shop stewards began to emerge who were generally allocated light duties, and allowed a degree of freedom of movement within the plant and regular access to the convenor's union office on the shop-floor. In the event of a serious dispute emerging on a section, the operation of Ford's new industrial relations policy meant the almost immediate involvement of senior stewards. Tony, a shop steward for over 20 years, chairperson of the Body plant stewards' committee and an independent socialist militant, related:

> There were that many stoppages of work that Ford did everything to utilize the senior stewards as 'policemen of discontent'. Consequently they were not on the job. They had to give them facility time to help them solve disputes (although the company blew hot and cold on this

issue). When they wanted to use the shop stewards to settle disputes, to exercise a restraining influence on shop-floor militancy, it suited them to allow even some sectional stewards virtually 100 per cent facility time. But if they thought the stewards were abusing their authority and leading opposition they would quickly put them back on the job.

Therefore, on the one hand, the decade after 1968 saw Ford opt for a strategy of accommodation and integration of the convenors and senior shop stewards within the Halewood plant. This was the 'carrot' part of the approach. On the other hand, the Halewood plant management simultaneously pursued a strategy of tight shop-floor discipline with the aim of securing high and continuous production. This was the 'stick' component of the approach and it was this element which was clearly the more dominant of the two as far as most of the stewards were concerned.

Management repeatedly took a confrontational approach to workplace industrial relations, for example operating a policy of laying off workers whenever the consequential effects of 'unconstitutional' stoppages of work by one section prevented another from doing their normal jobs. A senior employee relations manager in the Body plant outlined the predicament felt by supervisors and management at the time:

> As a production superintendent on the night shift, whenever a problem occurred the steward's answer, more often than not, would be, 'Well, give us another man on the line.' And with the only alternative being a stoppage of work you would bang a man in. That was fine on a temporary basis but once you'd put him in you couldn't get him out. Because of that we were heavily overmanned . . . A lot of supervisors felt demoralized because they had lost control, they knew they had lost control of the situation because every time they went in on an issue to get a change of some sort they were met with resistance or blackmail. So the place was running amok and the labour and the stewards were controlling it more than the management. It got so bad that locally the management said: 'If we go on like this we'll go under, we'll have to try something different.'

This tangible loss of managerial authority provided the rationale for a new set of policies towards the workforce. In 1976, frustrated with their lack of authority, management wielded the 'big stick' with tremendous ferocity. A new management team, mainly industrial relations managers from Dagenham, were drafted into the Halewood plant. The measures they took to 'regain' control of the shop-floor became known as the '2nd Riot Act'. Previously, sectional stewards had negotiated with supervisors; but the whole relationship changed as the new industrial relations managers started to go down on the shop-floor and, acting over the heads of front-line supervision, 'put the boot in' by insisting on strict adherence to the 'Blue Book' with no form of appeals procedure. The Body plant senior employee relations manager justified the approach thus:

> It was simply an intention on management's part to stand up to the issues and not run away from them, to take them on. We had to lose volume to restore control. So the shop-floor was flooded with personnel offices. Whenever there was an issue [where somebody refused a request from a supervisor] we introduced an 'off-pay' situation . . . But of course, when we took one guy off-pay the rest of his mates on the section went off-pay, went out on strike with him, maybe the whole line went on strike with him. So a lot of people got laid off. We went through a long period when they were in and out like fiddlers' elbows. Eventually, although it took a while, some sort of confidence began to build up within the supervision again and we went into a quieter period where we were more in control than we had been. It wasn't perfect but it was better than it had been.

Implementation of the '2nd Riot Act' lasted for a few months and produced numerous stoppages of work. As Tony explained:

> It was a bit like Germany in the 1930s. The IR were the 'Gestapo' and the production management the 'Weimar'. The position of the shop stewards was completely undermined. We felt the value of trade union representation in Halewood meant nothing to management.

Eventually the issue blew up into a two-week plant-wide strike initiated by the Halewood shop stewards in defence of basic workplace trade union 'representation', which was only called off after senior Ford UK executives and national union officials agreed on a new appeals procedure on discipline.

The 'stick' component of Halewood management's strategy remained a continuing feature during the late 1970s. An employee relations manager in the paint shop in the Assembly plant, arriving at Halewood in 1977 as a young graduate, remembered the old-style bombastic Ford manager:

> Rather than looking at the trade union rep as a representative of the men, they were looking at him as a person and saying, 'He's just a gobshite' . . . It was macho-style management in the 1970s . . . The view was that shop stewards were a nuisance. Shop stewards were not to be consulted . . . Management had the right to manage and you were a wimp if you made any conciliatory gestures to the trade unions. Junior levels of management and supervisors took the view that the only thing people responded to was the big stick. People were intrinsically lazy. On the moving line situation they had to be flogged into it. Everything was confrontational and the stewards reacted to that.

The senior employee relations manager in the Body plant also acknowledged that heavy-handed management was directly responsible for provoking much shop-floor militancy:

> This company has always been dominated by numbers, the number of cars you produce, the cost of it, the numbers employed. It's always been a numbers game. And there's always been a pressure on volume production. The managers in the '70s were obviously under pressure from their bosses higher up the tree to turn the volume out and if there was a risk that they wouldn't get it, they would resort to whatever measure they could to achieve it. A lot of them were tough, extremely autocratic and dictatorial. It wasn't so much the consultation or negotiation so much as, 'We're telling you that's what it's going to be.' And then you got the confrontation.

This was the strategy of the 1970s. As far as Halewood management was concerned both the 'carrot' and the 'stick', accommodation and confrontation strategies, were designed with the same objective: to break down the principal source of resistance to managerial authority, namely the union organization based around the stewards in both Body and Assembly plants. Clearly it was the 'stick' component of their strategy which predominated during the 1970s, although the impact of the 'carrot' component was more insidious. Yet, given there were dozens of sectional walk-outs in both plants on the Halewood estate during the 1970s (see Table 1, p. 208), it met with only limited success. Despite the sometimes dampening impact of senior stewards on workplace militancy, it is clear that quite powerful and independent shop steward organizations developed which were a constant source of concern to the Halewood management. Indeed, both Merseyside plants were at the centre of another nine-week national Ford strike in 1978 which succeeded in breaking through the Labour government's 'Social Contract' 5 per cent pay norm to win a 17 per cent increase, reflecting the confidence of shop-floor organization.

By 1980 a number of quite fundamental changes in several of the work processes at Halewood took place as the plant went through a retooling programme in preparation for the launch of a new model, the Escort Mark III. Ford's £205 million investment heralded the age of new technology in the plant. The advanced automated machinery was concentrated in the Body plant (and in the paint-spraying area of the Assembly plant) where 39 robots were installed – more than in any other car assembly plant in Britain. The Body plant was completely gutted and modernized as lines were thrown out and entirely different jobs introduced. As the Body plant became more capital-intensive the Assembly plant remained relatively more labour-intensive. Both shop steward organizations became preoccupied with the movement of labour as about 800 workers were either temporarily or permanently transferred from the Body to the Assembly plant. Management initially operated very cautiously; not sure how the new robots would function and with a new model about to be launched, they did not want to provoke any antagonism which might threaten production schedules. Nonetheless, numerous stoppages took place because so many jobs were disrupted and long-cherished customs and practices undermined.

In November 1980 a letter to all its British employees from Ford's referred to the 'appalling situation in the plants' with unconstitutional stoppages continuing unabated. At the centre of the problem were the Halewood plants. The company's own figures show the Merseyside complex accounted for a disproportionate amount of UK hours and sales losses between 1978 and 1982 (Marsden et al., 1985). Yet local management's renewed attempts to deal with the problem, new disciplinary procedures to raise the penalties for 'unconstitutional action' in 1979, a new work standards procedure in 1980, and the suspension of workers who could not meet new production targets in 1981 provoked sectional walk-outs and repeated lay-offs in both the Body and Assembly plants. Disputes in 1981 and 1982 gave Halewood respectively a 14.6 per cent and 12.6 per cent share of the British car industry's working days lost (Marsden et al.,

1985). By 1981 the introduction of new technology in the plant had led to a reduction of labour of 6.2 per cent, with many hundreds of voluntary redundancies. But management still found that shop-floor practices were difficult to reform.

The threat of foreign competition within Ford's core American and European markets, particularly from Japanese car manufacturers, made the task of reorganization more urgent. In the late 1970s there was a falling demand for British cars and a deep commercial crisis as the car industry began to suffer chronic overcapacity on a world scale. In 1981 Ford Europe's senior executive Bill Hayden visited Japan and later, in a detailed internal document, wrote of the ability of the Japanese producers to undercut Ford's most efficient operation in Europe by 30 per cent. This was a devastating document and set the tone for the decade. It was against this background that Ford coined a new calendar, called 'AJ', 'After Japan', to counteract the competition (Beynon, 1984).

Ford's initial response to the threat of Japanese competition was to push through rationalization and efficiency measures by traditional top-down methods, and in 1981 Halewood management reverted to the 'big stick' again by imposing Ford's new disciplinary code, known within the plant as the '3rd Riot Act'. It stipulated that if an employee had a grievance the employee was to be given up to 10 minutes off the line to talk to a supervisor and steward, after which if the problem had not been resolved and the employee refused to resume work that person was to be suspended for the rest of the day. If the shop steward organized a stoppage in his or her defence the section involved were to be immediately suspended for the following day's shift. An Employee Relations manager in the Body plant at Halewood explained:

> It was called 'Double Dosing'. Once they decided to take somebody off-pay and the rest of the section went on strike for the rest of the shift we suspended them for an equivalent amount of time. So any one-day strike became two days . . . It was like cutting off our noses to spite our faces, but it was another way of making it more painful for the employees to take strike action because it hurt people more financially.

Inevitably, because the policy meant large numbers of workers found themselves being laid off even though they had not been involved in any dispute, it caused tremendous anger amongst both stewards and members. Tony recalled the shop-floor response in the Body plant:

> The convenor and the stewards took a hard-line position in response to
> 'Double Dosing'. As soon as the company suspended anyone we
> reversed it and gave the company 10 minutes to take it back or we
> threatened a plant-wide stoppage. We took the position 'One's off-pay,
> we're all off-pay.' A lot of supervisors backed down. But eventually it
> blew up at the same time in both plants . . . we ended up recommending
> an all-out strike at mass meetings of the members.

Ford was forced to withdraw its disciplinary code completely after another
two-week strike paralysed production across the two Halewood plants,
providing the shop stewards with a significant victory.

Of course, the high strike levels in Ford's Halewood plants during the
1960s and 1970s were affected by other factors apart from managerial
intransigence. There was the alienating nature of work on a rigidly
organized assembly line work process, with a massive expansion and
influx of thousands of workers leading to enormous problems of turnover
and organization. There was the disruption caused by the introduction of
advanced robotic technology. There was the collectivist union traditions
of Merseyside and the influence of some left-wing shop stewards. Yet it
appears management's 'hard-line' stance was the principal contributory
factor to the day-to-day struggle on the shop-floor, which in turn helped
to shape the type of relatively powerful stewards' organization that
emerged and which was able to establish a significant degree of counter-
controls over managerial prerogative. Stewards administered overtime
rotas and monitored the movement of labour, strictly controlled through
a 'seniority system' based on the length of service of individual workers.
They also challenged management's authoritarian supervision of work
and disciplinary procedures. As Tony explained:

> In the '70s the role of the supervisor was being challenged every day,
> every hour, because people were confident. It was being challenged
> more by the workers themselves – it wasn't necessarily an organized
> co-ordinated action by the shop stewards. But the leadership was
> responsible for being seen to have the dominant role over who mans
> what job, who gets graded and that.

Thus, against the background of an aggressive managerial approach, the
shop stewards articulated rank-and-file workers' grievances, led shop-
floor struggles and built a relatively strong, combative workplace union
organization.

The 1970s: The Stewards' Weaknesses

Nonetheless, the extent of job controls and the strength of stewards' organization was by no means uniform across the Halewood site, nor unproblematic. This can be seen in a number of ways. Firstly, some sections of workers, such as the line-workers in the trim and final assembly departments of the Assembly plant and on the 'white lines' inside the Body plant, were able to take advantage of their strategic position in the production process to develop comparatively ambitious counter-controls. With many of these jobs being extremely repetitive, monotonous and badly paid, there was added incentive to engage in shop-floor resistance. Other sections bereft of significant leverage, such as non-line workers on sub-assembly work and janitors, tended to have less immediate control over the job, and their higher basic pay, access to greater amounts of overtime and/or generally less onerous work meant they tended not to engage in militant activity as readily. The uneven level of experience and activity of individual stewards was a notable influence on the degree of solidarity and cohesion among rank-and-file workers in different sections.

Secondly, another important factor influencing the balance of workplace power was the state of the product market. The motor industry is notoriously highly competitive and the dramatic restructuring of car manufacture which took place on a world scale during the 1970s, with imported cars taking an increasing share of the British market, placed even greater pressure on Ford for increased productivity and output. During periods of market boom, when the shop-floor were working high schedules, management often considered it not worth their while to challenge certain areas of job control. As the senior Employee Relations manager in the Body plant acknowledged:

> In the mid-'70s the car industry was booming and we needed every vehicle we could produce and there was a sense that when the market was high and management wanted cars the union felt it was in the ascendancy.

Challenges to job control carried the risk of a stoppage and lost production. But the product market had its troughs as well as its peaks and during these periods management were not slow to exploit the situation to their advantage, thereby limiting the extent and durability of shop-floor union controls. As Phil related:

> Ford were quite fickle in their industrial relations strategy. It used to come in waves. You would find that when the order books were full they

were quite willing to make concessions all over the place. They would overman sections, they would know people were working the 'welt', having extra tea breaks and so forth. But when there was a bit of a squeeze going on – either because the order books were tighter or there was a model change coming up and they could mark time a bit – they were quite willing to dig their heels in and a lot of disputes would occur. The thing *did* go in trends.

In this respect there was an ebb and flow to industrial relations in the plants reflected in the incidence of disputes and other forms of militant activity.

Thirdly, the combination of objective and subjective factors affecting the balance of workplace power and the type of shop stewards' committee that developed can be highlighted by comparing the differences between the two plants on the Halewood estate. Beynon's study (1973) concentrated virtually exclusively on the Assembly plant. Arguably, during the 1970s the relative importance of the Body plant was markedly enhanced. Although there was considerable overlap in terms of the level of shop-floor militancy, with both plants being in the forefront at different periods of time, the Body plant stewards' committee was probably a more unpredictable thorn in the side of management than the Assembly plant stewards' organization.

To begin with, the nature of the work process was more physically demanding and dangerous in the Body plant than in the Assembly plant. This tended to cause far more problems over issues of health and safety and led to numerous shop-floor disputes over the level of noise, amount of fumes and intensity of heat. Whilst the very highly disciplined organization of work in the Assembly plant also proved to be a constant source of conflict, the substantial changes to the Body plant's production system, particularly with the introduction of giant presses and new machinery in the late 1970s and early 1980s, created even greater pressures for workers' resistance. Moreover, there appear to have been more persistent hard-line management attempts to impose discipline and control over the pace of work and the level of absenteeism within the Body plant. Despite its periodic bouts of set-piece confrontations, there was a comparatively more co-operative day-to-day relationship established between management and senior stewards in the Assembly plant, where a larger number of managers than in the Body plant appeared to have practised a more consultative approach to workplace industrial relations.

The character of the shop stewards' leadership was also rather different. In the Assembly plant, there was a well-established union convenor, Trevor Wilson, who remained in office throughout the 1970s and was personally very influential in shaping a stewards' leadership. He was only prepared to take strike action 'as a last resort'. By contrast, in the Body plant, there was a less stable steward leadership with a succession of different convenors during the 1970s, including a Communist activist. At the same time, the Assembly plant stewards appear to have been more firmly integrated into official trade union structures. The TGWU Halewood factory branch committee was completely dominated by Assembly plant stewards who, despite their preparedness to act unofficially on occasions, tended to operate strictly within official union procedures. By contrast, in the Body plant the stewards' committee tended to operate more autonomously of the official union machine. In part, this was because TGWU shop-floor organization inside the Body plant was a much more recent phenomenon than in the Assembly plant. Only after the 1969 parity strike did the TGWU become the majority union, following the exodus from the GMWU of 2000 members disgusted at the behaviour of its full-time officials. Even then, until 1973 the convenor of the Body plant was a member of the engineers' union, the AUEW. Furthermore, there were a far greater number of craftsmen in the Body plant than in the Assembly plant, with their own independent power base of union organization. Indeed, a serious split between the TGWU and craft shop stewards in the Body plant (which led to the existence of a separate craft stewards' committee from 1973 to 1978, not formally recognized by the company or national union officials) meant shop-floor bargaining was invariably more fragmented and less stable than in the Assembly plant.

Fourthly, there were a number of sectional divisions which were a handicap to the development of strong shop stewards' organization. In the Assembly plant, the differentiation between line-workers and non-line workers, over such things as the nature of work, level of supervision, rate of pay and availability of overtime, was a traditional source of animosity. There was also some resentment amongst many line-workers towards the 100-plus women sewing-machinists who worked within the trim manufacture department. Although they only worked day shifts they were on a higher basic grade than most line-workers and they were viewed as women who only worked for 'pin-money'. Similarly, in the Body plant, a significant factor undermining shop-floor unity was the differences in job, pay and conditions between the two-shift and three-shift sections,

Table 1 *Number of stoppages in Ford Halewood 1976–1983*

1976:	310
1977:	264
1978:	116
1979:	69
1980:	116
1981:	52
1982:	73
1983:	34

Figures supplied by Personnel Development and Training manager, Ford Halewood, February 1989.

with the latter traditionally concerned to maintain their advantageous position. Another division was that between TGWU production workers and craftsmen (members of the AUEW and EETPU) who often crossed TGWU workers' picket lines.

Fifthly, the image of a militant and powerful shop stewards' organization in both plants at Halewood has to be qualified by consideration of the fact that for a great deal of the time rather uneventful bargaining took place resolving problems *without* confrontation. Even if Ford's constant reassertion of managerial prerogative left little scope for a deeply rooted accommodation between the stewards' bodies and management as a whole, the application of the 'carrot and stick' approach clearly had some success, at least in the long term. On the one hand, the (short-term) 'stick' approach often provoked disputes which could sometimes undermine plant-wide solidarity with its consequential lay-offs. On the other hand, the (long-term) 'carrot' approach, of involving joint works committee stewards in overseeing the formalized agreements, helped to create the basis for aspects of a 'strong bargaining relationship' and of a more 'professional' workplace trade unionism. Thus, the number of stoppages of work recorded by Ford, counted on the basis of disputes involving three or more workers stopping work for 15 minutes or more, shows a successive decline during the course of the 1970s (see Table 1). In some respects, this decline in the strike rate underlines the extent to which there was the gradual emergence of a somewhat more conciliatory relationship between stewards and management.

Finally, there was the weakness of what Beynon (1984) described as the stewards' 'factory class-consciousness', a highly developed understanding of the day-to-day conflicts on the shop-floor but with politics essentially limited to the confines of the factory and not generalized to wider political concerns. As Phil, one of the most prominent stewards of the 1960s, observed:

> We didn't have a very heightened political awareness. None of us were active in political parties. We were all accused of being every faction of 'Trot' when the truth was none of us really were. Almost naively in some respects our attitude was conditioned around the shop-floor. We got the trust from the lads and the support on the issues that became the priority. No one was ever able to say we were politically motivated maniacs. Although they tried that they weren't able to prove it.

Significantly, after leaving Halewood in 1970, Phil belatedly recognized the need for a political organization rooted on the shop-floor and joined the Communist Party. A handful of other stewards joined small revolutionary socialist organizations, such as Big Flame, which produced a newspaper aimed primarily at car workers and was based on Merseyside, and the International Socialists (forerunners of the Socialist Workers Party), who built a factory branch of about a dozen supporters in 1974–75. Others were 'mainstream' members of the Labour Party. Nonetheless, it necessary to note that active shop-floor political intervention was eschewed by some leading stewards. Phil reflected on the attitude of his successor as convenor in the Assembly plant during the 1970s:

> The Ford stewards didn't integrate themselves within the local labour movement, they bricked themselves in. Trevor Wilson was very different from me as a convenor. I think if my deputy had been elected he would have perpetuated a more progressive regime. Individuals do have an influence, it's a fact. When Trevor came in, radical newspapers and organizations came along and he censored them all, threw them all out. Anyone who wanted to carry a Ford banner who wasn't part of Ford was excommunicated. He cosseted and protected the stewards from the outside world.

The picture was rather different in the Body plant, where the handful of politically committed left-wing stewards seemed to wield slightly more influence within the stewards' committee compared with the Assembly plant. Yet, by and large, most of the stewards who emerged during the 1970s adopted a quasi-syndicalist approach, concerned only with immediate issues in the plants, with the Halewood stewards' bodies being essentially peripheral to the broader campaigns and issues taken up within the local labour movement. No doubt the fact that day-to-day improvements were achieved through shop-floor union organization encouraged the majority of stewards to believe they could rely on industrial muscle alone. But although this self-sufficiency reflected their sense of strength it also underlined an important political limitation which would become ever more apparent during the recession years of the 1980s.

Yet, all such qualifications aside, there is little doubt that the balance of workplace power was tilted to the relative advantage of shop steward organization in the Ford Halewood plant during the 1970s. It was built up in struggle against a management which, despite its limited initiatives aimed at incorporating a layer of senior stewards, worked to undermine the basis of any deeply rooted or stable accommodative relationship with the stewards' organization through its complementary and more dominant strategy of 'sticking the boot in'. Thus, despite aspects of co-operation the period can be generally characterized as being relatively conflictual.

Stewards' Relationship to Management: The 1980s/1990s

The Early 1980s: 'Jaw-Jaw, Not War-War'

During the early 1980s there was the beginning of a marked change inside Halewood, as the shop stewards increasingly became preoccupied with the fear of job loss and began to believe the plant would be closed unless workplace industrial relations were radically changed. To begin with, against the backcloth of a crisis in the world car market and with Japanese efficiency levels outstripping Ford's, there was the development of a 'Ford Europe' production system, as most plants now became identified with single models. Thus, Halewood was to produce only the one model, the Escort. At the same time, the introduction of internationally integrated sourcing ended the practice of single plants building single models for their own national markets; the same Escort model assembled at Halewood was now also produced in Saarlouis in West Germany, enabling Ford to switch production between plants and to make productivity comparisons between the two with the ultimate threat of closure unless effciency was improved. The mass media reflected this concern about possible job loss. Thus, in February 1981, under the headline: 'Ford Plans to Run Down European Plants', the *Guardian* reported that documents leaked from Detroit outlined Ford's plan to switch Escort production to Brazil by 1983, with Ford Europe left merely to supply the components; it suggested the European plant most likely to be affected would be Halewood (*Guardian*, 26 February 1981). Similar scare stories were run in the *Liverpool Echo*.

Meanwhile, with the installation of new technology in Halewood leading to a substantial reduction in labour requirements, Ford announced a voluntary redundancy programme in January 1983, with the loss of 3000 jobs sought over a period of two years. The steward committees were opposed in principle to job losses and, initially at least, few workers volunteered for redundancy. A major turning point appears to have been Halewood management's provocative sacking of a line-worker, Paul Kelly, for alleged vandalism of a small car bracket in April 1983. This resulted in a four-week Assembly plant strike in his defence and led to immediate lay-offs in the Body plant. In many respects the strike reflected general shop-floor anger at management's relentless drive for 'efficiency'. But management took the opportunity of plunging the knife even further by announcing within eight days of a return to work in the Assembly plant that they would be implementing a series of new working practices within the Body plant, prompting the Body plant shop stewards' committee to recommend indefinite strike action if Ford went ahead with its plans. Eventually, Ford's backed down from its bellicose stance. The Assembly plant workforce returned to work after the company agreed to abide by the outcome of an independent tribunal into Paul Kelly's sacking, which eventually led to his reinstatement, and although some efficiency changes were introduced in the Body plant, the stewards were able to forestall key aspects of their implementation.

It was another illustration that Ford could not just ride roughshod over shop stewards' organization in Halewood. But there was also a heavy price to pay in the aftermath of the strike, as a flood of mainly younger workers, fearing the possibility of eventual compulsory redundancy, opted to take voluntary redundancy and accept the relatively high payments being offered by the company. Frank, a rank-and-file union activist in the Body plant, where he has worked since the late 1970s, remembered:

> Quite a few young unmarried men took the redundancy. Some of them were the more militant people, particularly in my area. They felt the most insecure. They had been going through two years with the change in the model, unsure what their job or the future was going to be and when the strike happened over Paul Kelly – we believe the company instigated that because when the redundancies first showed nobody put their name down – when the strike began to bite, the people who had the least service and were unsure, they went.

The looming prospect of plant closure was greatly accelerated after the 1983 Paul Kelly strike, when Ford Halewood's operations manager took the highly dramatic step of going down on to the shop-floor to stop all the production lines and address the workforce about the drastic changes required if the closure of Halewood was to be averted. According to the production manager of the Trim in the Assembly plant:

> When he had finished no one said anything. There was absolute silence. But the clarion call didn't go out on the Friday and we all changed on the Monday. It took at least a year before attitudes really began to shift.

In part, the reason why attitudes did not change quickly was that there remained a view amongst workers that they would be able to defend themselves collectively.

Throughout 1983–84 management gave a number of presentations to shop stewards using graphs, charts and a torrent of statistics to illustrate the low level of labour productivity, the overmanning and poor labour relations in the plant that threatened its future survival. In particular, Ford made extensive use of productivity comparisons between their British and Continental plants to 'prove' Halewood was the least productive in Europe. According to a newsletter issued to the Halewood workforce in 1983, labour and overhead efficiency in the plant declined by 15 per cent between 1972 and 1978 whilst the Saarlouis plant in West Germany, which also produced the Escort, underwent continuous improvement of 41 per cent between 1972 and 1982 (Marsden et al., 1985). The constant theme was the need to cut labour, reform working practices, break demarcation, introduce wider flexibility, boost productivity and raise quality.

Meanwhile, as will have become clear from the two previous case studies, during the economic recession of the early 1980s Merseyside became synonymous with plant closures and redundancies. The closure of two massive car industry factories in nearby Speke, the Dunlop plant in 1979 (which was one of the best union-organized workplaces on Merseyside) and the BL Number 2 plant (following a prolonged strike over mutuality and manning levels; Beynon, 1979), had a particularly sobering impact on the horizons of many Ford workers. Senior stewards felt they were being taken to the edge of the abyss and shown how deep it really was. As John remarked:

> Whether it was true or not the Ford Motor Company constantly said, 'Halewood – you're under threat. Your record is bad. You've got an absenteeism problem, a labour relations problem.' So we were under tremendous pressure. We had just had the experience of the British Leyland plant up the road shutting down and we realized we were in direct competition with Saarlouis if we were going to survive.

This was complemented by a concerted attempt by management to lay the foundation for uncertainty and a sense of insecurity about the future. Billy, who has worked on the trim in the Assembly plant for 14 years, serving as a shop steward for two years in the late 1980s, and is a member of the Socialist Workers Party, noted:

> Management convinced them with the economics of the thing that the plants in Germany and Spain were producing cars more efficiently with less labour and less cost. Management were looking at it from a world viewpoint and Halewood was the least productive. So therefore in terms of long-term investment it made sense to put it where it was most productive instead of Halewood, which was prone to strike action. That convinced them that management were looking to running down Halewood if the situation didn't improve.

The key dilemma for the Halewood stewards, as they saw it, was whether to resist change completely, risking closure of the plant with catastrophic job loss, or to acquiesce to some changes in the hope of increasing the likelihood of survival, even though this would involve forfeiting hard-won gains. After much deliberation and argument (and under some pressure from full-time union officials) they decided on the latter option.

As a result, the convenors in both Assembly and Body plants approached management to pledge their willingness to be part of the 'saving of Halewood'. The convenor in the Body plant, Keith Hardcastle, spoke personally to Bill Hayden, Ford's UK director at the time, to indicate he was prepared to work with the company to save jobs for the future. Hayden visited Halewood and spoke directly to the senior stewards, insisting they had to change the strike-bound image of the plant constantly projected in the media. The only way to survive, he argued, was for everybody from the shop-floor to management to realize that 'working together' was the way forward. It was necessary to 'fight the competition, instead of each other'. As a gesture of intent, Hayden offered a new plastics project in the Body plant costing $11 million, but only if the shop stewards' bodies agreed to abandon their militant 'one-out, all-out' policy towards lay-offs. The 'one-out, all-out' had often been invoked in the past when management had laid off groups of workers who had not directly participated in, but were nonetheless affected by, stoppages taken by other sections of workers. Such action had resulted in numerous plant-wide shutdowns. But the Body plant convenor now used his authority and influence to convince the stewards to accept a new *selective* lay-off agreement, which would aim to maintain production in those areas not in dispute.

A simultaneous metamorphosis took place in the Assembly plant, where the convenor, Trevor Wilson, argued that to ensure Halewood did not close the stewards 'would have to do business in a different way'. Dave observed:

> When Trevor Wilson approached the company there was a hell of a lot of heart searching amongst the stewards because traditionally and historically we had a point of view towards management that they were not going to exploit our members. So we had to sit down and reappraise our approach and adjust to the fact that the company were going to make certain demands on us that were going to be in the long-term interests of the membership. But there was a hell of a lot of heart searching because we had to turn over 20-odd years' attitudes and we had to think differently.

A joint presentation was given at a mass meeting in the Assembly plant with the Operations Manager on the platform alongside Trevor Wilson and senior stewards. As John explained:

> What we said to the meeting was we don't want to give away any *fundamental* agreements like progression through seniority – which we'd

be prepared to man the barricades for – but we *do* realize that to make sure this plant is still open in the 1990s the stewards and members have got a different role to play with management. The phrase became, 'It's not war-war, it's jaw-jaw.'

Significantly, this change of attitude by the Halewood stewards roughly coincided with a recasting of Ford's corporate industrial relations approach in its British plants (Starkey and McKinlay, 1989). Recognizing that improvements in productivity and quality necessary to compete with Japanese car makers were unlikely to succeed if they maintained the traditional adversarial approach, Ford managers adopted a new labour relations strategy of 'Employee Involvement' (EI) imported from plants in the United States (Werther, 1985). Unlike the merely structural reforms of internal bargaining institutions that had been implemented during the 1970s, 'EI' also emphasized a gradual, processual approach to building a co-operative relationship between management and unions, with the aim of encouraging shop-floor workers' identification with company objectives and at harnessing their consent and commitment to organizational change.

Thus, from the early 1980s onwards, Halewood management slowly began to alter their confrontational approach in favour of what could be described as a rather sophisticated 'poisoned handshake' approach, aimed at establishing more conciliatory 'strong bargaining relations'. Two managers recently drafted into the Halewood plant had already begun to encourage a constant dialogue with the shop stewards, and over the next few years the principles of 'EI' were put into practice in earnest. John recalled the effect this had inside the Assembly plant:

Managers and supervisors started getting involved in actually *talking* to the stewards. I suppose we began to court each other a little bit. The attitude was: 'This strike business is doing us no good, we've got to change the image of Halewood and all pull together. Let's not go back to the '60s and '70s when we had to fight every day.'

As Tony explained, a similar process took place in the Body plant:

The approach to people on the lines by management and supervision became totally different. It didn't happen overnight. But whenever a grievance arose that could potentially lead to a stoppage the company would *back off* immediately. The problem would run and people would talk about it. The manager gave the steward the chance to talk to the members on the section. It took the pressure off. The whole atmosphere changed. Management would even go and chat to the lads on the line, 'What's the problem, let's have a working lunch.' The lads would go into the conference room with IR, the manager and a steward and there'd be pies and tea and sticky buns. They'd get their dinner and they'd get paid for sitting down and having a chat.

This was the beginning of a process of managerially inspired change, aimed at demobilizing the unions in the plant.

Over the next few years Halewood management adopted a variety of measures designed to change the adversarial nature of workplace industrial relations, with the aim of encouraging both shop stewards and rank-and-file workers to identify more closely with the problems confronting the company, and hence accept the inescapability of the policies proposed by them. The convenors' offices in both the Body and Assembly plants were moved off the shop-floor and transferred to the Personnel block next to the plant managers' offices. The vast majority of sectional shop stewards were effectively granted 100 per cent time off work to help resolve work-related grievances. The union was provided with more extensive facilities such as typing and printing provision, and a free supply of paper, pens and office equipment. A series of company video presentations outlining the 'state of the company' were screened first to the joint works committees, then the shop stewards and finally to the workforce. Management introduced 'training programmes' that took small groups of workers off the lines and provided tours around the Halewood site to show them how the car was built from beginning to end. 'Joint action groups' composed of stewards and managers in each area of the plant met informally to discuss volume and come up with agreed solutions to work-related problems. Some sections of the plants, particularly the shop-floor tea areas, were transformed with much-improved lighting and heating and the provision of framed pictures and potted plants, to help 'humanize' the working environment. An extensive programme of Saturday visits to the factory by workers' families, with the provision of free 'Ford Escort: Made with quality by my dad' T-shirts for children, were organized to encourage a wider sense of corporate identity.

Yet perhaps the most distinctive initiative was the financial investment the company made into organizing group trips abroad to visit other

Ford plants in Germany, Belgium and Spain. Two or three aircraft flew from Liverpool Airport each week, with different groups of Halewood workers accompanied by managers and shop stewards, on 36-hour round trips. The advantages, from management's point of view, to be gained from such an exercise were not lost on the Employee Relations manager in the paint shop of the Assembly plant:

> What that did was twofold: it showed how they did it abroad and it got them into contact – over dinner and a few drinks – with the managers. It formed relationships there – and so there was this forming of a bit of a bond.

About 500 Halewood workers, with delegations from every section of the plant, participated in these visits with the objective of encouraging an improvement in the efficency and productivity of Halewood in line with the Continental plants.

It is important to note that a number of stewards remained sceptical about Ford's 'poisoned handshake' strategy, interpreting it as a subtle attempt to mould workplace union organization into management structures. Ray Storey contrasted the attitudes of the *senior* stewards with the *sectional* stewards in the Assembly plant:

> The senior stewards accepted it hook, line and sinker. But there was tension with some of the sectional stewards who felt the senior stewards were accepting all kinds of things without consulting them. But because they didn't have the counter-arguments to challenge them they were gradually drawn more and more into it. So it seeped down. But I think orginally they were dragged into it by the senior stewards and Trevor Wilson. When we had stoppages the argument that 'We're all in the same boat and we've all got to work together' came up. So it was gradually absorbed. As the pressure from the shop-floor went away they were pulled more and more to embrace it.

Thus, management developed a policy of incorporating the senior stewards into the progress and ideology of change as a precondition to obtaining support from the stewards' bodies at large.

But whilst there was some differentiation between the convenors and senior stewards on the one hand, and the sectional stewards on the other, as well as between the Body and Assembly plants, it was essentially over the speed of the changes to work organization rather than any fundamental disagreement in principle over the need to make Halewood more 'competitive'. As Paul, a Body plant senior steward who worked in the plant from the early 1960s, noted:

> Everyone has matured, stewards and management. In the '60s the average age in the plant was about 28, but by the '80s it had become a lot older . . . Now, everyone seems to be working to one end: to make the plant viable and profitable. Now, 'profitable' was a dreadful word for a shop steward to be using because we used to say, 'That's management's jargon.' But it's not, you know, it concerns everybody – because if management are not making profits then they are not making motor cars, and then there's no work for people.

The increasing isolation and demoralization of the small left-wing forces inside Halewood meant the policy met little organized opposition. But there were also substantive material and ideological pressures underlining the more cautious approach adopted by most stewards and rank-and-file workers in the Halewood plant. Apart from the very high local rates of unemployment and wave of redundancies on Merseyside combined with the pervading threat of closure by Ford, the British trade union movement generally during this period was very much on the defensive with the 'new realism' further reinforced by the Conservative government's defeat of the 1984–85 national miners' strike.

In addition, the new co-operative relationship established between stewards and management led to a very significant decline in the number of stoppages of work, from an annual average of about 75–100 in the late 1970s to about 12 by the late 1980s (see Table 2). This had a noticeable impact because it meant an end to the recurrent lay-offs and reduced weekly pay packets that had prevailed in the past, and thus helped to encourage a new sense of job security amongst many workers. Billy pointed out:

> Because of the sectional stoppages people were getting fed up on the shop-floor. You didn't know whether you were going to be laid off from one week to another. So there was unrest about that and that's the way it was sold to the shop-floor. Getting a regular wage packet every week was a sense of security. And there was the feeling your job was safer from redundancy. Discipline over 'welt' working was overlooked to a

Table 2 *Number of stoppages in Ford Halewood 1980–1988*

1980:	116
1981:	52
1982:	73
1983:	34
1984:	31
1985:	12
1986:	13
1987:	12
1988:	17

Figures supplied by Personnel Development and Training manager, Ford Halewood, February 1989.

large extent so people openly flouted that. And people saw that as a gain. Also, they saw management were prepared to talk to them, so there was less aggro. They were prepared to listen and consider problems.

Management's new-found willingness to 'talk out' grievances, rather than automatically put their foot down and say 'No', also created a more congenial shop-floor industrial relations atmosphere than anyone could remember previously.

The invariable rule, as Jimmy (a left-wing militant shop steward in the Body plant) observed, became '*talk* first, second and last', with disputes frequently settled through the direct involvement of senior stewards:

Say there is a problem over an increase in line speeds. Before management will let you down on to the floor to say to your members 'Right, let's go' they'll sit you down around the table and get the senior steward in, the convenor, as many people as they can to argue a different line. They wouldn't increase the line speeds while you're talking – in the old days they would have done that – but they'll talk the dispute out. They'll say, 'We would like to do this' and we say, 'But we've got these problems.' So the company will try and address those problems but 75 per cent of the time they get what they want. They're getting an awful lot without conflict.

Halewood management viewed shop stewards throughout the 1980s as absolutely central to the process of achieving change and winning the co-operation of the shop-floor. As Billy acknowledged:

> Management's 'backing off' is a recognition that by involving the steward in trying to sort out problems it's delivering the goods. They think if they only spend the time explaining what the changes entail and make the steward feel involved, he'll understand the reasons and accept it.

In fact, management's more sophisticated 'poisoned handshake' approach to industrial relations succeeded in securing acquiescence to substantial increases in labour productivity and output involving an intensification of work effort.

Although productivity is an extremely difficult concept to measure and relies only partially on the exertion of workers (Nolan and Marginson, 1990), the average number of cars produced daily in Halewood increased from 786 in 1982 to 1100 in 1990 despite a simultaneous 40 per cent reduction in the number of jobs, as the workforce was cut by over 4000 during the 1980s (albeit through natural wastage and voluntary redundancy). Meanwhile, in 1985 Ford made an important breakthrough in securing the agreeement of the NJNC to more flexible working practices within its British plants. Although opposed by Halewood shop stewards and rejected in a ballot of the workforce nationally, a far-reaching two-year wages and conditions agreement was implemented at local level. It drastically reduced the number of job demarcations as workers became expected to be mobile around the plant, to carry out a wider range of tasks including simple maintenance and housekeeping of their workstations, and to have more responsibility for quality control. Paul drew out the implications:

> If we were to compete with the Japanese we needed to reduce the headcount, and the way to do that was to extend people's responsibilities and give them the necessary training. Members saw this as a weakening of their bargaining position – which indeed it was, there's no argument about that. If you're telling a forklift truck driver that after he's been trained to do a quality control job he's expected to drive the truck as well, then the people who got most out of this, obviously, were management because they were able to shed quite a number of people.

As a result, members were less likely to support any calls for national action or take action on their own behalf and initiative.

Thus, by the late 1980s the strong shop stewards' organization that had been prepared to give its backing to militant unofficial workplace stoppages a decade earlier had become considerably weakened as the balance of workplace power was pushed to management's advantage. The more conciliatory 'strong bargaining relationship' established between the stewards (particularly the senior stewards) and management had the effect of routinizing workplace trade unionism, demobilizing collective rank-and-file workers' self-activity and sapping the vitality of the stewards' organization.

The Late 1980s/Early 1990s: Potential and Limitations

Although the shop stewards' power was considerably undermined during the late 1980s, this did not mean workplace union organization was unable to forestall, influence or change developments. One important factor ensuring the stewards' organization was compelled to defend workers' collective interests was the fundamentally antagonistic relationship that underlay the apparent picture of shop-floor harmony. As Lee, a white collar employee and Manufacturing Science Finance (MSF) senior steward in the Assembly plant, commented:

> The Operations Manager is certainly unrecognizable from a few years ago. He was a very aggressive man. It was as if he had a baseball bat in his hand which he would beat you over the head with. Today he jokes he's still got it in his office, but it's on the wall in a glass case. It's a bit tongue-in-cheek, but it's like a fire-alarm, in case of emergency. That really is the mentality at Ford. They could change just like that. And we know it.

In fact, there was a continuing contradiction between Ford's long-term goal of 'EI' and the occasional short-term necessity of asserting managerial prerogative.

Although the basic relationship of conflict between management and shop stewards was often submerged below the surface, it did not disappear entirely. From time to time the 'big stick' or confrontational approach re-emerged in a variety of ways. For example, despite periodic attempts, management were still not able to crack the shop-floor control exercised over the movement of labour and manning of jobs based on seniority. This remained a major source of grievance as workers defended a hard-won unofficial 'custom and practice'. Likewise, stewards maintained control over overtime rotas and managed successfully to defend informally established 'early finish' practices. Equally, the company still faced an incessant challenge to imposed work standards and unilaterally revised timings of jobs and speed-up.

Continuing shop-floor resilience became evident during a two-week regrading strike by line-workers in both Body and Assembly plants in 1985. Sporadic sectional stoppages against attacks on work standards coalesced into a bitter explosion of anger at a national two-year pay deal, agreed despite a massive vote of opposition from most UK Ford plants – including a 70 per cent ballot vote rejection at Halewood. As soon as it became known that the anticipated extra pay allowance for line-workers was not to be forthcoming a spontaneous rank-and-file revolt pressurized even the senior stewards to give their blessing to a strike that effectively closed down most of the Halewood operation. Even though the strike eventually fizzled out, it was an illustration that shop-floor union organization was still alive and kicking.

Resistance was also evident when management tried to introduce 'quality circles' into Halewood in 1985. These 'problem solving' groups, involving meetings of supervision, stewards and the workforce in each section of the plant, were aimed at shifting the general emphasis away from the negotiation of change towards more consultative methods. Their successful implementation in the United States encouraged Ford to adopt the experiment within its UK plants (CAITS, *Teamworking: Same as Employee Involvement but Worse.* TGWU 1/1107 Branch, April 1988) and a management consultancy firm, W. P. Dolan & Associates, was brought into the Halewood plant to oversee their introduction. Yet with official TGWU support, the stewards successfully blocked the attempt to introduce 'quality circles' in Halewood on the basis that they threatened to bypass and subdue the traditional role of shop-floor union representation.

Another example of workers' belligerency was provided by the national Ford pay strike of 1988, the first for a decade. This strike was spearheaded by unofficial walk-outs from Halewood in protest at a proposed three-year agreement that provided for more flexible working practices. Billy related what happened when the company's offer was discussed on the trim lines in the Assembly plant:

We held a meeting on my section. Everyone wanted to do something. The meeting only lasted about 30 seconds. The steward told us the offer; he said, 'It's crap' and called a stoppage and we were out.

John added:

The strike proved that Ford misread the situation. They really believed the shop-floor would just about accept anything – but they've been proved wrong. The stewards were totally opposed to what the company were asking. We went to mass meetings and had two secret ballots: 87 per cent voted for strike action. The men knew how much they had given the company and how much they had turned it around and they knew what they were being offered was nowhere what they had achieved for the company.

This was a sign that the workforce was still willing to face up to the challenge posed by managerial approaches of the 1980s.

A number of different elements appear to have combined to create a sudden revival of militant struggle within the plant. There was the general feeling that Ford workers had taken enough; flexibility and speed-up had led to a worsening of conditions and the insult of a new pay deal that 'asked for their souls' but gave little back in return provoked a groundswell of bitterness. There was also the impact of the limited economic recovery on many workers' attitudes. The fall of unemployment nationally by 550 000 from its peak in 1986 was reflected inside Halewood by the ending of the recruitment freeze imposed in 1979 and the taking on of some new workers. The message that many workers had accepted for years, that any struggle over wages or conditions would threaten jobs, lost some of its credibility. Workers felt a change in the strength of their bargaining power. It was not too surprising, therefore, that along with booming company profits and high rates of productivity growth, the decline in unemployment gave Ford workers the incentive to fight for a better deal.

The strike exposed the vulnerability of Ford's highly integrated European 'just in time' single-sourcing operation, which left virtually no room for alternative production sources or the storage of strategic stocks, and resulted in immediate lay-offs at the Genk plant in Belgium (Oliver and Wilkinson, 1990). Ford UK executives backed down from their original hard-hitting demands and the revised deal increased pay above the level of inflation, reduced the length of the agreement to two years and conceded that new working practices could not be imposed without local plant agreement. It illustrated the way, at least in some respects, the shift in the balance of workplace power was associated more with adverse economic and product market factors than with any irreversible sea-change in the attitudes of most (sectional) stewards and workers.

Of course, shop-floor resentment towards management was usually not translated into action as workers rarely had the confidence and the means to take matters into their own hands. On a few occasions there were isolated sectional stoppages, for example in October 1989, when a strike over a health and safety issue laid off the entire Body plant for two days and forced management to make some concessions. Significantly, half of the strikers were 'new starters', young men who had only recently been hired. Similarly, 300 night-shift workers in the Assembly plant walked out over the introduction of new coiled air lines in November 1990. Billy related:

> They wanted to introduce a curly compressed line on the new model as opposed to the straight ones we used to have. There was little difference between the two but people were annoyed management had introduced them without consultation. The section stopped straight away and the senior steward called a meeting. He said there was no real reason management were making the change except they thought they could get away with it, but then half-heartedly said we should go back to work. He was voted down two to one and we came out for two nights. It ended in compromise with air lines that are part straight, part curly.

Clearly, these were important moments in the bleak climate of the 1980s, indicating that beneath the surface of appearance there was still a readiness to take direct action.

But despite these sparks of resistance the overarching accommodative relationship established between senior stewards and management continued to be a pervasive feature of developments throughout the late 1980s and early 1990s. For example, the 1988 pay strike did not really change the terms of this relationship with Halewood management. It was perceived as being a dispute with the Ford Motor Company nationally, rather than with local Halewood management. The dispute neither upset the cooperative relationship with management nor fed any greater confidence on the shop-floor to use strike action to fight over day-to-day issues. As Tony pointed out:

> The cosy relationship with management was maintained throughout the
> strike, inasmuch as management provided the pickets with a caravan and
> the stewards allowed certain people to go in and move things around.
> There was picketing but the senior stewards still went on discussing
> things with management as if it was just normal business. Although
> nothing was being produced the strike didn't interrupt normal
> relationships.

Another example of this sustained co-operative relationship occurred just
before the three-week plant summer shut-down in 1989. Ford had just
launched a £600 million four-year investment programme in Halewood,
in preparation for the launch of a new Escort model, and major reconstruction work had begun on retooling the plant with the latest technology and
production systems, particularly in the Body plant. Ford's reorganization
plans were suddenly threatened when the 200 sub-contract electricians
fitting the new machinery banned overtime in pursuance of a wage claim
with their employers. But TGWU full-time officials and senior stewards
jumped to Ford's defence by demanding the electricians call off their
dispute to allow the work to proceed. Billy explained:

> The attitude of the Assembly plant convenor was that the electricians
> were holding us to ransom. Delaying the introduction of the new
> technology meant we could be laid off without pay because it would be
> behind schedule. So it was a threat to T and G workers. He told the
> electricians they were no more than 'industrial gypsies'. He said *they*
> were all right, they move on, but their action would threaten our
> livelihoods.

The threat of lay-offs and pay penalties pushed the TGWU workers to
reject any appeal for solidarity with the electricians and to respond to the
convenor's criticisms of the electricians.

Even more damaging was the stance adopted by the Halewood steward
committees towards a strike by the plant's 600 AUEW and EETPU skilled
maintenance workers in February 1990. Although Ford's TGWU production workers had narrowly voted to accept a new national two-year pay
deal, the craftsmen at Halewood (and other plants across the country)
walked out on strike in protest at the strings attached to the deal, in the
process causing the laying off of both Body and Assembly plants for a
number of weeks. In response, many TGWU stewards condemned the

strike for being 'divisive', suspicious of the involvement of the EETPU, which had recently been expelled from the TUC for its 'business unionism' practices. (At the Ford Dagenham plant many electricians had left the EETPU to join a left-wing breakaway union, although this was not the case at Halewood.) The stewards echoed the arguments from full-time union officials that it involved a minority trying to dictate to the majority. Following pressure from management and union officials the Halewood steward committees called mass meetings and recommended their members to cross craft workers' picket lines and return to work, effectively breaking the back of the strike. Significantly, it was the first time in the Halewood plant's history that TGWU production workers had 'scabbed' on a strike. Yet, as at least a minority of stewards argued, the craftsmen were fighting against strings that increased differentials and would result in a loss of skills and jobs. From this perspective, a craftsmen's victory might have helped bolster production workers' bargaining position. Instead, by opposing the strike, it could be argued that the TGWU stewards only played into the hands of management and the right-wing leaders of the EETPU.

Further major challenges have confronted the stewards during the early 1990s. Britain's renewed economic recession led to another wave of redundancies and closures across the country, with Merseyside again hit very badly. The British car industry came under increasing pressure from plummeting sales, overcapacity and intensified competition from Japanese car makers Nissan, Toyota and Honda, all with newly established British plants. In response, Ford UK, which announced a record pre-tax loss of £587 million in 1991 (*Liverpool Echo*, 27 May 1993), introduced a drastic rationalization programme involving three waves of redundancies affecting thousands of workers across its British plants, particularly Halewood. Through a process of voluntary redundancy, early retirement and natural wastage, 600 jobs were lost in Halewood in 1990, 1000 were phased out in 1991 and another 1500 in 1992. Throughout 1991 and 1992 the entire Halewood site was put on short-time working for months at a time, involving either a four-day or three-day production week (although workers received 100 per cent lay-off pay, less bonuses and incentives). Daily car production was cut from 1060 to 810 (*Liverpool Echo*, 17 December 1992).

At the same time, Ford UK executives held crisis talks with full-time union officials and Halewood senior stewards to renew threats to close the Merseyside site unless it closed the gap with its competitors. A management 'Survival Plan' proposed 'bell to bell' working, the right to retime jobs without union agreement, job progression on merit – ending the policy whereby the longest-serving workers take the most senior jobs – and the abolition of fixed meal-times and tea-breaks. Finally, management pressed ahead with plans for a drastic reduction in the number of recognized shop stewards, particularly in the Body plant. In response to such challenges, the Body and Assembly plant convenors and senior stewards vigorously pursued their collaborative stance towards management, even going so far as to produce a joint union–management video and leaflet, pressing home the need to join together to beat the competition:

> We should all realise that we have to do the best we can in our work, our quality and our performance, as these things provide us with the most protection and help the company to sell more cars. We at Halewood are all in the same boat. We all need to pull together. (Halewood convenors' leaflet, 1991)

However, the depth of cooperation still had some limits, particularly when, in a desperate bid to achieve its plans for job cuts across its British plants in 1992–93, Ford threatened to impose compulsory redundancies (on statutory minimum severance payments) if not enough volunteers came forward (to accept enhanced payments). Faced with the first compulsory redundancies for 30 years, combined with a plan to impose a six-month wage freeze plus a 40 per cent cut in lay-off pay, there was a groundswell of anger on the shop-floor (particularly against the backcloth of country-wide anger at the Conservative government's October 1992 announcement of pit closures). Even TGWU and AEU full-time officers warned of a national strike ballot in response. Initially, the reaction of the stewards, especially in the Halewood Assembly plant, was rather sluggish, although they eventually distributed leaflets and held a mass meeting opposing management's stance. Billy commented:

> The news should have been met with immediate walk-outs. Instead, at the mass meeting we were told by the convenors to give any questions about the proposals to the stewards. But there was a bit of a change in mood with the anger over the miners. There was a bit more confidence. The Tories were under attack from all sides and it boosted people.

In the Body plant, after the stewards had organized canteen meetings on both the day and night shifts, 1400 workers walked out on a one-day unofficial protest strike. Even though stewards in the Assembly plant did not follow their example the action showed that, despite the recession, workers at Halewood were willing to fight, particularly when stewards gave a lead. Ford eventually withdrew its compulsory redundancy threat, claiming a sudden improvement in the British car market had led it to revise its plans. In reality, it was the threat of further strike action disrupting the launch of the new Mondeo model that led to the climbdown. Ironically, an unofficial one-day strike by 600 truck drivers at Ford's Dagenham plant, in response to a confidential company document warning that plans to put transport and maintenance services out to tender with the loss of 1150 jobs in Britain could lead to industrial action that 'would probably result in the progressive closure of all Ford European manufacturing plants within three days' (*Financial Times*, 4 March 1993), confirmed Ford's own worst fears of what could happen. Its climbdown was a testimony to the power of Ford workers to beat back management's attacks.

As for the future, the challenge of a redesigned integrated production system, with its demands for wider flexibility, team working and the erosion of traditional demarcation lines separating production from maintenance workers, unskilled from skilled workers and blue-collar from white-collar workers, will pose new problems for stewards' organization in Halewood. Management will be keen to introduce even more efficiency changes and have already indicated their intention to sub-contract all non-core production jobs, such as security, driving and services. The ongoing response of the stewards and members and the nature of the struggle over workers' representation will shape the future direction of events. Although shop stewards' organization has been significantly weakened in recent years the 1988 strike and the 1993 Body plant stoppage show the potential for future resistance.

Stewards' Relationship to Members: The 1970s–1990s

The 1970s: 'Walking the Tightrope'

As we have seen, during the 1970s there were numerous stoppages of work within Halewood. John recalled: 'The quote was, "If you brought your sandwiches to work you were an optimist." ' The reason for the high level of strikes was primarily the 'big stick' approach adopted by Halewood management. Jimmy remembered the situation inside the Body plant:

> It was a militant shop-floor in those days, very militant in some cases. But justifiably so because of the way we were being treated. We had a dog of a management. On the white lines area we had three dog-rough people, a senior foreman, a superintendent and a manager. It was 'effing and blinding' every time they went on to the floor and they got the same reaction from the labour.

In the Body plant, Tony remembered the way new, young shop stewards were encouraged by their more experienced, battle-hardened colleagues:

> The first thing we were told is you've got to have a blazing row with the foreman in front of all your workmates on the shop-floor – and be seen to stand your ground, no matter how weak the foreman is. Don't have any mercy – just go for him. You've got to be seen battling things through, winning disputes.

Confrontation and militancy were very much part of the life of the Ford worker. Even though many of the disputes, over the speed of the lines, the movement of labour, job timings, discipline and so on, were initiated by spontaneous outbursts of rank-and-file members, the shop stewards always had to be seen giving a lead:

> Some of the arguments we used then just wouldn't stand up today. We were finding arguments for absolutely anything at all. If a man asked for a sub of his wages and the company refused, his mates on the line would immediately stop work. If a person was disciplined and given a verbal warning there would be a strike. The stoppages of work were regular and if the steward didn't lead the strike he would be open to question. He had to be seen up front having a go. Even when the senior steward advised the steward on the section to back down on the issue he usually couldn't afford to, because he wouldn't have been a steward much longer. The section was very confident, they had the power and they used it.

Individual shop stewards 'cut their teeth' on sectional militancy, in the process not only helping their members carve out some control over the job and bolstering their bargaining authority *vis-à-vis* management, but also strengthening the esteem of the steward bodies as a whole. As Jimmy commented:

> The shop-floor instilled confidence into the shop stewards and the stewards knew they could rely on the shop-floor at the drop of a hat over certain issues.

This was a highly confident, active and militant rank-and-file, constantly pushing the 'frontier of control' in their favour via their stewards.

Management had a different view of the situation. Rather than seeing a union membership pushing legitimate interests via their representatives, they attributed the militancy of the membership as a weakness of the stewards and convenors. As the Employee Relations manager in the paint shop of the Assembly said:

> Many of the stewards were . . . manipulated by their members on the floor, some of whom were just mischievous in some of the things they did. I mean really mischievous. They were disruptive just for the sake of stopping the line and having a blow. There was no real control by the senior stewards.

Throughout the 1970s there was a massive influx of labour, with the number of workers in the plant reaching its peak of 14 000 in 1978. Many brought with them their rich experience of trade unionism on the Liverpool docks and elsewhere and were keen to establish some counter-controls to managerial authority. The close scrutiny of stewards' activities placed them under a direct form of democratic accountability in which the challenge of alternative ideas and personalities was a constant feature. Jimmy noted:

> In the white line area there was a high turnover of stewards. There was two stewards for about 300 men and there was that many different issues going on – mainly timings, work methods, mobility of labour – that if a steward let down on a certain issue he'd get challenged. He'd see his term of office out, but inevitably he'd face a challenge – particularly in the high-profile areas like the moving lines.

Stewards' positions were usually contested at election time by more than one candidate and there was quite a high turnover of personnel; for example, in the Body plant most sectional stewards' tenure of office averaged only four to five years, although it was longer for senior stewards.

The sectional stewards often found themselves having to walk the tightrope of trying to work full-time alongside their members on the line, at the same time as taking up grievances and carrying out union duties. On the one hand, Ford's reluctance to let stewards off the job to negotiate sometimes led to stoppages of work, although management were also under pressure to grant stewards facility time so they could help resolve disputes quickly. On the other hand, whilst rank-and-file workers recognized the need for their steward to have time off work to represent them, they also often complained when they felt they were spending too much time off the shop-floor in the convenor's office. As a result, many stewards tried to remain on the job for at least some of the time by having reliefs or working on a 'Mickey Mouse' job which they could get away from without too much disruption of work. As Tony explained: 'It was amazing. It meant you had to be seen to be working alongside people, to be there on the job, and not be there at the same time, if you were going to be able to represent them properly.' Such demands placed stewards in an often unenviable position, as workers and as workplace leaders.

Of course, it is also necessary to take account of the rather problematical (volatile, vulnerable, non-strategic and contradictory) features of workers' self-activity in relation to which, and even sometimes against which, shop stewards' leadership operated. The tension between sectional shop-floor militancy and the steward committees' plant-wide concerns was ever apparent. John added:

> Quite a lot of times people went home against the advice of the shop stewards. They probably got carried away with the euphoria of how to win things. On some occasions it became quite indisciplined, silly strikes that should never have taken place. The stewards weren't always in control of the shop-floor.

Moreover, it would be mistaken to picture all the stewards in Halewood as 'militant' during this period. Dave recalled the situation inside the Assembly plant:

> We were always the ones accused of causing strikes but it wasn't true. I'd say 99 times out of 100 it was the steward who was trying to dampen things down, to resolve the dispute. We would find ourselves

the lads in the middle – on one side, we would have the 'macho managers' and on the other side we had our undisciplined members – and we were in the middle, constantly dealing with the lads, trying to get them back to work and resolve the problem that way.

On many occasions the stewards felt obliged to support their members even if they took action against their advice. Nonetheless, evidence of the stewards' willingness to try to get disputes settled as quickly as possible was provided by their adoption of what became known as the 'one-hour notice'. Of major concern was the way a stoppage of work by a handful of workers often led to thousands of others being laid off elsewhere in the plant, which in turn threatened lay-offs in the adjoining plant. Even though the specific grievance could potentially be settled within the space of an hour or two, *before* lay-offs occurred, it was quite common for striking workers not to bother waiting for stewards' intervention, but to walk out of the plant and go home for the remainder of the shift. As Tony explained: 'This blew the company's brains. They couldn't do anything if people weren't there – there was no way of resolving the situation.' However, in the late 1970s, the stewards agreed to a 'one-hour notice' which gave the company an 'eleventh hour' during which striking workers became obliged to wait to see if it could be resolved before they left the plant.

The role of the senior stewards on the joint works committees was rather more complex. By the mid-1970s the convenors in both the Body and Assembly plants were on a permanent day shift, provided by management with union offices and paid to be the full-time union representatives on the site. Spending much of their time in negotiations with plant management or co-ordinating the activities of the stewards, they were generally less visible to rank-and-file members, although they were intimately involved with day-to-day issues affecting the shop-floor. Similarly, most of the senior stewards who were on the joint works committees did not have even a nominal job on the shop-floor – enjoying 100 per cent time off work to conduct union business – although unlike the convenors they followed the alternating shift patterns of their respective members. But whilst the responsibility of their position at times encouraged them to take a rather more cautious attitude towards the periodic stoppages that flared up, this had to be balanced with the direct pressure they encountered from members in their own individual constituencies.

Meanwhile, Ford's long-term policy of incorporation of convenors and a layer of senior stewards succeeded in gradually formalizing bargaining procedures within the Body and Assembly plants and creating a slightly more stable framework within which workplace industrial relations could be conducted. There was a concentration of decision making within the top tier of senior stewards, with a tendency for JWC members to negotiate all the substantive issues in the plants while the sectional stewards merely administered within the boundaries already laid down. Senior stewards, like Paul, made efforts to restrain the 'unofficial, unofficial' disputes, those that occurred without even the support of their steward:

> Often my role as a senior shop steward was to put the fire out, withdraw to a room and talk about the situation. We tried to instil this into shop stewards, to dampen down the flames, to get the fellas back to work with an assurance that we would take up their case – and usually we were able to make a compromise solution. But if the steward had no control over his section then it was down to the senior stewards like myself to tell them, 'The consequences are you'll be out for four days and you won't get the backing because you haven't gone through the procedure.' And there were times you were lucky and you got them back in . . . The stewards' committee thought long and hard about how to solve these wildcat disputes – but we voted against manning up jobs when it was put to the vote.

With the emphasis on procedure and the centralization of negotiations there was a concerted move against 'wildcat' disputes on occasions by senior stewards.

The formation of a militant national rank-and-file organization during the 1978 national pay strike known as the 'Ford Workers Group (Combine)' was an indication of the disquiet felt by some shop-floor union activists at the insidious process of integration amongst the convenors and senior stewards. But generally during the 1970s, the frequent sectional and plant-wide disputes, often initiated by the Body and Assembly plant steward committees themselves, provided little basis for any deep-seated or long-term accommodation between stewards and management and had the effect of encouraging a relatively close, accountable and democratic relationship between stewards and members.

A specific illustration of this relationship was the adoption in 1974 of the 'one-out, all-out' policy towards lay-offs caused by sectional disputes. The shop stewards took the view that if management laid off a group of workers because of a dispute occurring elsewhere in the plant they should threaten an all-out strike in response. Of course, in practice the policy was applied only irregularly – for example, between six to ten times a year across both plants – and usually over issues of discipline. Its *threatened* use was usually enough to force management to back down. But it was a powerful bargaining lever that successfully handicapped managerial attempts to 'mould' stewards into their way of operating.

Meanwhile, the TGWU Ford Halewood branch linked the stewards' day-to-day activities on the shop-floor with the wider activities of trade unionism. The branch met monthly and was attended by an average of about 80 workers – including a number of stewards – although depending on the issues being discussed there could be a few hundred in attendance. Significantly, the composition of the branch committee was always dominated by stewards from the Assembly plant, where TGWU organization had been established over a longer period. The majority of union members attending branch meetings also tended to be from the Assembly plant. Branch meetings were a key forum for debate and argument over the strategy adopted by the steward committees, with the steward bodies being, formally, subordinate to branch decisions, and a number of younger rank-and-file workers became active in branch affairs, some of them acting as 'opinion leaders' back on the shop-floor.

But the most important arena for contact between the stewards and members was the shop-floor itself. Throughout the 1970s section, shift and mass meetings of the membership were a regular occurrence, usually called in the event of a dispute or stoppage of work or when lay-offs were imminent, although sometimes held merely for information purposes, to allow the stewards to relay news of ongoing negotiations, possibly as a prelude to action in the future. Factory leaflets, produced by the steward committees and distributed on the sections, were also a common feature of the relationship between stewards and members.

Significantly, Beynon's study (1984) drew attention to the way shop-floor activism differentiated stewards from the mass of their members. Involvement in day-to-day struggles and contact with events across the plants created within both shop steward committees a more radical critique of management than existed generally within the factory. Even if some senior stewards, occupying central organizational roles within the plants, on occasion opposed strikes, their representation of workers' grievances in face of managerial intransigence tended to encourage a more political orientation to workplace industrial relations. Not that, as we have seen, in the majority of cases this translated itself into much beyond a 'factory class consciousness'. Apart from the handful of stewards and workers who joined the revolutionary socialist groupings, Big Flame and the International Socialists, the Labour Party was the most influential political organization in the factory. Yet the vast majority of stewards were not affiliated to any political party. Even so, formally, the stewards were, by and large, to the left of their members. But their close contact with the members and their willingness to mobilize rank-and-file activity in the face of management inflexibility meant the gap between them was relatively narrow, particularly in comparison with the 1980s.

The 1980s/Early 1990s: 'A Bit Like the Borgias'

Not surprisingly, the 'strong bargaining relationship' established with management during the 1980s had important repercussions on stewards' relationship to rank-and-file members. The abandonment in 1983 of the 'one-out, all-out' policy towards lay-offs in favour of 'talking out' disputes was a reflection of this change. Instead of attempting to link together the uncoordinated sectional stoppages of work that constantly broke out across the plants into unified action against management, the senior stewards effectively agreed to isolate and neutralize their impact by adopting a more conciliatory approach towards lay-offs. Many workers, frustrated at lost earnings and the uncertainty of their long-term job prospects, welcomed the stewards' new agreement on the basis that it was 'better to lose a few hours' production than a whole day'. The impact of the agreement is indicated by Billy:

> It's a lot harder now to get a sectional stoppage because you don't feel as confident as a few years ago. With the 'one-out, all-out' it gave sections protection, it gave them a lot of power because a dispute could lay the whole plant off within a matter of hours. But the stewards accepted a new *selective* lay-off agreement under which management try to keep the rest of the plant working for up to three days. It's reduced the sectional power of the shop-floor. It's made them feel more isolated because they have virtually no protection now.

In the long term it had the effect of undermining the strength of shop-floor union organization.

Another reflection of the changed relationship between stewards and members was the notable decline in the number of sectional stoppages.

Partly, this was a reaction to objective pressures such as mass unemployment, the fear of plant closure and the retreat of the trade union movement generally. In addition, with the introduction of new technology leading to thousands of voluntary redundancies (with the loss predominantly of younger workers), the average age of the workforce in Halewood generally became much older, and many workers, with family responsibilities and teenage children, became heavily dependent on maintaining a regular weekly wage packet. But the convenors and senior stewards also played a crucial subjective role throughout the 1980s in consciously intervening to pre-empt threatened strike action. Billy emphasized the transformation that occurred inside the Assembly plant:

> There were almost daily stoppages when I first started at Ford. Lines would be stopped for half an hour or an hour – there used to be loads of gaps on the line because of the shortage of car bodies. But today you rarely get a gap on the line from eight o'clock in the morning until quarter to five. It's almost continuous production now . . . The stewards are quite pleased with that. They've patted themselves on the back saying, 'We've kept you in and saved you money.' Ten years ago the stewards' role was trying to resolve disputes – except there were a lot more disputes and they were under much more pressure to solve them satisfactorily to the rank-and-file. Disputes could get out of their hands very quickly, whereas today the stewards are much more in control.

The attitude of compromise – so as to change the image of Halewood as a strikebound plant – prevailed, with the phrase 'We've got to keep our ammo dry' constantly used by the stewards.

What disputes did occur became more institutionalized and procedures even more formalized, with the senior stewards involved immediately whenever the threat of strike action arose on a section. The employee relations manager in the paint shop of the Assembly plant confirmed the extent of the stewards' change of attitude:

> The stewards realize they can't win everything. They realize now that you can't just stop the plant over a small, minor, sectional issue. They take more guidance from the senior stewards. They think to themselves, what will be the consequence of stopping the plant? What will it do in terms of politically embarrassing our national trade union officials? Or when the vice-president of manufacturing gets on to them and says,

'What the hell are you people doing at Halewood?' – sorts of considerations they wouldn't have cared about in the past.

An extreme example of such constraint took place in the Body plant in 1987 when, following a meeting with their steward, ten line-workers with a grievance over work arrangements walked off the job and went home. According to Tony:

> When the Operations Manager found out he hit the roof. He went beserk: 'It's the end of Halewood.' The massive pressure of competition means the company can't afford to be seen allowing strikes to take place, they have to be stopped. So they sent out a car with a senior steward and an IR manager to visit each individual's house to get everybody back to work. They knocked on people's doors and said the trade unions had agreed to call the strike off. Most lads did go back but they were bloody upset. It was unbelievable, something I would never have dreamt could happen.

Such procedures became one extreme feature of the late 1980s.

Meanwhile, the isolation of the left-wing activists inside Halewood became pronounced during the late 1980s. For example, the convenor's position in the Assembly plant, which had been occupied between 1970 and 1987 by Trevor Wilson, a middle-of-the road Labour Party member, was filled by a more 'moderate' supporter. A number of other stewards who were members of the Labour Party were critical of Neil Kinnock's right-wing leadership but believed the most important priority was to get a Labour government elected; until then, all that could be done was damage limitation. This meant not 'rocking the boat' or jeopardizing Labour's electoral popularity. The handful of left-wing stewards were marginalized, and the situation was no different inside the Body plant.

The impact of the ideas of 'new realism' within the trade union movement became evident, with many stewards accepting management's view that Halewood had to be made more 'competitive' in order to have a future. Billy related an argument that occurred at a TGWU branch meeting attended by stewards and shop-floor union activists, many of whom were Labour Party supporters:

> We talked about the lines being speeded up. The stewards were saying this is a good thing, we're building more cars at Halewood, it means

Ford are unlikely to close the plant. When I said: 'Well, I work on the line and I don't think it's a good thing the line speeds are going up – we're working hard enough already as it is', I was just ridiculed. They said: 'Don't expect Ford to produce cars and not make a profit.' And I said: 'Well, that's *their* philosophy, but it shouldn't be *ours*.' Anyway, profits don't guarantee jobs, they haven't stopped the head count going down at Halewood. But that's what the stewards lack: any wider, general politics that provide counter-arguments to those of management.

The important point was that that in the late 1980s there was increased acceptance of the ideology of competition and efficiency.

Although stewards might have wanted to put up a fight against management their ideological acceptance of notions of 'competitiveness' restricted their ability to fight back in practice and led them, on occasion, to act in conflict with the interests of their members. An example of this occurred in the Body plant in 1989. Tony takes up the story:

There was a safety problem with people working on rickety boards and demanding they be replaced. They waited five weeks – that's a sign of the co-operation, in the past that would never have happened, people would have stopped work and demanded it be fixed there and then. But what happened was the lads wanted to stop work demanding this thing get fixed. So there was a meeting of the stewards, and the steward for the section said, 'No, management have promised the work will be done over the weekend.' His attitude was that the members' behaviour was a disgrace. The company did start correcting it over the weekend but on the Monday night the shift just walked out because it hadn't been done properly. The steward never came in on the Monday night because he knew what would happen – and he's brilliant at surviving like that. Everyone was back the next night because the company worked like thunder to get the flooring right. But when the steward met the section on the Tuesday night he maintained they'd been right out of order.

Although compromise was the style of this steward, the example illustrates the way some stewards came to defend managerial concerns, at times unwittingly.

A number of other factors worked to impoverish the close relationship that previously existed between stewards and members. Because the constant influx of new people into Halewood had ceased and the number of stoppages had declined, the constant challenges to the stewards' position from the shop-floor also evaporated. Tony related the situation inside the Body plant:

> By and large, stewards stay in the position for much longer now than they used to in the past. Most stewards have been in the job for about ten years and have worked for the company for 15–20 years. On my particular shift there are 14 stewards. Excluding two that have just come in – the last newly elected steward was in 1977 – 80 per cent of the stewards have remained the same as those who came in during the mid-1970s . . . There's been a slow stagnation of the same faces.

An employee relations manager in the Body plant reflected on the significance of this 'stagnation' for management–steward relations inside the Assembly plant:

> The average age of the stewards has increased, they're all about 40-odd now. Eric Kennedy [the convenor] is 50-odd. He's been a shop steward for over 18 years. The deputy convenor became a steward about the same time. There is a number who've been stewards a long time and their whole attitude has changed. Certainly, the ageing factor has changed everybody. We've all grown older, maturer, mellower, more experienced.

The second edition of Beynon's study emphasized the pivotal role of long-standing and experienced senior stewards in Halewood, by quoting one worker:

> It was a bit like the Borgias. They had so much experience you couldn't tell them anything. If you went over with a complaint, 'This is wrong, that's wrong', they always had the answer. It was impossible to oppose them really. If you tried, they'd cut your head off. (Beynon, 1984, p. 350)

As Billy explained, this tension between stewards and members became even more accentuated during the late 1980s and early 1990s:

> There is a lot of anger and bitterness at management and people feel the union isn't fighting. But the members don't challenge the stewards

> more because, although they attack them – 'You're not doing this,
> you're not doing that' – they don't have the confidence they could do
> the job themselves. It's a vicious circle – the stewards don't feel they
> could get support from the shop-floor and the shop-floor don't feel they
> can get back-up from the stewards.

The circularity of this position was reinforced by the relative stability of
the workforce and the stewards in a situation of increasing uncertainty.

At the same time, many stewards became more and more removed
from the day-to-day work intensification experienced by their shop-floor
members. Whilst the senior stewards tended to spend an increasing
amount of their time in meetings with personnel and plant management,
the granting of 100 per cent time off work for sectional stewards (who of
course did not wear blue work overalls like their members) encouraged
many to spend a disproportionate amount of their time in the union office
talking with each other and to senior stewards rather than with their constituents. Only in the Body plant did a few left-wing stewards still work on
the line, for example working the 'welt system' with a workmate who
would cover for them when they were on union business. Generally,
however, stewards' accountability was under less direct scrutiny than in
the past and it was this which allowed stewards a wider freedom to act more
independently, if not more bureaucratically.

A severe decline in the frequency of sectional or mass meetings within
the plants took away an important forum for democratic debate and
decision making, while at the TGWU branch attendance fell considerably. With factory leaflets becoming few and far between, rank-and-file
members received scant information about shop steward decisions and
activities. The convenors and senior stewards tended to negotiate changes
with plant management, often informing the rest of the stewards' body
only after the event, leaving the onus on individual stewards to communicate with their members, most of whom were left in the dark. It was
a process which helped to foster a passive membership.

In broad terms, the more the stewards became linked to management
in a cautious 'pragmatic' bargaining relationship the more distant they
became from the workers they represented on the shop-floor. Nonetheless,
there were also important *counter-pressures* and informal workplace sanctions to those acting solely to bureaucratize shop stewards. Every steward
was still obliged to go down on the line to deal with issues on a daily
basis – meaning they were in frequent dialogue with their members and

judged by their ability to resolve issues satisfactorily. Whilst often the relationship appeared highly agreeable, despite its quiescent nature, on occasions the applecart would be overturned. As Tony pointed out:

> At the end of the day you're only as good as your last job. You can be a brilliant steward, give people everything, but the next day when they turn you get the shock of your life.

An example of the members 'turning' was the 1985 line-workers' regrading strike. For the previous two years senior stewards had successfully acted like firemen by pouring cold water over most of the sporadic sectional stoppages that threatened to puncture the co-operative relationship established with management. As Billy remarked:

> Dispute after dispute was lost – because of the role of the senior stewards. People started to think, 'What's going on, we aren't winning anything at the moment.' Even though sectional stewards had given their backing to the stoppages the senior stewards managed to sit on them by giving an assurance that line-workers would be regraded as part of the national pay agreement that was being negotiated by national officials.

In fact, although national TGWU leaders had raised expectations that regrading was on the cards, no such agreement was ever signed, and when line-workers discovered they were not to receive any extra allowance they spontaneously walked out on strike in the Assembly plant. Significantly, the strike began while the Halewood convenors and senior stewards were away in London at NJNC negotiations on the pay deal. Billy recounted how the strike began:

> We had a mass meeting in the Empire Theatre and there was a demand from the floor for all the stewards to get up on the platform and say where they stood on the strike. One by one they were forced to get up. Even the senior stewards made it clear they were for a continuation of the strike. It showed they're still responsive to the shop-floor.

However, because even *senior* stewards are also *sectional* stewards this two-week rank-and-file revolt effectively compelled them to swing completely around in favour of militant action against the company, even in defiance of national union officials. The 1988 national pay strike, in which

Halewood played a central role, also underlined this continuing responsiveness of the stewards' leadership. Again, the initiative for the strike came from below, from rank-and-file members, and successfully encouraged the stewards to take the lead in organizing a major strike, in defiance of the wishes of the national union leadership.

A stoppage by almost 200 Assembly plant workers in December 1991 further illustrates the point. The dispute arose as a result of a manager's allegedly abusive attitude to an operator who was threatened with disciplinary measures. The operator's workmates on the section immediately threatened to walk out in his support if the threat was not withdrawn and an apology provided. The sectional steward's attempts to resolve the dispute were dismissed by the manager. This was the impetus for the steward to agree to spread the dispute. A mass meeting was organized by stewards in other departments, halting production. Plant management were completely taken by surprise at the response of the shop-floor and immediately backed down. The disciplinary threat was withdrawn and the manager apologized to the operator. No doubt the planned visit the following day of Albert Caspers, Ford's European Vice-President, to confirm an export order for Halewood to produce 25 000 vehicles for Europe panicked Halewood management into a 180-degree turn to avoid the embarrassment of having to explain why the production lines had been halted. But the dispute sent a clear message to managers that the shop-floor was still capable of flexing its muscles.

Indeed, such incidents suggested the fact of the members' 'turning' in opposition to management (the 1993 Body plant walk-out over compulsory 'voluntary' redundancies being another example) provided an important safeguard against an immutable set of bureaucratic features becoming locked into place inside the stewards' organization. Even if management were able to get away with many things they wanted they still felt obliged to take workplace union organization seriously, in part because there was continuing pressure from the shop-floor and they knew that if they introduced changes without union agreement there was the possibility of a disruption to production. Significantly, the convenor Eric Kennedy only narrowly survived a challenge to his position in the Assembly plant during 1992, in a vote that reflected a growing discontent amongst a number of sectional stewards with his handling of management attacks.

All the same, the general atrophy of stewards' organization during the 1980s proved a major handicap to a reinvigoration of the relationship between stewards and members. Whilst the stewards held together union organization through a difficult period, during which most members were relatively passive, they tended to lose confidence in their ability to lead battles within their own sections and could often be more conservative than the members they represented. Another problem was the way left-wing stewards in the Body plant made the mistake of attempting to split the Ford Halewood TGWU branch, looking for short-cuts to the task of rebuilding shop-floor strength to fight management. Traditionally, the branch was dominated by stewards from the Assembly plant, with Eric Kennedy and the senior stewards holding the bulk of branch committee positions. Not surprisingly, the policy of co-operation with management adopted in the early 1980s was reflected in the 'moderate' industrial and political stance taken at union branch meetings, as attendance dwindled to about 30–35 members. A handful of left stewards from the Body plant became increasingly frustrated, particularly when their attempts to offer support to strikes that occurred in the Assembly plant were blocked on the basis that it was 'shop stewards', not branch, business'.

In response, during the late 1980s some of these left-wing activists collected 38 signatures from the 44-strong Body plant stewards' committee in favour of having their own separate TGWU branch, even receiving the backing of local left-wing full-time union officials. Eventually, after three years' wrangling, and with some help from TGWU officials, they managed to secure a ballot of the Body plant's union membership on the issue. According to Billy, it was a bad tactical mistake, diverting the energies of the militants down a blind alley, and even the left stewards in the Assembly plant opposed the plan:

> My argument was if you don't think the branch is doing what you want then you have to operate within it to change it. I don't think some of the people arguing for splitting the branch had really done that, some of them hadn't even attended the branch meetings. There's no reason the PTA [Paint, Trim and Assembly plant] should control the branch, it's just that they've been more successful at getting people to meetings . . . They accused the right wing of using bureaucratic manoeuvres to get their way but they adopted the same tactic: they wrote to regional officials to help them, they relied on the official machine. The PTA stewards argued [that] the regional officials supported splitting the branch so they could build their own little power base, because they resented the power the Ford TGWU branch has and wanted to cut it down to size and control it.

Not surprisingly, the Assembly plant senior stewards campaigned against the split, distributing leaflets through the auspices of the branch committee to the Body plant's workforce prior to the ballot. They were also able convincingly, and with some justification, to present themselves as the defenders of unity and strength:

> Brothers, you have your own branch, the one you're in now and you should defend and support it by voting YES in this vote. Ask yourself why this ballot is going on. Ask yourself who stands to gain. Ask yourself why outside influences are involved. Ask yourself why only part of your branch is getting a vote. Two different branches of the TGWU members could easily carry different policies on wage claims of site importance causing major disputes and unnecessary demarcation and friction. Ask yourself why local and senior officers are working so hard to split your branch. The reality is that certain people want to politicise your branch. Because they have been unsuccessful they seek a split by conning people to believe they are being deprived. What a lie . . . If the Ford Motor Company were to draw up a plan to split the shopfloor they couldn't have done a better job. The slogan of your branch banner is 'Unity is Strength'. Let's stay that way . . . Vote YES for UNITY (TGWU branch leaflet).

Although the left activists in the Body plant also distributed leaflets, a sizeable number of the 38 stewards who had originally been signatories to the call for a separate union branch gradually withdrew their support. Tony reflected:

> The branch created the fear that we were 'Lefties' who wanted to politicize people. We would have control of the money, be able to order them out on strike even if they didn't want to. And the membership bought it.

The ballot result produced a two-to-one vote in favour of retaining the existing branch and served to boost the authority and confidence of the right wing on both steward committees, as well as within the TGWU branch, a major beneficiary of which was Halewood management.

During the 1970s, faced with an intransigent management and representing a combative workforce, militant stewards at Halewood had been preoccupied with building up the strength of *shop-floor* union organization. Even if the TGWU branch was constitutionally the premier union body in theory, the left understood that day-to-day factory issues were the key concern in practice. The left activists were involved in both, but the emphasis was tilted towards shop-floor organization. However, with management's 'poisoned handshake' approach and the downturn in workers' struggles in the 1980s, some union militants looked to the TGWU branch as a short-cut solution to advance workers' interests, side-stepping the hard slog of trying to restore morale and rebuild an organized core of opposition to management within each section, utilizing the branch as a secondary forum in that task.

Perhaps the most serious future long-term threat to the relationship between stewards and members at Halewood is 'team-working'. By the early 1990s each section of the Assembly plant had been divided up into small groups with 'group leaders' recruited from the shop-floor, and paid £20–£25 extra weekly to take on a supervisory role for ensuring all jobs are manned, for arranging breaks and organizing simple maintenance. Part of the aim is to improve job flexibility, although, as Billy explained, it is also to by-pass the stewards' organization:

> The group leader is paid about 10 per cent more – he's like a chargehand at the moment. People accept things off the group leader because he's seen as one of them which they wouldn't accept from the foremen. But he's in a bit of an ambivalent position, because he gets his ear bent by management. On any big problem you would still involve the foremen and the steward. But it's undercutting the steward to a certain extent because if you have a minor problem you see your group leader. As for the future, it depends on whether management use the group leaders to tighten up on the quality of work.

The danger is that the group leader could begin to substitute for the steward, at least on work organization issues.

Although there is a danger of team working and the group leader system acting to undermine stewards' traditional representation of members, there remain contradictions in such management strategies which can be exploited. Thus, in some sections in the Body plant attempts have been made to have the group leader position rotated regularly amongst shop-floor workers. In the future, it might be possible for some stewards to alter their constituency so as to encompass a number of teams within a section of a plant. As Jimmy pointed out:

> There *has* been a change of attitude at Halewood – it's more
> co-operative now because the face of management has changed to the
> people on the shop-floor – but the underlying strength of the steward
> organization is still there. People still look towards their steward to
> represent them even when the company tries to get a group of people
> together. That is a fundamental thing that the lads do insist on whatever
> the problem is. The company haven't been able to bang that out of
> people's heads.

Ironically, Halewood management's decision in 1992 to end 100 per cent
facility time for most sectional stewards in both plants, so that they are now
only occasionally granted release from the job, could have the effect of
counteracting to a certain extent the gap that has developed between
stewards and members in recent years.

Stewards' Relationship to Full-Time Union Officials: The 1970s–1990s

The 1960s/1970s: Establishing Lay Representation

The Ford Halewood stewards were relatively independent of local full-
time TGWU officials during the 1970s. Traditionally there was close contact between the two, especially as local union officials were often ex-Ford
Halewood workers themselves. Phil described the role of the local official
during the early 1960s, when the plant was being unionized:

> Although full-time officers shouldn't be seen as very important in the
> scheme of things, Sam Glasstone was a good old-fashioned
> blood-and-thunder trade unionist who was just what the doctor ordered
> to stand up to the bullies at Ford. We loved him. But he used to have an
> ambivalent view of things. 'He's just a glorified shop steward', other
> officers used to say. When he addressed a meeting he'd say: 'Look lads,
> I've got to tell you this, you're out of procedure, so nothing is gonna be
> made official here. Now I don't blame you. If I was in there I would have
> been out a bit fucking quicker.' So we used to say: 'We don't expect
> any of them to be made official, we ain't going back, so you can go in
> there and tell them that.' And he'd say: 'Fair enough, I like that.'
> Management would tell him his members were out of order and he'd
> say: 'Well, I've told them that, but they're not coming back to work,
> unless and until.'

The position dovetailed with the emergence of a relatively independent form of union organization in the plant.

After the establishment of a well-organized shop steward structure in the late 1960s the relationship with local officials became much more autonomous. The stewards had the organization, resources, experience and confidence to handle a variety of grievances and negotiations within the confines of the plant. For example, until his death in 1987, Trevor Wilson was convenor of the Assembly plant for 17 consecutive years, his experience rivalling the local officials'. In these circumstances, there was little reason to call for *external* assistance, except to perform those tasks which only a full-time official was authorized to carry out, such as giving formal ratification to any bargaining agreements or taking a major dispute into procedure. Thus, the vast majority of stoppages of work were 'unofficial' and were dealt with *internally* by the Halewood stewards themselves, without the involvement of local union officials.

There were, however, some exceptions to the autonomy of the stewards, particularly when either plant faced lay-offs or on those occasions when management saw an advantage in using the officials to sort out unruly sections of workers, as a Body plant employee relations manager recalled:

> I can remember one incident around 1976 or '78, when the regional organizer of the T and G was brought in. We had a lead booth. It was always a troublesome area because it wasn't an easy or likeable job – because the guys had to wear spacesuits and respirators. It was one of the most famous places in the Body plant where 'welt working' was rife and the booth was in and out on strike by the minute over all sorts of issues. We involved the officer and we fired all the lead diskers and after an appeal we agreed to reinstate them provided they sign a declaration that they would be good guys in the future. But we didn't reinstate all of them, some of the militant ones stayed dismissed. Now, that was with the knowledge and concurrence of the officer. So he recognized that whilst he would always have to support his members things were running out of control and something had to be done for the greater good of the greater number of his members.

Such connivance was quite rare, particularly since the local union organization was such that it could negate such action by full-time officials. On the whole, the shop stewards operated relatively autonomously of the local officials, without their involvement in the details of workplace industrial relations.

Much more problematic was the stewards' relationship with *national* union officials, particularly those represented on the NJNC. Ford had formalized its negotiating procedure in 1955, earlier than most British companies, when it signed a procedure agreement with full-time national union officials from the 21 unions with members in the British plants. This ratified centralized negotiations over the major questions of pay and conditions of work and led to a separation between *plant-level* shop stewards and the *national* officials who represented the unions on the NJNC. Throughout the 1950s and 1960s, Ford was able to maintain this collective bargaining regime, dealing exclusively with national trade union officials and ignoring the shop stewards, except for local bargaining purposes. Thus, at the Dagenham plant, a powerful but extremely autonomous shop stewards' committee developed, with few links with the NJNC or with the formal trade union structures (Beynon, 1984).

By contrast, the Halewood plant was characterized by the emergence of a shop stewards' organization determined to forge links and alliances within the official structures of the TGWU. This was influenced by the negative experience of Ford Dagenham, where an isolated plant organization suffered a severe setback after the successful victimization of its leading stewards in 1962, and by the positive experience of the nearby Dunlop plant in Speke on Merseyside, where stewards had gained considerable influence within the TGWU with represention on key union committees. The 'Dunlop way' seemed to offer the possibility of using the official trade union structures 'but without illusions' in its 'bent' national officials and it was this approach that was adopted by the Assembly plant stewards. By the late 1960s Ford stewards were represented at regional level and on the national executive committee (Beynon, 1984, p. 83).

At the same time, a 'devolution of power' to shop stewards had been openly encouraged by sections of the TGWU leadership (particularly the general secretary Jack Jones), with a more central role in shop-floor negotiations for stewards and far closer links between them and official union structures (Undy, 1978). Devolution may be seen, at least in part, as a pragmatic response to the position which shop stewards had achieved informally in many areas of the TGWU's membership, as at Ford Halewood in the late 1960s. Nonetheless, growing rank-and-file discontent at the Labour government's incomes policy during this period encouraged fierce verbal resistance to the pay norms, and the union machine increasingly shifted to the left politically as a 'new breed' of national and district union official took office, particularly in Merseyside.

The development of regular contacts between the Halewood and Dagenham shop stewards led to the formation of a Ford national shop stewards' combine committee and a campaign to democratize the company's corporate bargaining structure that concentrated all effective decision making in the hands of full-time union officials. The Ford national convenors' committee, a body comprising convenors from each of Ford's UK plants, organized lobbies of the NJNC meetings in London and demanded the referral of all national decisions for ratification in the plants. Phil recalled:

> As far as national officers were concerned we quickly learned – mostly through the experience of the Dagenham people, who hated the national officers and felt so badly let down by them – the corrupt bastards they were on the National Joint Negotiating Committee. They used to have their meetings in the Café Royal in London. There wasn't any democracy or accountability or opportunity for the wishes of the membership to be transmitted, you weren't allowed to have any say in the compilation of the pay claim or other issues. Even though we had developed quite good structures in terms of shop steward organization and in terms of getting resolutions passed through the TGWU, no one took any notice of us at the NJNC. So stewards and convenors used to be outside the Café Royal lobbying the national officers. That was the relationship we had with the national officers at that time. We had disdain for them.

Although the gains made by establishing a national shop stewards' combine committee had limited success with the NJNC, it was an important initiative as far as the stewards were concerned.

A national unofficial delegate conference of shop stewards from all Ford plants in the UK was instituted, known as the 'Coventry Conference' because it met at the TGWU's Transport Hall in Coventry, to decide general policy and formulate immediate demands. Policies agreed at these delegate conferences were binding on all plants and the national convenors' committee was given the task of securing the implementation of decisions reached. Again, Halewood stewards were centrally involved; and in 1969 it was the convenors and stewards in the Assembly plant who took the initiative in organizing plant-wide walk-outs in response to Ford's proposed package deal containing 'penalty clauses' aimed at curbing 'unconstitutional action'. The unofficial stoppages quickly spread to a national Ford strike and brought to a head the whole problem not only of industrial relations in the plants but *also* the relationship between the union officials on the NJNC and the plant-based shop stewards.

Despite the backing given to Ford's package deal by the NJNC, dominated by right-wing trade union officials, the strike was given official support by the recently elected left-wing TGWU general secretary, Jack Jones, and AUEW president Hugh Scanlon, and their national executives, reflecting the internal differentiation within union officialdom. As a result, the structure of the NJNC collapsed and the chairperson of the trade union side of the committee and the TGWU's own national official both resigned their positions. After the strike, which forced Ford to water down its 'penalty clauses', the NJNC was reconstituted with a more proportional distribution of seats between the various unions and, for the first time ever, lay representation from the plants. Four convenors (including the two TGWU convenors from the Halewood plants) were admitted into its structure. Phil drew out the significance of the change:

> It was a tremendous advance. The lay representation at least ensured we had some say on the agenda. We didn't make any difference to the actual style of negotiation. That was still conducted through the chair and union secretaries; Reg Birch [AUEW] and Moss Evans [TGWU] would do the talking, and we would just sit there like we were in a goldfish bowl. But we were there to observe and carry back and it made a significant difference, it was a breakthrough. For example, we put 'parity' on the agenda. Ford weren't happy with the development.

Meanwhile, 2000 Halewood workers from the Body plant left the GMWU, disgusted at its failure to back the strike, and joined the TGWU, which now became the majority union in the plant and on the stewards' committee. Thus, the 1969 strike represented a significant victory for shop stewards' organization in the Halewood plant. It proved itself to be highly responsive to the demands of a confident rank-and-file membership and able to act as a powerful counter-weight to the bureaucracy of official trade union structures.

Of course, this independence from the national union leaders was a *relative* phenomenon, as was illustrated in 1971 when Ford plants across the country voted to join those at Halewood and Swansea who had walked out on strike in response to Ford's pay offer of a £2 increase on the basic rate.

This second national strike was aimed at establishing 'parity' with the earnings of Midlands carworkers and lasted for nine weeks until the 'terrible twins', Jack Jones and Hugh Scanlon, secretly concluded a deal with Ford's UK chairman (which prohibited further strikes over pay for the next two years), by-passed the NJNC (of which they were not members), and presented the agreement as a *fait accompli* to the official negotiators and plant shop stewards (Matthews, 1972). Instead of allowing mass meetings of the membership to decide whether to go back to work they insisted on a secret ballot of the workforce, exactly as the Conservative government's hated Industrial Relations Act demanded. Although the pay settlement was higher than the government would have liked, Ford had found that collaboration was still possible, even with so-called 'left-wing' union leaders, and within a matter of days Halewood management were clamping down on shop-floor organization, sacking John Dillon, a steward in the Assembly plant.

Significantly, the opening up of the NJNC was also double-edged in some respects. The 1969 strike had initially posed a serious threat to the NJNC itself and its preservation as an authoritative joint union–management bargaining forum became the company's top priority. Paradoxically, the widening gap between the national union officials and shop stewards within the plants gradually persuaded Ford that it would be better to deal with accountable shop-floor leaders who could be held responsible for their side of a negotiated agreement rather than be reliant on national officials alone. Thus, during the 1970s they began to make a virtue out of what had previously been a necessity, taking a series of initiatives aimed at further democratizing the NJNC and progressively involving wider layers of plant convenors and senior stewards in an institutionalization of conflict within formalized company–union procedures. The admission of all 21 Ford British plant convenors to the trade union side of the NJNC in 1978 was more than a symbol of the transformation of industrial relations in Ford; it reinforced the authority of the NJNC and demonstrated how far the company was prepared to go in its attempt to incorporate the senior full-time shop steward leadership in the plants (Friedman and Meredeen, 1980).

Although the NJNC did not usually directly intervene in domestic plant issues, except those relating to national pay agreements, the involvement of two Halewood convenors in more or less regular contact with Ford UK managers and national full-tine union officials inevitably had a significant effect on the conduct of steward organization on the site. Ford encouraged them to take a more active part in persuading their stewards and members to remain at work and 'talk out' grievances rather than 'walk out' without allowing formalized procedures to operate. To assist them in this, senior stewards on the joint works committee were granted much more leeway to take time off work to conduct union business, and a variety of facilities were granted. Moreover, the convenors increasingly came under the pressure of full-time trade union officials who expected them to 'carry the plants' in support of formal commitments and agreements made nationally.

In fact, pressures towards their 'assimilation' encouraged the formation, a few weeks prior to the 1978 national pay strike, of a small militant national rank-and-file organization (the 'Ford Workers Group (Combine)') disaffected with the way the convenor system linked contact between the plants directly through the official channels of the NJNC. The 'Combine' successfully established a network of activists within a number of Ford plants across the country, with one of the largest groups of about a dozen unaligned left-wing militants, including a handful of shop stewards – based at Halewood. Formed with the object of campaigning for a rank-and-file controlled strike the 'Combine' produced many thousands of leaflets, stickers and 'Fraud' badges parodying the Ford logo, and kept up constant pressure on the NJNC by organizing regular lobbies of the London negotiations, with up to 150 workers in attendance from across the country. Although operating within official union structures, it aimed at building militant unofficial opposition to the union officials and to those convenors and senior stewards who were becoming more distant from the shop-floor; and during the dispute it tried to play the role that a fighting national strike committee might have undertaken by, for example, organizing 'flying' pickets to the docks, car transporter depots and Ford dealers.

Nevertheless, even if most plant convenors on the NJNC were connected to the union officials' subsequent recommendation to accept a deal far short of the £20 and 35 hours claim, Halewood proved to be the exception. It was the only Ford plant in the country where the steward committees recommended a protest vote of rejection, although given their isolation the membership voted to return to work. After the strike, the 'Combine' supporters in Halewood produced a few copies of a duplicated bulletin named *The Halewood Worker*, which aimed to 'break down the isolation and the lack of communication between workers in the plants' (*Halewood Worker*, Christmas edition 1981). But the group withered away with the downturn in workers' struggles during the mid-1980s.

It would be a mistake to assume that the process of incorporation of the convenors and senior stewards at Halewood was unproblematic. Certainly, the tradition of fighting semi-independently of the full-time officials, firmly established in the 1960s, was not lost overnight during the 1970s, even though there were rather different levels of autonomy between the steward committees in the Body and Assembly plants. According to Tony:

> The most important difference in historical terms is that the Assembly plant was always more under the *official* line of the union, whereas the Body plant conditioned itself to attempt to run *outside* and within the official line. We always saw that when the officials came in it was to smack our hands because we'd acted just as workers and the union was something distant, although we were always under the union's protection and we were acting out policies of the union and making greater demands as a shop stewards' organization. But the Assembly plant would adhere and recognize the official union line, when we were just not bothered with it.

Thus, the stewards' organization had an ambivalent relation with the officials.

But it was the lack of a deeply rooted and stable accommodative relationship between stewards and management in either of the Halewood plants that ensured there were powerful countervailing factors operating against the attempt by national union officials to win backing for policies of restraint. Essentially, it was the level of shop-floor militancy during the 1970s that made sure they were held directly accountable to their rank-and-file members and retained a high degree of independence from union officials. Significantly, the Halewood stewards tended to be more militant than in other Ford plants across the country, invariably recommending the rejection of nationally negotiated pay agreements, often taking the initiative in organizing strike action without waiting for official union sanction, and usually being the last plant to return to work following a national ballot.

The explanation of why this was the case cannot be sought solely in terms of the Halewood plants themselves. It is also necessary to place the Halewood stewards within the wider context of Merseyside, its distinctive economic, political, social and cultural traditions. The key point here is that it further illustrates that, compared with most other Ford plants in Britain, the Halewood stewards retained a high degree of autonomy from full-time union officials during the 1970s.

The 1980s/Early 1990s: Transmission Belt of Influence

Not surprisingly, from the early 1980s the relationship between the Halewood shop stewards and full-time union officials underwent a marked change. The downturn in workers' struggle within the plant left its imprint on the willingness and ability of shop stewards to act autonomously of the national union leadership. Whereas in the 1970s there had been a quite powerful shop-floor organization with a tradition of action without relying on the union officials, in the 1980s the plant convenors and stewards were increasingly drawn into a more institutionalized relationship with both the company and national union leaders. Economic recession, mass unemployment and the threat of factory closure sapped the militancy of shop-floor workers, which in turn undermined shop stewards' confidence to act independently of the officials.

The extent of the dependence that developed began to become evident in 1981, after the Halewood '3rd Riot Act' or 'Double Dosing' strike. Ford withdrew its 'disciplinary code' only after a reconvened meeting of the NJNC had agreed to a 'detailed commitment from union leaders to improve self-discipline on the shop-floor'. Thus, TGWU national organizer Ron Todd sent a personal letter to Ford workers calling on them to demonstrate 'self-control'. It stated:

> The trade union's aims in negotiations on behalf of Ford workers are too often inhibited by our failure to honour the agreements that we sign on your behalf. We therefore require our members to reinforce our commitments to ensure that our agreements are observed. Unless we operate as a disciplined and united trade union force we can never direct our efforts against the major problems facing our future – new technology, predicted job losses, foreign penetration of our markets – all of these require our individual attention if we are to safeguard our future interests. (Freeman, 1984, p. 225)

That meant twisting the arms of the shop stewards and members.

During the early 1980s the entire weight of the official union bureaucracy, with its 'new realist' philosophy that militant strikes were a thing of the past, was consistently placed on the Halewood convenors and stewards, as TGWU full-time officials joined the chorus of those warning that Halewood faced closure and catastrophic job loss unless the stewards 'put their house in order' and ended the 'unconstitutional stoppages'. Whilst powerful material factors were already pushing in this direction, such external pressure appears to have been of crucial significance in giving the Body and Assembly plant convenors the legitimacy necessary to convince their respective steward committees of the need to adopt a new co-operative approach with Halewood management. It was a reflection of the more general defeatist attitude adopted by national union leaders in face of a hostile Thatcher government and employers' offensive. Virtually every initiative taken by Halewood management throughout the 1980s, aimed at involving shop stewards in a collaborative drive to boost efficiency and productivity, was given wholehearted backing by TGWU full-time officials. Thus, even though the Halewood stewards retained quite a high degree of autonomy *vis-à-vis* the *local* TGWU officials, they generally became more and more subservient in their relations with and ideological acceptance of the policy emanating from *national* union officials.

Another problem was the activities of some Halewood senior stewards within the higher echelons of the TGWU machine. Tony emphasized the significance of the 'moderate' Assembly plant senior stewards' dominance of the Halewood TGWU branch:

> The branch is one of the largest in the country with 6000 members, so obviously it's an important stepping stone within the T and G, and the right have got it stitched up. The Assembly plant convenor and chairman of the joint stewards' committee is a representative from the branch to the district committee; he's the national trade group representative for automotive workers in Britain and he's on the national executive committee. The deputy convenor is a member of the district committee and from that he's the representative on the national automotive group.

Of course, during the 1970s there had been stewards from Halewood represented at various levels of the TGWU's machinery. But generally, they had tended to be left-wing-influenced stewards concerned to push the union towards a more combative stance to employers. For example, they played a part in overturning in 1977 the union's initial backing of the Labour government's 'Social Contract' in favour of a return to free collective bargaining, which in turn was a prelude to the national Ford pay strike of 1978 which broke through the government's 5 per cent pay limit. But by the late 1980s, the transmission belt of influence, although always a two-way channel, moved much more forcefully from above. Certainly, despite the lay character of the TGWU's governing bodies, there was a lot of pressure to rely on the full-time officials for guidance on the major national issues. Moreover, although the faction-riven 39-seat national executive committee was traditionally controlled by the left, during the late 1980s the influence of the right became much stronger. Within this framework the convenor of the Assembly plant, Eric Kennedy, played a particularly important role in consistently pushing 'moderate' official union policies downwards into the steward committees and on to the shop-floor.

Notwithstanding such developments, it is important to recognize that there were significant countervailing pressures operating on the shop stewards during the 1980s, despite the general decline in struggle. Thus, the 1983 Paul Kelly strike, the 1985 line-workers' strike and the 1988 national pay strike showed that steward organization was much more responsive and accountable to rank-and-file pressure than the full-time union leadership. In 1988, because national TGWU officials were seen by many workers to be too placatory in negotiations with the company, failing to respond to the growing anger amongst their shop-floor union members, there were unofficial stoppages of work at Halewood leading to a national strike, which forced the stewards to provide some leadership despite the repeated attempts of TGWU and AEU officials to obtain a return to work (amidst no fewer than three 'final offers'). The enormous power of Ford workers was convincingly demonstrated when the Ford plant in Belgium was closed and the plants in Spain and West Germany were forced to work part-time, after a little less than two weeks of strike action. However, the opportunity to use this power to inflict a decisive victory over Ford was squandered. Full-time national union officials were quickly able to regain the initiative, switching from opposition to strike action to supporting the action but on their terms and under their control. This enabled them to defuse the initial surges of militancy and get the strike called off after recommending acceptance of only a slightly improved deal which conceded increased flexibility in the plants, albeit subject to local agreement.

But if the union officials played their characteristic conservative role their action was undoubtedly made easier by the erosion of strong shop stewards' organization in Halewood (and in the other Ford plants) as a result of the years of collaboration with management. At first, Halewood shop stewards, under direct pressure from their members, provided leadership to the unofficial strike wave. But, as Billy complained, they failed to involve the majority of workers in activity once the plant had been entirely stopped:

> All the way through the strike nothing was done to involve people. Anyone who wasn't a steward was discouraged from going on the picket line. The convenors wanted it passive, to keep the picket lines down to a minimum. The argument that dominated was that we could win just by sitting tight, nothing more. But as the picket line was the only meeting point for the workforce during the strike that left the majority of people isolated at home where they were vulnerable to pressure to return to work as soon as another ballot was arranged by the officers.

The union leaders were able to convince the NJNC into accepting a deal which was well below what could have been achieved. Even though both shop steward committees' at Halewood recommended rejection they failed to inspire any confidence that more could be gained, not least because the plant convenors refused to break publicly with the official return to work directive. Jimmy recalled:

> A lot of people wanted to carry the fight on. But the officials seemed determined to accept whatever offer the company came up with. There were three final offers. Mick Murphy called one of them 'an historic deal'. It was an hysterical deal as far as we were concerned. People thought we could have got more out of it. The shop stewards' committee did reject the offer but the way the convenors put it to the meeting didn't inspire people. It was total defeatism . . . There was a lot of disgruntlement at the way the officials called it off.

Equally, the members were not ready to push a more active response in the face of a relatively tepid lead from the stewards.

The pervading influence of union officialdom was also displayed in 1990, when the national automotive organizer of the TGWU, Jack Adams, wrote a personal letter to Halewood workers urging them to break the picket lines of striking craftsmen, on unofficial strike over a national pay deal. Having concluded an agreement with Ford's the union officials argued any disruption could lead to the company fulfilling its threat to withdraw investment at British plants. The notion that 'If it's good for the company it's good for the union' led TGWU stewards at Halewood to authorize 'scabbing' against the EETPU and AEU members. Again, the union officials' stance was carried directly into Halewood by the senior stewards.

Thus, in general terms it is clear that the Halewood stewards had a much more dependent relationship with union officials than in the past, although the 1988 strike, as well as the 1993 unofficial strike against 'voluntary' compulsory redundancies, illustrated that the problem of dependence was not necessarily of a permanent nature. They showed the risk that Ford run of launching an offensive that could provoke an unofficial backlash in which the rank-and-file and a reinvigorated shop stewards' organization make the running, not the union officials.

Some Issues and Themes

Many of the issues and themes raised in Huw Beynon's *Working for Ford*, as well as in the previous two case studies, resurface in this account of shop stewards' organization in Ford Halewood. Of particular significance is a comparison of different managerial strategies and their impact on the development of stewards' organization.

On the one hand, strong workplace union organization develops through collective struggle against management's 'hard-line' confrontational strategy, although stewards cannot afford to challenge management at every turn as sometimes outright conflict might leave workers vulnerable. Hence the need for strategic stewards' leadership. On the other hand, there is the opposite danger of 'playing the game' through a co-operative bargaining relationship in which the 'soft line' invites routinization and a settled professionalism within stewards' organization, with its own vulnerabilities in undermining the vitality of workplace unionism. Both pressures were evident within Ford during the 1970s, although the balance between them changed considerably between the 1970s and the 1980s and early 1990s.

Again, as with the previous case studies, there were complex dilemmas and limitations for plant-level based forms of union activity in the face of corporate restructuring, particularly against the backcloth of product market crises and constant threats of closure. But in the stewards' response to such dilemmas it was possible to discern an important distinction between 'having to compromise', in circumstances that were not favourable to shop-floor union organization, and the active 'celebration of retreat', which tended to embrace managerial logic to such an extent that it contributed even further to the disarming of union strength that followed.

Also it was possible to see a direct connection between the level of shop-floor confidence, activity and combativity *vis-à-vis* management and the relatively close and democratic relationship that existed between stewards and members during the 1970s. Thus, the generally combative stance of the stewards encouraged the active participation of rank-and-file members in union affairs. By contrast, during the 1980s and early 1990s there was a link between the relatively low level of shop-floor resistance towards management and the increasing bureaucratization of relations between stewards and members that ensued. In the context of rank-and-file members' demobilization and relative passivity, stewards became more remote from the direct forms of accountability and democratic scrunity that had previously prevailed. Nonetheless, sporadic and spontaneous shop-floor rebellions were an important safeguard against an invulnerable bureaucracy becoming locked into place.

Other principal themes included the narrow ideological and political horizon of the shop stewards, the inability of the left to provide a coherent alternative to the politics of the strike-free running of the plant, and the growing integration of convenors and senior stewards into company and official trade union forums.

The next chapter explores some of these features of workplace relations in greater detail and makes a comparative assessment with the experiences of the Birds Eye and Bemrose plants, drawing out the implications for workplace unionism more generally.

7 ASSESSMENT AND IMPLICATIONS

Introduction

Each of the preceding case studies suggested that relatively powerful shop stewards' organizations were built up during the 1960s and 1970s but were considerably weakened during the 1980s and, in the case of the surviving plant, Ford, the stewards' organization continues to face formidable challenges during the 1990s. The qualitative changes in the strength of the stewards' organizations were the result of both objective and subjective factors, both external and internal to the workplace. The product market crises of the early 1980s dealt a blow to shop-floor power and presented stewards with immense strategic and tactical difficulties that could not easily be overcome. The shift in the balance of workplace power toward management was inextricably linked to the hostile economic and political climate within Britain generally and within the Merseyside regional context in particular. The downturn in workers' struggles within the British labour movement, deepened by the defeat of the miners' strike in 1984–85, was another debilitating influence on the strength of the stewards' organization. The ideological embrace of 'new realism' within the TUC, involving the discouragement of industrial militancy in favour of a more co-operative stance with employers and the Conservative government, was paralleled in the pressure placed on shop stewards by full-time union officials to make wide-ranging pragmatic concessions to management within the three Merseyside workplaces. Many convenors, sectional shop stewards and rank-and-file workers, anxious to minimize job losses and prevent plant closure, embraced aspects of 'new realism', albeit in a more varied, uneven and contradictory fashion than many national union officials. The absence of a coherent ideological or political alternative leadership from the left was a further impediment to any other outcome.

In this concluding chapter there is a brief assessment of the limits of generalization from the case studies. This is followed by a comparative assessment of the shop stewards' organizations at Birds Eye, Bemrose and Ford, which relates the case study findings to a critique of the Labourist/reformist analytical approach of Eric Batstone outlined in Chapter 1, with the aim of drawing out some wider implications about the underlying dynamics of shop stewards' organization, activity and consciousness. This involves a summary and evaluation of some of the principal common themes – with reference to stewards' relationship to management, members and full-time union officials. Finally, consideration is given to some of the underlying implications of how to rebuild the strength of workplace unionism in the future.

Level of Generalization

How far is it possible to generalize from the distinctive experiences of three manufacturing plants in Merseyside? Obviously there are important specificities which it would be mistaken to ignore, namely the way the general balance of class forces in society can potentially affect different sections of workers across the country in varying ways. For example, Martin (1992) has shown the way in which the distribution of bargaining power in three industries – hotels and catering, motor vehicles, and white-collar local government – are very different according to various environmental, contextual and organizational factors. The case studies above would suggest that geographical location and local union traditions are especially important. Thus, the Merseyside shop stewards appeared to be much better organized and more defiant towards management than in many other plants within the same company or industry elsewhere across the country; for example, taking the initiative in setting up a stewards' combine committee (Fords), establishing superior pay and conditions of work (Bemrose) and often rejecting management pay offers only to be out-voted by their counterparts elsewhere (Birds Eye).

In assessing such differences it is necessary to take account of the significance of the economic, political, social and cultural context of Merseyside. Chapter 2 argued that there are related contributory factors which go some way to explaining the region's distinctive collectivist traditions. The case studies suggest that workplace militancy during the 1970s was encouraged by, amongst other things, the relatively deprived economic and social conditions, hard-line confrontationist management and the role of influential militant shop stewards. By contrast, during the 1980s, the downturn in workers' struggle and stewards' more co-operative relationship with management was probably influenced more than anything else by the impact of the economic recession, in a city where manufacturing industry was hit disproportionately hard and where the rate of unemployment remained consistently much higher than the national average. Thus, the specificity of the case study material, given the important corporate, sectoral and regional variations within any general picture, has to be taken into account.

Nonetheless, as noted previously, this does not preclude a level of *analytical* generalization being made about the general contours of shop stewards' organization. In this respect the case studies documented a variety of dilemmas faced by many stewards inside the British labour movement over the past 20 years. For example, how to deal with threats from both frontal managerial attacks on workers' job controls as well as from attempts at the incorporation of workplace unionism, and how to reconcile the tension between the battle for workers' immediate day-to-day grievances and the stewards' committees plant-wide strategic perspective are widespread and recurrent dilemmas confronted by shop-floor union representatives across all industries and localities. Thus, the common themes contained within the case study experiences are of much wider relevance, even if specific conditions need to be constantly borne in mind. Moreover, the closure of two of the plants examined in no way makes obsolete many of the problems explored, quite apart from the value of historical analysis in its own right. In fact, in many respects the case studies provide some insights of value not only for an assessment of the *past* but also for an understanding of *contemporary* developments as well as possible *future* trends, with implications for workplace unionism more generally.

Stewards' Relationship to Management

All three case studies illuminated the contradiction between resistance and accommodation that lies at the heart of the shop stewards' relationship to management. Certainly, the evidence appears to confirm the view that shop stewards' attitudes to, and expectations of, management should not be conceptualized in a one-dimensional negative sense of 'primitive rebels' hell-bent on permanent confrontation (Ackers and Black, 1992). Of course, for a minority of stewards the legitimacy of management was often rejected and the possibility of co-operation for mutual benefit usually denied, leading to the advocacy of the maximum exercise of shop-floor power when opportunities arose. By contrast, some of the other stewards more often than not had quite positive expectations of management's role in providing strong and effective leadership concerned with achieving profitability and of the merits of maintaining harmonious workplace industrial relations. However, most of the stewards tended to adopt a complex and shifting blend of conflictual and consensual frames of reference, depending on the issue and context. What was most striking was the changing balance between resistance and accommodation reflected within the steward bodies *as a whole* between the 1970s and 1980s. Whilst in general terms stewards adopted a relatively conflictual approach towards management during the 1970s, this became much more consensual during the 1980s.

Essentially this shift occurred because of the changing nature and extent of shop-floor struggle, reflected in particular in the level of workers' confidence and combativity *vis-à-vis* management. This assertiveness was itself the result of many factors, including the wider economic and political context, product and labour market conditions, managerial strategies and nature of steward leadership. Rather than merely summarizing the combined impact of such factors on the ebb and flow of workplace struggle inside the three plants and on stewards' relationship to management, it is useful to isolate in more detail one important (although by no means exclusive) factor, namely the approach adopted by managers themselves towards shop stewards. Such a narrow focus can be justified on the basis that it helps to shed light on some of the underlying processes involved, although it is necessary to avoid any implication that this is either the only, or the most important, factor affecting shop stewards' contradictory relationship to management. Of course, the extent to which companies can be said to have coherent industrial relations 'strategies' which are integrated into overall business or organizational strategies is questionable, and there are a wide variety of constituents to corporate profitability, not all of them centred on labour control (Littler and Salaman, 1982; Purcell and Sisson, 1983; Marchington, 1992) Nonetheless, managers *do* often utilize a variety of strategies and tactics to control and motivate shop-floor workers, with shifts and variations in the relationship between force and consent. Focusing attention on how such different managerial strategies in the three case study workplaces helped to influence the development and character of the steward organizations simultaneously underlines the nature of the balance between resistance and accommodation in the stewards' response.

Thus, on the one hand, shop stewards sometimes faced a 'hard-line' managerial approach which compelled them to respond in conflictual terms. Ford provided a sharp example of the circumstances of this type of approach. During the 1970s the 'stick' component of Ford's strategy involved the assertion of the right of an unfettered managerial stance and the pursuance of tight shop-floor discipline with the aim of achieving high and continuous production levels. It was this aggressive approach which helped to precipitate the constant stoppages of work, and which encouraged stewards to articulate rank-and-file grievances, lead shop-floor struggles and build a strong, combative and independent shop stewards' organization. A similar process, albeit less sharply delineated, occurred at Birds Eye. Of course, in neither workplace were there uniform processes. They varied according to the differential bargaining leverage exercised by sections of workers, the contrasting experience and leadership of stewards and so on. Moreover, stewards sometimes felt they could not afford to challenge management on every occasion, as outright confrontation could leave workers vulnerable and risk serious defeat. Nonetheless, 'hard-line' management at Ford's and Birds Eye did contribute to the process whereby stewards were encouraged to mobilize their members in terms of a resistant relationship which challenged managerial authority.

On the other hand, both plants illustrated how shop stewards can also sometimes face a co-operative 'soft line' from management, aimed at incorporating them into accommodative relationships. Again, Ford provided the most acute example of this process. During the early 1980s, in the context of a changed economic and political climate, management's 'poisoned handshake' approach led to a 'backing off' whenever a shop-floor dispute arose, aimed at talking out issues without confrontation. In the long term this led to a more accommodative relationship between stewards and management, to the routinization of workplace trade unionism and the demobilization of collective rank-and-file self-activity. A similar development occurred at Birds Eye. Again, this was not necessarily a uniform picture. Whilst, in some respects, the more co-operative relationship with management was grounded in real, albeit limited, concessions, this did not preclude occasional battles with management. But what Birds Eye and Ford showed is that where accommodative relations have become established over a prolonged period of time, there can be a danger of stewards, and to a lesser extent workers, becoming socialized into accepting management's viewpoint.

All the same, the tension between resistance and accommodation (as with most stewards' attitudes towards management) did not express itself in a either/or scenario. The same management could apply different strategies at the same time. Thus at Ford during the 1970s the 'carrot' component, indicated by the attempt to incorporate workplace union organization by democratizing the NJNC and granting senior stewards extensive plant-level facilities, complemented the more assertive strategies implemented at the same time. Similarly, at Birds Eye there was a contradiction between a relatively aggressive plant-level management approach, often encouraged by corporate Birds Eye intervention, and the more consensual approach of many departmental managers. This same overlap was also evident during the 1980s. For example, at Ford, management's long-term 'EI' strategy clashed with their short-term need to reassert the 'big stick' on occasion, which provoked rank-and-file resistance. At Birds Eye, the apparently new co-operative approach soon gave way to an attempt to force draconian new working practices in the shape of 'Workstyle', which led to outright stewards' hostility.

Perhaps the most graphic example of the mix of conflictual and consensual relationships between stewards and management was demonstrated in Bemrose. Thus, during the 1970s, management had a twofold strategy. On the one hand, they regularly threatened to close the plant down (particularly whenever contracts came up for renewal) unless productivity was improved. On the other hand, given the nature of the product market, it often made little short-term financial sense to resist chapel demands and jeopardize production, so they were prepared to make significant concessions to win consent (even though the plant was ostensibly consistently unprofitable). As a result, whilst powerful chapel committee organizations developed, able to carve out a series of counter-controls to those of management, there was also quite a high degree of co-operation between the two, for example over the maintenance of production levels. It should be noted that a significant difference between shop-floor industrial relations at Bemrose compared with Birds Eye and Ford was the comparatively low level of workers' struggle. The chapel committees' strength came much more from advantageous market pressures, workers' strategic relationship to production and an institutionalized pattern of craft job control than from the daily battles on the shop-floor which generally characterized the others. Nonetheless, the same contradictory pressures of resistance and accommodation, influenced by managerial strategy, were evident.

However, the contradiction between resistance and accommodation was never equally balanced in any of the three workplaces. In Ford during the 1970s, it was the 'stick' component that was the predominant managerial strategy, promoting a relatively high level of workers' struggle and a combative steward–management relationship which provided little basis for any deep-seated or long-term accommodation. By contrast, during the 1980s, Ford's 'poisoned handshake' approach, whilst punctuated by occasional use of the 'big stick', encouraged a quite different co-operative relationship with shop stewards. Likewise, in Birds Eye during the 1970s, management adopted a much more antagonistic approach to stewards' organization than during the early 1980s, until the pendulum swung back again in the late 1980s. Even in Bemrose, despite management's much more complex, ambivalent approach, the day-to-day shop-floor relationship with the chapel committees was relatively more conflictual than co-operative during the 1970s when compared with the 1980s (notwithstanding the set-piece confrontations that occurred on a plant-wide level during the 1980s).

The differences in managerial approach can be explained primarily by their response to changes in product and labour markets, the influence of corporate strategy on plant-level managers and the perceived strength of shop-floor union organization. A crucial issue then concerns the influence of management policies and tactics on the nature and character of steward organization. Clearly, there was no automatic convergence between managerial approaches and shop steward responses. As was mentioned above, it depended on the wider economic and political context, on product and labour market conditions, on the level of rank-and-file confidence and activity and on the nature of stewards' leadership. Thus, Birds Eye management's more conciliatory approach following the 1978 lock-out did not lead to a more co-operative relationship between stewards and management. Paradoxically, although the stewards suffered a severe setback, they found that management's hesitancy in the face of production problems associated with the new technology provided them with the opportunity to rebuild some shop-floor strength, in the process pushing up manning levels and engaging in plant-wide strike action in defence of two sacked colleagues. By contrast, Bemrose management's adversarial stance over flexible working practices during the early 1980s did not spur the chapel committees into militant resistance.

The relationship between managerial strategy and the nature of steward organization is not a simple or mechanical one; there are enormous complexities involved, with the level of workers' confidence and combativity *vis-à-vis* management being a critical ingredient. At the same time, this is obviously only *one* factor amongst many influencing both the ebb and flow of workplace struggle and the nature of stewards' relationship to management. Clearly, during the early 1980s the product market crises, which influenced managerial strategy, were crucial in shaping stewards' qualitative change of approach towards management compared with the 1970s. Nonetheless, what the focus on managerial strategy does underline is the tension between resistance and accommodation at the very heart of steward–management relations in all three workplaces.

What also became apparent were the pitfalls of 'strong bargaining relations' between stewards and management, of workplace union strategies that respond pragmatically to managerial initiatives by means of a 'flexible' bargaining approach (Batstone *et al.*, 1977; Jones and Rose, 1986). As was noted in Chapter 1, Batstone assumed that by moderating their goals stewards could achieve more for their members than they could through a more combative perspective. This might mean that in specific instances the gains won by stewards would be less than they might have been, but equally there would be other occasions when procedural routes achieved gains (or minimized losses) where outright conflict would suffer resounding defeats. Thus, the moderation of demands involves a rational estimate of the balance of gains and losses and the formulation of the most cost-effective strategy. Of course, in some respects Batstone's whole notion of reformist workplace trade unionism and pragmatic bargaining underlines the manner in which shop stewards necessarily operate on a terrain which inevitably involves compromise and trade-offs. As has been mentioned, it is not a question of individual stewards adopting an adversarial *or* a conciliatory stance; most stewards adopt both approaches, depending on the issue and the context, although the balance can vary considerably. However, what the case studies showed is that the adoption of a 'strong bargaining relations' approach by a shop stewards' committee as a whole (or at least its centrally placed stewards) over a prolonged period of time, notwithstanding its supposed 'rationality' and apparent benefits, had serious limitations. These limitations were apparent both in terms of obtaining substantial material improvements in workers' conditions and in terms of maintaining the vitality of workplace union organization.

Obviously, the broader context in which such relations unfold is of some relevance. It is useful to make a comparison between the 1970s and the 1980s. Clearly, there were aspects of 'strong bargaining relations' in both Birds Eye and Ford during the 1970s, but because of managerial intransigence there was little foundation for any deep-rooted accommodation. Instead, amidst a relatively favourable economic and political climate, it was militant shop-floor activity enacted from below (rather than carried out from above) which succeeded in carving out a significant element of counter-control over the immediate work process and providing the basis upon which strong workplace union organization could be built. For example, in Birds Eye it was sectional stoppages of work that achieved improved bonus payments, condition rates and job evaluation, which won the guaranteed working week and May Day holiday, and which prevented the loss of bonus payments when machinery broke down. Such activity also had the merit of forging the strength of the stewards' organization. A similar picture was evident at Ford.

Undoubtedly there were difficulties with this combative approach in both workplaces, relating to the precariousness of some disputes and the volatile, vulnerable and sometimes non-strategic features of workers' self-activity. But overall the setbacks and defeats suffered during this period were not *because* of the relatively oppositional shop-floor approach, but *despite* it. Even in Bemrose, where 'strong bargaining relations' were much more firmly rooted, management were obliged, owing to the peculiar nature of the product and labour markets, to concede very high rates of pay, considerable control over the movement of labour and high manning arrangements, because they feared the shop-floor power of chapel committee organization and the threat or use of sanctions to disrupt production. Nonetheless, whilst 'strong bargaining relations' in these circumstances ensured the balance of workplace power lay to the advantage of the stewards, there was a very low level of struggle and some serious shortcomings in the cohesion of union organization.

Significantly, Batstone appears to have assumed that 'strong bargaining relations' were only to be found where there was a broad balance of power between stewards and managers (Terry, 1986b). In fact, as will have become apparent, similar kinds of relationships can exist not only in situations where the bargaining power of stewards is greater (as in

Bemrose during the 1970s) but also where it is less (as in Birds Eye and Ford during the 1980s). The latter two are particularly significant. Crucially, Batstone failed to take suffcient account of the problems which arise when the institutional framework of bargaining relations becomes insecure or unstable as a result of product market pressures or economic recession (as during the 1980s). Because, in these circumstances, the 'rules of the game' changed, the options open to stewards through shared rules and understandings and 'give and take' were rather different than previously. Relying on 'strong bargaining relations' – whatever its estimate of costs and benefits at one point in time – could no longer be guaranteed to deliver the most cost-effective strategy when judged in terms of the defence of established jobs, working conditions and strong work-place union organization.

As the case studies showed, the consequence of stewards adopting 'strong bargaining relations' during this period invariably meant making wide-ranging concessions to management that would not have been considered in more favourable circumstances. Of course, it was understandable that during the 1980s, faced with the threat of plant closure, some stewards felt it necessary to abandon the comparatively militant strategy of earlier years to adopt a more flexible and co-operative relationship with management. It could be argued that shop-floor militancy was really not an option and could only anyway have had detrimental, if not catastrophic, consequences. By contrast, the stewards' pragmatism was the most realistic strategy, whatever the short-term costs there might have been. Certainly, such pragmatic bargaining provided a number of immediate shop-floor gains, for example in Birds Eye a reduction in the working week, and in Bemrose the parity of craft rates. Moreover, the very fact that jobs were maintained for so long in both plants, and the Ford factory remained open, could perhaps be interpreted as testimony to the success of the strategy overall.

But there is no doubt it also had serious disadvantages. Thus, most of the shop-floor gains were actually double-edged, with the reduction in the working week and parity of craft rates, for example, achieved only through an increase in workers' productivity and an intensification of work effort. It was also a strategy that continued to meet resistance from sections of workers and stewards who appeared to make an important distinction between 'having to compromise', in circumstances that were not exactly favourable to shop-floor union organization, and the active 'celebration of retreat', which embraced a managerial logic to such an extent that it contributed significantly to the demobilization of collective rank-and-file activity and facilitated the disarming of union strength that followed. Thus, the 'strong bargaining relations' strategy threw away some important opportunities for union advance. For example, at Birds Eye it handicapped the stewards' potential ability to utilize the high demand for the MenuMaster range and their control over the new technology substantially to improve wages, manning levels and working conditions. Furthermore, ultimately, in Birds Eye and Bemrose it helped to lull workers into a false sense of job security and ill-prepared them to resist the enforced closures of the two plants.

Moreover, it is important to note that whilst the 'flexible' bargaining strategy adopted by stewards at Birds Eye, Bemrose and Ford has certainly been replicated in many other workplaces across the country during the 1980s, evidence from a few recent studies (Spencer, 1989; Cohen and Fosh, 1988; Heaton and Linn, 1989; Coyne and Williamson, 1991; Fairbrother, 1988, 1989, 1990; Darlington, 1993) has emphasized the resilience and imagination of at least some steward organizations in attempting to respond more assertively to restructuring, the threat of redundancies and new managerial techniques. Although the specific circumstances confronting the stewards in the workplaces examined in these studies differ somewhat from those in Birds Eye, Bemrose and Ford, the overall dilemmas remain the same, and what they demonstrate is the manner in which pushing the frontier of resistance against management can actually be much more advantageous to the defence of workers' interests than a 'strong bargaining relations' approach.

Thus, Spencer's study of workplace unionism in 'Newbrewco' in Merseyside documented the manner in which, despite economic recession, a stewards' organization with a proven record for toughness, an active and involved membership and external links with the wider labour movement was able to retain its considerable bargaining power. Spencer concluded:

> It would be simplistic to assume that because steward organisation is facing major problems like large scale redundancy it is not able to fight on other issues which may be important for the maintenance of site morale. (Spencer, 1985, p. 4)

Heaton and Linn's study of nine manufacturing plants in Humberside revealed how, even where workplace union organization had been initially defeated and the balance of workplace power had shifted sharply towards management, stewards were still able to re-establish themselves. They also showed that whilst the employers' aim may have been to circumvent the stewards and to communicate directly with workers, through such devices as quality circles and team briefings, the outcome of such measures was by no means definite, and could even result in the opposite of that intended.

Coyne and Williamson's study of two workplaces in Merseyside facing major changes in work organization (including the Vauxhall car plant) showed how stewards have developed strategies to counter the effects of new management techniques on their organization, developing a coherent idea of their own members' needs whilst maintaining a healthy cynicism towards management's promises. Fairbrother's studies of the impact of restructuring in some public enterprises and post-privatized industries in the Midlands highlighted the opportunities for a 'renewal' of workplace unionism towards more active and participative forms than previously existed. Darlington's (1993) study of local union organization within the Royal Mail in Liverpool has also underlined the enduring resilience of traditions of collectivism and solidarity. In other words, despite the immense specific obstacles confronting the stewards at Birds Eye, Bemrose and Ford, there is at least some limited evidence from workplaces elsewhere to suggest that their 'pragmatic' strategy – which involved a very high price in terms of the strength of workplace union organization – was not the *only* feasible or 'cost-effective' response that could have been adopted.

Of course, even if it is accepted that the level of resistance might have been somewhat greater, the experience at Birds Eye, Bemrose and Ford could still be interpreted as support for a 'strong bargaining relations' approach. It could be argued that, no matter how structurally strong or militant, the limitation of workplace trade unionism is that it is not in a position to encroach systematically rather than episodically on managerial prerogative, especially when faced with attempting to thwart large-scale redundancies or plant closure. There was the problem of convincing workers that militant resistance could be successful despite managerial threats to close the factories down. There was the impact of economic recession in a region where manufacturing industry was hit disproportionately hard and where the rate of unemployment was consistently higher than the national average. There was the problem of the overall acquiescence to 'new realism' within a generally defensive British labour movement amidst the lack of any wider industrial and political mobilization that could provide a source of external encouragement. There was the problem of attempting to win solidarity action from other plants within the same company to avoid possible isolation and defeat. There was the problem of confronting the cautious preoccupations of full-time union officials.

Nonetheless, arguably there was no *inevitability* about the tyranny of market forces, in the form of corporate restructuring, riding roughshod over shop stewards' organization. It would be mistaken to assume an iron law of development which somehow predetermines how stewards will react. Indeed, the danger of an economically determined view of the power and resources available to stewards is that it disguises the potential for challenge which exists even in a hostile climate. Thus, Ford's climb-down over 'voluntary' compulsory redundancies in 1993, when faced with the threat of (so-called 'old-fashioned') national strike action, was a pointer to the possibilities for a much more belligerent response. Whilst it would be foolhardy to assume outright resistance would have been guaranteed to succeed it is possible industrial action could have significantly influenced and constrained the area of management discretion, both at corporate and plant level. Moreover, even if militant resistance had failed, at the very least the nature and experience of the defeats might have been rather different and a positive tradition of defiance maintained for others to emulate elsewhere.

One intriguing feature of the case studies was the variety of approach towards management adopted by individual convenors and shop stewards within each of the three workplaces. In particular there was a marked division between the relatively adversarial approach of Martin Roberts, Ray and Terry (Birds Eye), Alan Hebden and Mark (Bemrose), and Tony and Billy (Ford) on the one hand, compared with the more conciliatory stance of Steve and Jack Boyle (Birds Eye), Geoff (Bemrose), and Trevor Wilson and Eric Kennedy (Ford) on the other. This naturally raises the crucial question of whether a different *political* leadership within the stewards' bodies could have made a difference to the actual course of events or not, an issue which is explored in more detail in the following section.

As far as the debate on the 'state' of shop steward organization in Britain is concerned, the experience of Ford Halewood during the 1980s and early 1990s would indicate that the substantive nature and strength of stewards' organization has undoubtedly been seriously undermined, with Batstone's notion that 'nothing much has changed' being grossly mistaken. Nonetheless, the process of change has been uneven and has co-existed with important continuities. Not only have management changes usually been introduced through long-standing procedures of collective bargaining but the basic structure of stewards' organization has remained essentially intact. Even if the balance of workplace power has firmly shifted towards management they still feel constraints on their 'right to manage'. Furthermore, not only have many sectional stewards and shop-floor workers resented aspects of the restructuring process but they have been able to resist, amend or undermine managerial initiatives on some occasions and win concessions on others.

Finally, what of the future? Can shop stewards at Ford rebuild a strong workplace union organization and push the balance of workplace power to their advantage? Has the new climate of 'responsible' workplace industrial relations really become ingrained or will it evaporate as the company struggles to maintain momentum in fiercely competitive markets? At Ford the significance of the 1988 national pay strike, as well as the 1991 Assembly plant and 1993 Body plant stoppages, is that they offer a glimpse of how a renewed sense of workers' confidence to fight might be felt at some stage in the future depending on particular, changing, circumstances. Thus, a new car model, an urgent order, or a slight upturn in the British economy and lowering of unemployment could all have the effect of helping to boost workers' bargaining leverage. Similarly, Ford's future attempts to make fundamental changes to work organization could undermine the Halewood convenors' and senior stewards' co-operative relationship, particularly if workers and sectional stewards force the pace from below. In other words, the revitalization of stewards' organization and a return to a much more combative stance in Halewood cannot, by any means, be ruled out. Certainly, there appears to be little justification for assuming the present weaknesses of the stewards' organization will be either permanent or irreversible or that recent changes in shop-floor power necessarily represent a secular transformation towards a 'new industrial relations' rather than largely a cyclical phenomenon (Kelly, 1990).

Stewards' Relationship to Members

A number of commentators have drawn attention to the contrast between 'participatory' and 'representative' forms of democracy in shop stewards' relationship to rank-and-file members (Hyman, 1979; Terry, 1983a). One version of the argument has suggested that during the 1950s and 1960s, stewards were genuine workplace delegates, deeply immersed in the activities and preoccupations of those they represented; policies emerged out of regular discussion and debate within the workplace and stewards were directly accountable to their members, liable to be dismissed in the event of an inadequate performance. By contrast, during the 1970s and 1980s, following the emergence of a lay élite of full-time senior stewards, there was the development of more professional, hierarchical and centralized stewards' organizations which became increasingly differentiated from the members, arising in part from the implementation of the Donovan Commission's recommendations (Hyman, 1979; Terry, 1978, 1983b). What the case study material above would suggest is that tendencies towards democracy and bureaucracy in many respects co-existed with one another throughout both periods, an argument closer to that advanced by other commentators (Fairbrother, 1984; Cohen and Fosh, 1988; Fosh and Cohen, 1990). Thus, as Beynon revealed, even in the heyday of shop-floor militancy at Ford Halewood during the late 1960s, the shop stewards found themselves 'torn between the forces of representation and bureaucratization' (1984, p. 209). But the case studies also suggest it would be mistaken to assume, as Batstone did (Batstone, 1984, 1988b; Batstone and Gourlay, 1986), that 'nothing much has changed', that steward organization today is basically as centralized and 'sophisticated' as it ever was in the past and that the 'bureaucratization of the rank-and-file' thesis (Hyman, 1979) is misconceived. In each of the three workplaces studied it is clear that the relationship between stewards and the members *did* undergo a qualitative shift between the 1970s and 1980s. Arguably, the most important issue is not whether stewards either have a 'representative' or 'participatory' relationship to their members (in Batstone's terms 'leader' or 'populist') but what the balance is at any one time between these two co-existing and contradictory tendencies and what pressures are pushing in each direction.

In both Birds Eye and Ford during the 1970s, there were tendencies towards 'representative' democracy, with senior stewards sometimes using their 'power for' the members as a 'power over' them by restraining workplace militancy (for example, at Birds Eye participating in management's break-up of the powerful cold store department). But the pendulum was pushed much more towards the 'participation' component, partly as a result of the pressure from below, the high level of rank-and-file struggle, itself a response to hard-line management, and partly as a result of the active intervention of stewards bargaining on the shop-floor themselves. Although the steward committees retained a degree of autonomy from the shop-floor, the day-to-day struggle ensured they did not become too isolated from the practical needs of their members. In other words, there was a direct connection between the level of shop-floor confidence, activity and militancy *vis-à-vis* management and the relatively democratic relationship that existed between stewards and their members. There was also a direct link between workplace union democracy and the shop stewards' goals and objectives. The generally combative stance of the stewards encouraged the active participation of rank-and-file members in union affairs in the workplace. Again, the experience in Bemrose was more complex. On the one hand, chapel committee representatives maintained a relatively close and democratic relationship with their members; whilst there was not a high level of struggle there was a lot of confidence on the shop-floor *vis-à-vis* management and there was quite a degree of involvement in chapel and union branch affairs. On the other hand, the sectional nature of chapel organization, underpinned by the 'strong bargaining relationship' established with management, facilitated the development of a highly centralized and semi-bureaucratic form of union leadership concentrated in the hands of the FoCs. But even here there were strong elements of participatory as well as representative democracy.

All this was in sharp contrast to the 1980s, a period when the weight of the relationship between democracy and bureaucracy swung towards the latter component in all three plants. Again, it was possible to see a linkage between the low level of shop-floor confidence, activity and militancy *vis-à-vis* management and the relatively more bureaucratic relationship between the shop stewards and members that ensued. The 'not rocking the boat' stance towards disputes, encouraged by product market crises, dissipated the mood to fight and sapped shop-floor morale and confidence. In the context of rank-and-file demobilization and passivity, stewards became more remote from the direct forms of accountability and democratic scrutiny that had previously prevailed. It was also possible to see a connection between the shop stewards' much narrower goals and horizons and the lack of participation of their members. 'Strong bargaining relations' with management encouraged stewards to act much more on their members' behalf; there was little need to involve them in activity or decision making, and the links binding the stewards to the members were loosened. Again, it was not entirely a one-way process. The stewards still took up members' day-to-day interests and were placed under some scrutiny; and the spontaneous rank-and-file rebellions that erupted from time to time were an important safeguard against an immutable set of bureaucratic features becoming locked into place. Nonetheless, the atrophy of stewards' organization generally proved to be an important handicap to the reinvigoration of a direct form of accountability between stewards and their members.

Although workplace unionism faces both external and internal pressures towards both democracy and bureaucracy, the distinction between a 'representative' and 'participatory' form of relationship between steward bodies and members remains a useful one. For Batstone a 'sophisticated' shop stewards' body is organized on the basis of a layer of 'leader' stewards who owe their position to their knowledge and expertise and who maintain a steady downward flow of communication to the members. In such a workplace the membership at large have very little responsibility for the active development and pursuit of policies or objectives, nor would stewards see any virtue in such involvement. But the case study evidence suggests that without active participation by the members a shop stewards' structure is something of a sham as far as workplace union democracy is concerned. Because the whole logic of trade unionism is collective, workplace union democracy should be a democracy in which everyone is encouraged to take an active part. From this vantage point, a 'participatory' form of union democracy is not some abstract ideal model but the most effective practical route to the development of a strong, independent shop stewards' organization able to obtain real concrete gains for the members and ensure a vibrant form of workplace unionism. Recent research (Cohen and Fosh, 1988; Fosh and Cohen, 1990) has underlined the manner in which a local union leadership style characterized by a commitment to collectivism and members' participation is actually more effective in handling local issues than Batstone's 'top-down' approach. What this involves is not a simplistic model whereby local leaders merely mouth members' aspirations, however unrealistic, but rather an interactive process between local union representatives and members, whereby local leaders to a significant extent mould members' demands, sometimes moderating them and sometimes increasing their scope, but with the main thrust of members' expressed interests taken account of.

Ironically, Hyman's emphasis (1984) on the manner in which bureaucracy pervades trade union practice at every level seems to ignore the fact that democratic relations must be similarly pervasive. Whilst his analysis raises important questions about an understanding of full-time union officialdom which cannot be explored here, it also runs the risk of fatalistically accepting the 'inevitability' of bureaucratization when related to shop stewards' organization. For example, whilst it would be shortsighted to refuse the granting of workplace facilities by management, a variety of means could be adopted to counteract their negative features, such as avoiding where possible all stewards being on 100 per cent release from work, by organizing regular section and mass meetings of the members, and so on. In other words, the balance between 'representative' and 'participatory' forms of workplace unionism is not fixed; it is extremely dynamic.

Another interesting theme evident in the case studies was the way in which in all three workplaces there was a tension between sectional rank-and-file workers' militancy and the shop steward committees' plant-wide strategic perspectives. On the one hand, the strength of workplace union organization arises from sectional power and the battle for workers' immediate day-to-day grievances. On the other hand, there was a need to protect the interests of the majority of workers across the plant as unco-ordinated activity threatens the cohesiveness and bargaining authority of the stewards' body as a whole. Clearly, individual stewards and groups of workers can act in a parochial manner which obstructs the interests of other groups and which precludes the pursuit of issues that require a collective response on the part of the workforce as a whole. Yet the co-ordination of activity by shop steward organization, particularly where senior shop stewards have become divorced from the realities of shop-floor life, can sometimes be a form of hierarchical control. In essence, it raises the question of the relationship between spontaneous shop-floor activity and a collective trade union identity, between sectionalism and generalization, and the often crucial role played by shop stewards.

Certainly, sectionalism represented a major obstacle to a unified and collectivist response to management in all the three workplaces, especially Bemrose. Yet sectionalism was not a predetermined state of affairs, as is sometimes assumed (Terry and Edwards, 1988). On the contrary, the basically antagonistic nature of the labour process gave it a dynamic, uneven and contradictory character, as the shop-floor practice of 'welt working' vividly illustrated. Even though the existence of discrete sections of workers within each plant – divided by the nature of work, by skill, by department, by gender and so on – created the basis for fragmentation and disunity, there were also factors promoting collective trade union attitudes and organization amongst people who worked together and shared common interests (Thompson and Bannon, 1985). Moreover, as Batstone himself revealed, whilst organizational and institutional factors help shape sectional work group behaviour and attitudes, the social networks that inform argument and initiative and through which 'leader' shop stewards promote 'trade union principles' of unity and collective identity are also significant (Batstone *et al.*, 1977, 1978). Batstone's underlying assumption that rank-and-file members are only sectionally orientated, that they require a 'responsible' and 'sophisticated' steward leadership to control and, to some degree, manipulate their undisciplined militancy, was misconceived. But his analysis did have the merit of focusing attention on the relationship between workplace activity, union collectivism and the intervention of shop stewards.

Beynon (1984) also probed the extent to which the shop stewards are the catalysts of collective workplace trade unionism. But compared to Batstone, Beynon had a much more positive view of the contribution made by rank-and-file self-activity. He revealed the dialectical interplay between the day-to-day struggles of shop-floor workers on the one hand, and the distinctive form of 'factory class consciousness' developed by an experienced shop stewards' leadership on the other, that generates a basic collectivism and opposition to management and through which effective workplace union organization is developed and sustained. This involves stewards both 'listening to the lads' and arguing with them, sharing their experiences on the assembly line and giving a lead.

What the case studies confirmed in many respects is the way in which sectional militancy is the bedrock of strong plant-wide stewards' organization. Its success depends upon the ability of stewards building up the power of union organization by fighting over the immediate issues that confront their members and involving them in activity, whilst at the same time forging a sense of collective identity between different sections of workers by linking the grievances of the most confident and best organized with those of the less sure and well organized. For example, at Ford during the 1970s, individual shop stewards 'cut their teeth' on sectional militancy, in the process not only aiding rank-and-file members to carve out some control over the job and bolstering their bargaining authority *vis-à-vis* management, but also strengthening the power and esteem of the stewards' committee within the plant as a whole. A similar picture emerged at Birds Eye. Whilst the push for collective activity of this kind often came from the committed shop steward or left-wing political activist, such minorities were effective in mobilizing the members and overcoming sectionalism only because the conception of a more generalized, class-wide trade unionism was, at least to some degree, part of workers' consciousness. The 'factory class consciousness' in Ford's was one expression of this and the solidarity strikes in Birds Eye were another. Admittedly, such solidaristic sentiments swam alongside and were often in competition with other more limited ideas about work and politics, but it was something that could be appealed to and developed.

However, during the 1980s the Ford stewards' previously generally sympathetic attitude towards sectional militancy evaporated under the policy of co-operation with management. Instead of attempting to link together the uncoordinated stoppages of work that broke out across the plant into a united strategic challenge to management, the stewards adopted a more conciliatory attitude in favour of 'talking out disputes'. This had the effect of isolating and undermining sectional power, and, in the long term, weakening the stewards' organization across the plant. Again, there was a similar picture at Birds Eye. At Bemrose, the isolation of any action to the particular section of an individual chapel merely had the effect of reinforcing departmental and chapel sectionalism, and again it threw away the opportunity of forging shop-floor union links and building up a unified approach towards management. Whilst the lack of such a joint stance in Bemrose may not have appeared to have seriously hampered the power of union organization during the 1970s there is no doubt it underlay the erosion of the strength of the chapels during the 1980s.

Clearly, the contours of workplace struggle are tremendously uneven, so that workers who are passive one day can just as easily be driven to shop-floor militancy another. Management often tries to divide and rule, picking off those troublesome areas which need sorting out at any given time and counting on the passivity of the rest to bludgeon the aggrieved minority into submission. Arguably, the best response to this by shop stewards is not the bureaucratic 'unity of the graveyard' – in which sparks of rank-and-file militancy are immediately extinguished from above – but an attempt to break the sectionalism by spreading the action and involving other groups of workers in fighting together; levelling *upwards* to the active minority rather than *downwards* to the lowest common denominator of the passive majority. In other words, although material and ideological forces within capitalism pull workplace trade unionism towards a limited and sectional horizon, whether or not it stays there is determined to a significant extent by the rhythms of struggle and by the effectiveness of the shop stewards' leadership to which rank-and-file workers are exposed.

Another principal theme explored within the case studies concerned the limitations of the stewards' political horizons and the failure of the left (broadly defined as including those militant trade unionists who held a basic socialist and class commitment without any fixed political affiliation as well as those influenced by either Labour left or revolutionary socialist ideas) to provide a coherent organizational and political alternative to the pragmatism of 'Labourism'. Obviously, there were substantial material obstacles to the translation of shop-floor activism into a broader political (let alone revolutionary socialist) perspective, including internal fragmentation and sectionalism. Yet arguably, the influence of 'mainstream' Labourism, even if not formally embodied in political organization on the shop-floor, was an important factor reinforcing the constraints and compromises of workplace unionism within the three plants. From a reformist perspective Batstone assumed (as do Labour Party leaders and most union officials and shop stewards) that workers can improve their position and obtain reforms within the framework of the capitalist system without directly challenging the nature of that system. Clearly, as long as capitalism seems relatively healthy there is a logic in this, as important concessions can be won through workplace bargaining.

During the 1960s, much workplace militancy did not have a directly political character; at its best there was what Beynon (1984) described as stewards' 'factory class consciousness', a politics essentially limited to the confines of the workplace and not generalized to wider concerns. Only during the early 1970s, amidst the onset of economic crisis, a political offensive by the Conservative government and the rising combativity of the working class movement generally, did the influence of the left grow within the stewards' committees in Birds Eye, Bemrose and Ford (although it remained a minority influence). Whilst a handful of stewards joined small revolutionary socialist organizations, many others, although often to the left of traditional Labourism, tended to separate economics and politics, and operate merely as militant trade unionists in a quasi-syndicalist fashion. This did not prevent them from giving a lead to shop-floor struggles and building up the strength of union organization. In fact, it was often their initiative that pulled other, less militant stewards and members into action. Nonetheless, the advocacy of trade union militancy alone, whilst it tore the veil from the illusion of unanimity, proved to have severe limitations in the recession years of the early 1980s, when the fear of unemployment strengthened management's arguments about the need for 'efficiency' and made workers wary of entering struggles which might threaten the survival of the factory. Certainly, the logic of Labourist and reformist politics in this situation was to hold back from fighting, to seek compromises with management and even to become committed to the strike-free running of the plant (a process which was reinforced by most full-time union officials).

Recent studies by Terry (1989) and Marchington and Parker (1990) have confirmed the manner in which product market crisis can serve to align union concerns with management priorities by providing management with the opportunity to convince workers of the need to make major concessions in working practices as the price of plant survival. However, the argument has to be made in particular circumstances, which however favourable to some outcomes rather than others is by no means necessarily an inevitable process. It would be mistaken to underestimate completely the part that conscious intervention by individual militant stewards, capable of arguing with their fellow workers and pressing a course of action different to that proposed by the pragmatists, was able to play (for example, within the three-shift area in Birds Eye).

Throughout the 1980s sections of workers in all three workplaces sometimes showed a readiness to oppose management, even if their opposition often took the form of passive resistance. What they tended to lack was the crucial subjective element needed to turn a defensive action into an offensive one. Ironically, some of those stewards, like Jack Boyle in Birds Eye, who subsequently complained of workers' unwillingness to fight, were not entirely free of responsibility for this. Workers' activity is not like a revolver that can be kept unused for years in the leaders' pockets and then taken out and fired at will. To overcome the inertia, in part the product of lack of confidence and the debilitating effect of 'leave it to us' leadership, workers had to have confidence in themselves and in the stewards who organized and led them. In many respects, neither union officialdom nor Labour Party leadership could be relied upon to provide the catalyst for this vital self-activity of workers. But arguably, the left shop stewards also failed to provide the type of alternative political leadership that might, potentially, have influenced a much wider number of workers and drawn them into struggle. Whilst the case study material provides no strong positive evidence to substantiate such an assertion, it seems reasonable to point to the very real possibilities that existed for pushing the limits of workers' resistance much further than actually happened, although what is undoubtedly more speculative is whether the existence of sizeable groupings of revolutionary socialists in each of the three workplaces would have made any fundamental difference to the actual outcome of events. Despite the fact that empirically the case studies provide no basis for a definitive answer to this question, an exploration of the issue is both justifiable and necessary.

Some attention has already been given to the question of socialist organization and the role of various political groupings, an aspect of workplace unionism which many commentators often treat only in passing and with disdain, and which Batstone's work tended to ignore. Yet, at the very least, the case studies signalled the way in which the political inclinations of individual shop stewards can be an extremely influential, although by no means an exclusive, factor shaping the nature of workplace relations. Thus, it is no coincidence that some of the main individuals who sustained and developed shop-floor union activities in all three workplaces were committed socialists of one description or another. Inevitably this raises the broader question of whether the isolation and weakness of socialist organization made a crucial difference to the outcome of workers' struggles.

During the 1970s, the 'vacuum on the left' in Merseyside, created by the relative weakness of the Communist Party's base in the region, was not filled by the small revolutionary socialist organizations, which despite some influence remained quite small and marginalized. During the 1980s, the downturn in struggle further isolated the left. On occasions the approach of some frustrated workplace militants contributed to their own isolation. Thus, in Ford the left was never particularly strong, although it did have a base within both the Body and Assembly plant stewards' committees. In Birds Eye, the influence of the left was much more evident, albeit isolated within the three-shift area during the 1980s. Only in Bemrose was the left more firmly rooted, at least within the SOGAT chapel, and in a more advantageous position to help shape the course of events. Yet in none of the three plants was there a sufficiently coherent group with the ideological and political resources that might, potentially, have enthused workers to fight back.

Of course, it is clear that whatever the political complexion of the shop stewards' leadership, the obstacles to a more combative and successful challenge to managerial plans were immense. The problem of a purely plant-based locus of action and the absence of mass political mobilization inside the British labour movement more generally were graphically exposed. But to acknowledge the immense obstacles is not necessarily to reject the possibilities that might have existed for mounting some effective rearguard action which could potentially have significantly altered shop-floor developments, albeit only temporarily. Certainly, this was an inter-pretation drawn by some stewards, if only a minority, who pointed to the manner in which the 'pragmatic' strategy was actually implemented in practice.

For example, at Bemrose, whilst Mark acknowledged the necessity for compromise and organized tactical retreat (which maintaining basic trade union principles intact) he believed this should have been done on the basis of not denying the consequences of this for union organization and by attempting to claw back lost ground by seeking to raise the level of resistance whenever opportunities arose or circumstances became more favourable. Thus, whilst he accepted that generating militant resistance to the redundancy package in 1987 was problematic, he recognized how a rearguard action over the company's use of TNT transport could have rekindled some confidence, which in turn might have created the momen-tum for a fightback over jobs. By contrast, stewards such as Jack Boyle in Birds Eye saw the need for compromise quite differently, effectively making a virtue out of necessity by stamping out any sparks of workers' militancy, ideologically accepting the parameters set by management and actively collaborating to win workers' consent to managerial objectives; at the same time, presenting all of this as an advance of workers' interests.

In some respects Jack Boyle from Birds Eye and Mark from Bemrose personify the difference between a *reformist* and *revolutionary socialist* perspective within the workplace. Even if this distinction is somewhat less sharply polarized in the case of the independent or non-aligned socialists such as Tony (Ford), some of the Labour left activists such as Martin Roberts (Birds Eye) and Alan Hebden (Bemrose), and some of the quasi-syndicalist stewards such as Ray and Terry (Birds Eye), it does help focus attention on the contrasting types of political approach adopted. Significantly, the differences between shop stewards like Jack Boyle and Mark revolve not merely around ultimate objectives, such as the type of society desired, but also concern day-to-day practical questions of strategy and tactics on the shop-floor. In particular, they are reflected in the distinctive approach each has to the struggle for reforms, in demands for better wages, improved working conditions and job security. 'Reformism' of the shop-floor variety is a difficult phenomenon to pin down because it is defined by its internal contradictions. It expresses a complex mixture of opposites, contesting some of the effects of management power, usually through reasoned argument and 'strong bargaining relations' although on occasion through shop-floor mobilization, whilst simultaneously accommodating to capitalist power in general, by invariably containing protest and opposition within the established 'rules of the game'. Herein lies the essence of reformist workplace trade unionism, namely the attempt to reconcile the antagonistic interests of management and workers, exemplified in many respects by Batstone's model of 'sophisticated' shop steward organization.

By contrast, the revolutionary socialist shop steward believes the interests of workers and management are incompatible and is concerned above all to build strong workplace organization and to encourage the development of a combative rank-and-file, on the basis that the more confident workers are the more likely they are to reject managerial ideas and to embrace class-wide, socialist arguments which can help advance both the immediate fightback and the struggle to transform society. Thus, the struggle for reforms is viewed as a means by which workers can build the organization, consciousness and confidence to challenge and ultimately overthrow the capitalist system. From this perspective – emphasizing the pivotal role of the self-activity of workers – the active co-operation of shop stewards with wide-ranging changes in flexibility and job loss to make a factory 'efficient' involves a disabling compromise. The alternative is being prepared to acknowledge the need for compromise and retreat, particularly in unfavourable objective circumstances, but not by hiding or minimizing the consequences of this from rank-and-file workers or abandoning attempts to raise ideological and political opposition and encouraging shop-floor resistance whenever opportunities allow.

The distinction between a reformist and a revolutionary socialist approach in the workplace is important. Of course, in practice some individual stewards may vacillate between the two positions and, depending on the specific issue and circumstances, quite different types of steward may appear to act in similar ways on occasions. Nonetheless, in broad terms the distinction is important because it poses the question as to whether a sizeable and organized group of revolutionary socialists might have been able to have exercised a decisive, and rather more successful, influence on the activities and struggles of shop-floor workers than otherwise was the case. Even if, ultimately, it would not have changed the outcome of events it might have made the critical task of challenging the influential role played by full-time union officials somewhat easier.

Stewards' Relationship to Full-Time Union Officials

Batstone and Gourlay (1986) emphasized the mutual interdependence between shop stewards and full-time union officials which ensures there is no real divorce between a 'democratic' workplace union organization and a 'bureaucratic' official trade union machine. Despite sources of conflict, concerning their contrasting definition of members' interests and responsibilities for achieving objectives, there is broad agreement on general goals and 'trade union principles'. Ironically, whilst Hyman (1979) has insisted that the presentation of the relationship in terms of a dichotomy between the 'bureaucracy' (signified by a stratum of full-time union officials) and 'rank and file' (workplace members and their shop stewards) is 'absurdly oversimplified', it is doubtful whether Batstone would even have accepted Hyman's own more qualified notion of bureaucracy as 'a set of social relations that permeate the practice of trade unionism' (Hyman, 1979, p. 181).

It will have become evident that the accommodative and bureaucratic tendencies that are sometimes identified simplistically only with full-time national union officials actually operate in different forms and to different degrees at all levels in the representational structure of trade union organization – affecting local full-time union officials, convenors and even sectional shop stewards. Nonetheless, the failure common to many commentators (Roberts, 1976; Kelly, 1988; Watson, 1988; Heery and Kelly, 1990) to acknowledge the existence of a distinct and basically conservative social formation inside the unions, whose material position and social relations provide a set of interests qualitatively different from and opposed to those of the mass of their members, ignores some of the most fundamental features of the relationship between convenors and shop stewards on the one hand, and full-time union officials, both local and national, on the other. A few general observations can be drawn from the case study material underlining the limitations of prevailing conceptual frameworks.

To begin with, there are the underlying contradictory tendencies towards independence and dependence which can radically alter the character of stewards' relationship to union officials. This is particularly evident in the case of stewards' relationship to *national* full-time union officials. Thus, in all three workplaces during the 1970s, although there were aspects of both independence and dependence the balance was undoubtedly tilted towards the former. The study by Boraston *et al.* (1975) identified a number of factors which might affect the degree of independence from, or reliance on, full-time officials, including the size of the workplace, the cohesion and experience of the membership, and the scope and structure of collective bargaining. Whilst these were significant the most important factor encouraging a relatively independent relationship to full-time national union officials in Birds Eye and Ford was the high level of shop-floor militancy and the stewards' committees' combative approach to management. Such rank-and-file confidence and activity boosted the strength of stewards' organization and encouraged the degree of self-reliance and initiative which acted as an important counterweight to the sometimes restraining influence of officials. Similarly in Bemrose, although there was little overt shop-floor militancy, the powerful bargaining strength *vis-à-vis* management buttressed the chapel committees' relatively independent stance towards both branch and national officials.

By contrast, in all three plants during the 1980s, economic recession, threats of factory closure and the stewards' co-operative relationships with management sapped workplace militancy, undermined stewards' ability to act autonomously of the officials and resulted in a more formalized and dependent relationship towards them. Even though the tradition of acting semi-independently was not entirely lost, the national officials' 'new realist' philosophy played a key role in encouraging stewards to adopt conciliatory bargaining relations with management on the basis that industrial militancy had become outmoded and counter-productive in the changed economic and political climate. The Ford stewards' backing for official union 'scabbing' on striking craft workers in 1990 showed the extent of this dependence. Certainly, the gap between the convenors and full-time union officials sometimes became blurred at Ford.

Nonetheless, it is significant that the political shift to the right amongst national union officials during the 1980s, on occasion and over some issues, went so far as to create a gap which could be exploited by militant initiative from below. An example of this was the way union officials concluded a 'final' pay settlement with Ford in 1988 only to be wrong-footed by rank-and-file militancy. This created a situation which allowed a minority of shop-floor activists temporarily to seize the advantage. It showed the way in which unofficial action and organization could begin to emerge when the officials failed to respond to growing anger amongst the members. However, it also showed how such organization was shaped by the influence of 'new realism' inside the trade union movement. This allowed the officials to regain control over the union organization, switching from opposition to strike action to supporting action, but on their terms and under their direction, enabling the officials to defuse the initial surges of militancy and to isolate and demoralize the activists. Despite this, it also suggested that in the future it may be possible for workers' struggle to escape the control of officials in ways which a revitalized stewards' organization could potentially exploit.

Batstone failed to acknowledge how often, despite close ties of sentiment and practice, differences between stewards (and convenors) and full-time officials over policy issues and objectives arise because stewards tend to assign primacy to substantive interests, wages, conditions and job security, whilst the officials tend to be much more concerned with procedural issues such as the preservation of stable bargaining relations with management and the organizational interests of the union machine. Thus, at Bemrose during the 1970s, this conflict of interests was apparent in the contrast between the SOGAT chapel's ability to use its workplace bargaining strength to win extremely advantageous wages and conditions and the minimal role played by union officials (both local and national), which had the effect of threatening the officials' *raison d'être*, authority and self-esteem in the eyes of chapel members (and other union members across the country). Matters were eventually brought to a head in the 1980s over contrasting attitudes towards shop-floor manning levels and the need for flexible working practices, which resulted in the expulsion of Alan Hebden from SOGAT and his removal as FoC.

At Birds Eye, the union officials' instruction to stewards to accept what amounted to capitulation terms for a return-to-work agreement to end management's lock-out in 1977 was another example of a fundamental divergence of interest. At stake for the officials was the fear of a loss of union membership through plant closure combined with a desire to end a protracted dispute that was embarrassing to the union's local and national credibility. But for the stewards involved, it was a question of attempting to maintain shop-floor workers' conditions and union organization intact. Again, when the plant was threatened with closure in the late 1980s, although the stewards went along with the officials' muted strategy of resistance it was ultimately *they* and not the officials who paid the price in terms of jobs.

It should be noted there were some distinctions between officials at *national* and *local* level and between *left*-wing and *right*-wing officials. Thus at Birds Eye, the stewards' attitude towards local officials was much less antagonistic than to national officials. While local officials were involved in corporate union–company bargaining that usually secured poor pay deals, their involvement was merely in an advisory capacity, unlike national officials, who played a key role in negotiations. At the same time, it was because local officials were much less physically removed from the stewards' workplace organization and were usually more susceptible to pressure. Often they were themselves ex-shop stewards who retained close links with the local labour movement. By contrast, national officials were invariably more remote and likely to be more concerned with the interests of the institutional security of the union and the maintenance of a con- ciliatory relationship with the company; hence the TGWU regional organizer's ambivalent attitude to his union's instruction to return to work to end management's lock-out. Indeed, the local official during the late 1970s, Phil Donovan, was a left-winger who was very supportive of the stewards. But even a sympathetic left-wing local official was no guarantee of the defence of workers' specific and immediate interests, as the stewards' subsequent reliance on Kevin Dobson's flawed strategy of opposition to plant closure demonstrated.

Finally, Batstone completely ignored the problem of how shop stewards often need to contest and overcome the damaging role of full-time union officials. In all three workplaces during the 1980s the weight of the official union machinery was consistently placed on the stewards to encourage them to collaborate with managerial drives for efficency. It exposed in sharp relief how building the strength and independence of workplace union organization does not mean absolving official union leaders of all responsibility for the conduct of affairs. However, although the left stewards subjected the officials to sharp criticism they tended merely to dismiss them as a reactionary bloc instead of placing concrete demands on them which could have focused attention on how to take the struggle forward. For example, if the more militant stewards at Birds Eye had demanded that Kevin Dobson and the national officials call for immediate strike action to resist the threat of plant closure, it is possible that under some pressure he and they might have responded. It is also possible that the workforce by this time was so demoralized that they would have rejected this approach. However, the point is that the stance by the national officials precluded the democratic possibility of workers support- ing action or pursuing some alternative.

The placing of demands on the officials would have fitted the situation where there was a fine balance between the widespread shop-floor anger at the company's plan to shut the plant and the lack of confidence to take the initiative in fighting back. Even though they might have only acted half-heartedly, a campaigning lead from the officials might have provided the potential basis upon which stewards could have won the arguments for strike action. If the officials had not responded to such calls for action, at the very least the making of the demand would have revealed their unwillingness to fight and would have justifiably placed the main responsibility for the defeat of the campaign against closure not on the members but on ineffectual official union leadership. This argument has much broader implications, not only in terms of the lack of fightback within all the three workplaces but also across the British working class movement generally during the 1980s. Arguably, notwithstanding the hostile economic and political climate, it was the consistent refusal of the national trade union leadership to rally and co-ordinate the forces of organized labour, above all during the miners' strike of 1984–85, which led to a number of unnecessary defeats of workers' struggles and seriously weakened workplace union organization.

Significantly, Spencer's study (1989) of workplace trade unionism in three Liverpool workplaces emphasized the importance of shop stewards' links with the official structures of trade unions to ensure support for any possible action undertaken at workplace level. Although acknowledging many of the problems of bureaucratic union officialdom, he maintained that, as long as stewards can influence union policy and as long as unions are prepared to decentralize some of their decision making, stewards are best served by making demands on official union structures whilst simultaneously building horizontal links with other stewards' organizations. Whilst his analysis has the merit of focusing attention on how pressure can be exerted not only *downwards* from union officials to workplace union organization but also *upwards*, his assumption that stewards can continue to provide effective resistance to management by mutually supportive trade union action does not deal with the basically antagonistic structural and ideological linkages between stewards and full-time officials. Unfortunately, he falls into the error made by Batstone, namely liquidating the whole concept of bureaucratization so as to render the term virtually meaningless. Yet not only does this obscure the real conflicts of interest inside the unions, it also effectively lets union officials completely off the hook.

Whilst Beynon (1984) is justified in attempting to locate the 'sell-out' of union officials within the wider context of the dilemmas of workplace trade unionism under capitalism, this should not, as could be implied, mean fatalistically accepting the behaviour of officials and ignoring strategies which, to an important extent, could begin to transcend their limitations. In this context, even Fairbrother's identification (Fairbrother 1990; Fairbrother and Waddington, 1990) of a tension between bureaucratically effective forms of unionism at national level and those based on collective participation at workplace level fails to address the ways and means by which this tension might be overcome, as well as underestimating the importance of full-time officials in defining the contours within which any potential 'renewal' and revitalization of workplace unionism might take place.

Rebuilding Strong Stewards' Organization

Finally, some general implications can be drawn from this study. Although the basic structure of shop stewards' organization at Ford Halewood in the early 1990s remained intact, the picture was qualified by the experience of cumulative retreat which sapped the ability of rank-and-file workers to respond to the threats they faced. The comparatively much stronger stewards' organization of the 1970s was forged through struggle, small victories which consolidated workplace union organization, in which the members played an active role. By the early 1990s any disputes that may emerge come after years of demoralization and will require a reforging of workplace-based union organization. Hence the contradiction between the occasional sparks of workers' militancy and the continued dominance of the ideas of 'new realism'. This means that the job of rebuilding the strength of stewards' organization, of raising the level of self-confidence and workplace union democracy, is likely to be a long, hard haul in Ford (and within the British labour movement more generally).

Arguably, the best defence of workers' interests is strong workplace union organization which, despite the need for compromise, is both willing and able to engage in militant struggle against management. To secure the involvement of their members, stewards have to be fully accountable – by means of full report-backs of negotiations with management, by regular section and mass meetings, and by working alongside their members rather than relying upon 100 per cent time off work (except possibly for one or two senior stewards). Nonetheless, a revitalization of stewards' organization is likely to come most effectively through workplace struggle. This underlines the task of restoring morale and rebuilding an organized core of opposition on the shop-floor, by putting management regularly to the test within each section, and by recognizing that in the course of struggle it is possible for an active minority to overcome the unevenness in organization and ideas and to lead the less active majority. From this vantage point every issue needs to be approached with the aim of raising the level of rank-and-file self-activity and increasing the extent to which the fight of a section is generalized across the plant as a whole, whilst constantly looking beyond the factory gate to the struggles of other workers elsewhere. It means recognizing that neither relying on full-time union officials (even left-wing officials) nor condemning them out of hand is a substitute for relatively independent stewards' organization able to use the union leaders when they issue a call for action and to tackle them when they refuse to fight – a strategy of working with the officials at the same time as being prepared, if necessary, to work against them.

The question of political organization and consciousness is also of paramount importance. Arguably, as long as the shop stewards' political horizons are limited within the dominant tradition of Labourism their ability to make fundamental advances in workers' interests is likely to be severely hampered. Certainly, Batstone's 'strong bargaining relations' model of shop stewards' organization is an essentially reformist perspective which merely serves to reinforce the limitations and compromises of workplace unionism within capitalist society. But even some of the alternative left-wing models of workplace unionism which have been offered are problematic in terms of providing a sufficent basis for revitalizing stewards' organization. Thus, Fairbrother's syndicalist-type perspective on local union democracy and membership activism (Fairbrother 1989, 1990; Fairbrother and Waddington, 1990), echoed in the above case studies by a layer of the most active stewards tending to separate economics and politics, avoids the issue of how to counter the influence of the union officials and Labour Party leadership. Ironically, Militant's strategy in Bemrose highlighted the opposite danger, of looking to short-cut solutions, such as concentrating on capturing control of the lower echelons of the union machine and of attempting to make the Labour Party a vehicle for working class advance, to the neglect of independent workplace activity and political organization. Even Beynon's celebration of shop-floor militancy in Ford (1984) provides no real indication of how the shop stewards' 'factory class consciousness' might be broadened into a more 'class-conscious' perspective. By contrast, the case studies could be interpreted as signalling, even if they provide little direct positive confirmation of, the need for revolutionary socialist organization which is able to link broad socialist arguments with a practical day-to-day shop-floor strategy that can successfully challenge the influence of reformist leaders and provide an alternative political pole of attraction to workers. Although the Upper Clyde Shipbuilders work-in in the early 1970s occurred in quite different circumstances (and under the influence of a Communist Party imbued with the tradition of Stalinism), the study by Foster and Woolfson (1986) has the merit of showing the relevance of a network of workplace militants linked to socialist organization. A more recent study of the 1984–85 miners' strike (Green, 1990) reinforces the point.

In conclusion, the experience of Ford Halewood suggests that the legacy of the past decade or more will not be washed away overnight and that the 'strong bargaining relations' approach shared by the majority of shop stewards will continue to act to constrict the development of future workers' struggles. Even amidst a painstakingly slow revival of confidence, the old traditions of sectionalism and reliance on union officials will also cause difficulties for socialist militants who try to capitalize on workers' resistance. But it is possible that during the 1990s the mood of shop-floor bitterness against the previous years of work intensification, vented through spontaneous rebellions, could provide revolutionary socialists with a few inches more elbow room to gain the sort of influence that might play a decisive role in the long term.

APPENDIX 1: THE INTERVIEWEES

All the interviewees have been given pseudonyms, as have most other individuals who appear in the text, except for some of known national significance: for example, company chairmen, full-time national union leaders and one or two other individuals.

Birds Eye

CAROLE: TGWU member in two-shift area of Unit 2 department.

HARRY: TGWU member in engineering department.

MARION: TGWU member in beefburger/steaklet department.

PETER: TGWU branch secretary and shop steward in butchery department.

RAY: TGWU shop steward in three-shift area of Unit 2 department.

RITCHIE: TGWU shop steward in three-shift area of Unit 2 department.

STEVE: TGWU deputy convenor and shop steward in two-shift area of Unit 2 department.

TERRY: TGWU member in three-shift area of Unit 2 department (and shop steward for two years).

TOMMY: TGWU member in two-shift area of Unit 2 department.

Other Important Persons Referred to:

JACK BOYLE: TGWU convenor, 1980s.

KEVIN DOBSON: TGWU local official, late 1980s.

MARTIN ROBERTS: TGWU convenor, 1970s.

PHIL DONOVAN: TGWU local official, mid-1970s to mid-1980s.

SIMON KING: TGWU convenor, 1976.

Bemrose

ALAN HEBDEN: SOGAT chapel FoC; president of Merseyside SOGAT branch.

BILL: NGA '82 process chapel FoC; chairperson of federated chapel.

GEOFF: NGA machine chapel FoC.

MARK: SOGAT committee member in machine room; secretary of federated chapel.

PAT: SOGAT committee member in finishing department.

ROB BAKER: SOGAT committee member in finishing department; secretary of federated chapel.

PETER: SOGAT member in machine room.

VAL: SOGAT member in finishing department.

Other important persons referred to:

WILL FOWLER: NGA Liverpool full-time branch secretary.

STUART HENDERSON: SOGAT Merseyside full-time branch secretary.

TONY MULHEARN: NGA composing room deputy FoC.

Ford

BILLY: TGWU member, Assembly plant.

BRIAN: MSF senior steward, Assembly plant.

DAVE: TGWU senior shop steward, Assembly plant.

FRANK: TGWU member, Body plant.

JIMMY: TGWU senior shop steward, Body plant.

JOHN: TGWU senior shop steward, Assembly plant.

PAUL: TGWU senior steward, Body plant.

PHIL: TGWU convenor, Assembly plant, 1968–70.

TONY: TGWU senior steward and chairperson of Body plant shop stewards' committee.

EMPLOYEE RELATIONS MANAGER: Body plant.

EMPLOYEE RELATIONS MANAGER: Paint shop, Assembly plant.

SENIOR EMPLOYEE RELATIONS MANAGER: Body plant.

PRODUCTION MANAGER: Trim Assembly, Assembly plant.

Other important persons referred to:

ERIC KENNEDY: TGWU Assembly plant convenor, 1987 onwards.

KEITH HARDCASTLE: Body plant convenor, 1980–83.

TREVOR WILSON: TGWU Assembly plant convenor, 1970–87.

APPENDIX 2: THE FIELDWORK

Introduction

The bulk of my research material was obtained during 1988–93 through extensive semi-structured tape-recorded interviews with a number of strategically placed informants in all three plants, mainly shop stewards and rank-and-file union members but also managers and local full-time union officials. Such interviews often involved discussion and questioning that lasted two hours or more. This was supplemented by detailed analysis of a range of documentary and secondary material.

Birds Eye

Unfortunately, despite repeated formal approaches, it appears that the top-level decision by Unilever to close the Birds Eye plant provided the local management with the pretext to refuse point-blank to grant access or offer me assistance of any kind whatsoever for my research. Instead, I had to rely upon informal approaches to sympathetic trade union 'insiders' able to facilitate the process of 'getting in' (Buchanan *et al.*, 1986). It was the subsequent three-month campaign launched by the shop stewards' committee against the factory's closure that enabled me to establish a close relationship with a number of leading shop stewards and union activists, which was not only of tremendous assistance in reconstructing an account from one set of combatants but also in helping to fill in some of the gaps their protagonists left.

I was allowed to observe a number of mass meetings of the union membership during the campaign against closure, invited to weekly meetings of the Birds Eye Support Group from which stewards and rank-and-file union members built up shop-floor and community resistance to the shutdown, and provided with invaluable chronological and documentary material in the form of meticulously kept minute books of the shop stewards' committee and the TGWU branch and branch committee, stretching from the period of 1960 right up until 1989. It was from such close collaboration that I was able to carry out in-depth interviews with a number of the key 'actors' (although not, despite repeated promises, with the convenor, Jack Boyle).

Bemrose

In researching into Bemrose I was provided with some access to minute books of the SLADE and NGA '82 process chapels, to house agreements of both the SLADE and the federated chapel, as well as a variety of union, federated chapel and company documents. Again, repeated requests to interview industrial relations managers were turned down; it seems that although individual plant managers would have been happy enough to assist my research News International was not, and the parent company's disposition prevailed. Despite these obstacles I attempted, so far as was possible, to reconstruct the rationale behind management's policy towards workplace union organization.

Because of the complexity of the trade union organization in Bemrose attention was concentrated on the SOGAT chapel committee. On the one hand, any understanding of shop-floor industrial relations in Bemrose requires a consideration of *all* the major separate chapels, and this is something I attempted to do, particularly in terms of their relationship to management (excluding the NGA composing chapel, which was disbanded in the early 1980s). On the other hand, it proved useful to narrow the focus of inquiry so as to provide the necessary flesh to the bones of an account of chapel committee organization. My choice of the SOGAT chapel was made for a variety of reasons. Firstly, SOGAT consistently organized the largest number of workers in the plant. Prior to the 1987 redundancy exercise SOGAT had over 700 members, compared with the NGA '82 process chapel's 225 and the NGA '82 machine chapel's 185. Secondly, the SOGAT chapel, unlike any other, had members in every department of the factory, which provided its members with an invaluable overview of developments across the plant as a whole. Thirdly, in the course of my research, I found within the SOGAT chapel a wider pool of experienced union activists, both able and willing to be interviewed, than existed in other chapels. Fourthly, I discovered that developments inside the plant had a dramatic impact on the SOGAT chapel committee which helped to illuminate the underlying processes at work generally. Finally, unlike the other chapels, SOGAT organized the non-craft and unskilled workers and was most akin to the shop-floor production workers examined in the two other case studies.

Ford

Ford granted me permission to visit the Halewood complex in 1988 and 1989 to conduct interviews with some employee relations managers from both the Body and Assembly plants, as well as some senior shop stewards. In addition, in-depth interviews with a cross-section of union representatives and members were conducted outside of working hours between 1988 and 1993. This was supplemented by analysis of secondary material (much more of which was available than for the two previous case studies, particularly in relation to managerial strategy).

Of course, the research into the Halewood plant is greatly indebted to the pioneering study of managerial control and shop-floor challenge conducted during the late 1960s by Huw Beynon (1984) and draws substantially on his analytical approach. However, I have sought to provide a much more detailed account of the underlying processes and key events that occurred during the mid- to late 1970s – the period that immediately followed the era described in the first edition of Beynon's book (1973) and which is only briefly commented upon in his second edition (1984). In documenting the most recent events of the late 1980s and early 1990s I have extended the account beyond even Beynon's updated edition, providing a useful basis from which to place contemporary trends within their historical context. Significantly, Beynon chose a methodological device that utilized the stewards' organization and consciousness as a 'prism' through which the broader dynamic of class relations could be focused and understood. It is this which provided the basis for the close analytical symmetry between his own account and the perspectives of the stewards (Elger, 1986). By contrast, I have attempted to stand far more detached from the senior stewards' vantage point in assessing the overlapping, but sometimes contrary, concerns of stewards and their members. Finally, I have endeavoured to draw out the wider analytical implications of my empirical material more explicitly, for example in terms of the relationship between the volatile nature of rank-and-file sectional activity and the coherence of the stewards' strategic perspective (providing some comparative assessment in Chapter 7).

BIBLIOGRAPHY

Ackers, P. and Black, J. (1992) 'Watching the detectives: shop stewards' expectations of their managers in the age of human resource management', in *Skill and Consent: Contemporary Studies in the Labour Process*, eds A. Sturdy, D. Knights and H. Willmott, London: Routledge, pp. 185–212.

Anderson, P. (1967) 'Limits and possibilities of trade union action', in *The Incompatibles*, eds R. Blackburn and A. Cockburn, London: Penguin, pp. 263–80.

Aughton, P. (1990) *Liverpool: A People's History*, Preston: Carnegie Press.

Barker, C. (ed.) (1987) *Revolutionary Rehearsals*, London: Bookmarks.

Bassett, P. (1986) *Strike-Free: New Industrial Relations in Britain*, London: Macmillan.

Batstone, E. (1984) *Working Order: Workplace Industrial Relations over Two Decades*, Oxford: Blackwell.

Batstone, E. (1985) 'The durability of the British shop steward', *Personnel Management*, October, pp. 46–8.

Batstone, E. (1986) 'Bureaucracy, oligarchy and incorporation in shop steward organisations in the 1980s', in *Technological Change, Rationalisation and Industrial Relations*, ed. O. Jacobi *et al.*, London: Croom Helm, pp. 137–60.

Batstone, E. (1988a) 'The frontier of control', in *Employment in Britain*, ed. Duncan Gallie, Oxford: Blackwell.

Batstone, E. (1988b) *The Reform of Workplace Industrial Relations*, Oxford: Clarendon Press.

Batstone, E., Boraston, I. and Frenkel, S. (1977) *Shop Stewards in Action*, Oxford: Blackwell.

Batstone, E., Boraston, I. and Frenkel, S. (1978) *The Social Organization of Strikes*, Oxford: Blackwell.

Batstone, E. and Gourlay, S. (1986) *Unions, Unemployment and Innovation*, Oxford: Blackwell.

Bean, R. and Stoney, P. (1986) 'Strikes on Merseyside', *Industrial Relations Journal*, Vol. 17, No. 1, pp. 9–23.

Beaumont, P. B. (1987) *The Decline of Trade Union Organisation*, London: Croom Helm.

Belchem, J. (1992) 'Introduction: the peculiarities of Liverpool', in *Popular Politics, Riot and Labour: Essays in Liverpool History 1790–1940*, ed. J. Belchem, Liverpool: Liverpool University Press, pp. 1–20.

Beynon, H. (1973) *Working for Ford* (first edition), Harmondsworth: Penguin.

Beynon, H. (1979) *What Happened at Speke?* TGWU 6–612 Branch, Merseyside.

Beynon, H. (1984) *Working for Ford* (second edition), Harmondsworth: Pelican.

Beynon, H. (1987) 'Closures: the threat and the future for Labour', in *The Politics of Industrial Closure*, eds T. Dickson and D. Judge, Basingstoke: Macmillan, pp. 96–115.

Beynon, H., Hudson, R. and Sadler, D. (1991) *A Tale of Two Industries: The Contraction of Coal and Steel in the North-East of England*, Milton Keynes: Open University Press.

Blyton, P. and Turnbull, P. (1992) *Reassessing Human Resource Management*, London: Sage.

Boraston, I. G., Clegg, H. A. and Rimmer, M. (1975) *Workplace and Union*, London: Heinemann.

Broad, G. (1983) 'Shop steward leadership and the dynamics of workplace industrial relations', in *Industrial Relations Journal*, Vol. 14, No. 3, pp. 59–67.

Brown, W. (ed.) (1981) *The Changing Contours of British Industrial Relations*, Oxford: Blackwell.

Brown, W. (1983) 'Britain's unions: new pressures and shifting loyalties', *Personnel Management*, October, pp. 48–51.

Buchanan, D., Boddy, D. and McCalman, J. (1986) 'Getting In, Getting Out and Getting Back', in *Doing Research in Organizations*, ed. A. Bryman, London: Routledge, pp. 53–67.

Buroway, M. (1985) *Politics of Production*, London: Verso.

CAITS (1986) *Flexibility: Who Needs It?*, London: Polytechnic of North London.

CAITS (1988) 'Teamworking: same as employee involvement but worse', TGWU 1/1107 Branch.

Callinicos, A. (1982) 'The rank and file movement today', *International Socialism*, Vol. 2, No. 17, pp. 1–38.

Callinicos, A. and Simons, M. (1985) *The Great Strike: The Miners' Strike of 1984–85 and Its Lessons*, London: Socialist Workers Party.

Cavendish, R. (1982) *Women on the Line*, London: Routledge & Kegan Paul.

Chadwick, M. G. (1983) 'The recession and industrial relations: a factory approach', *Employee Relations*, Vol. 5, No. 5, pp. 5–12.

Clarke, T. and Clements, L. (eds) (1977) *Trade Unions under Capitalism*, Glasgow: Fontana/Collins.

Cliff, T. (1970) *The Employers' Offensive: Productivity Deals and How to Fight Them*, London: Pluto Press.

Cliff, T. (1979) 'The balance of class forces in recent years', *International Socialism*, Vol. 2, No. 6, pp. 1–50.

Cliff, T. and Gluckstein, D. (1986) *Marxism and Trade Union Struggle: The General Strike of 1926*, London: Bookmarks.

Coates, D. (1984) *The Context of British Politics*, London: Hutchinson.

Coates, D. (1989) *The Crisis of Labour: Industrial Relations and the State in Contemporary Britain*, Oxford: Philip Allan.

Cohen, S. and Fosh, P. (1988) *You Are the Union: Trade Union Workplace Democracy*, Studies for Trade Unionists, Vol. 14, No. 53, London: Workers' Educational Association.

Coyne, G. and Williamson, H. (1991) *New Union Strategies*, Liverpool: CAITS/MTUCURC.

Crick, M. (1984) *Militant*, London: Faber & Faber.

Cronin, J. E. (1989) 'The "rank and file" and the social history of the working class', *International Review of Social History*, Vol. 14, pp. 78–88.

Daniel, W. (1987) *Workplace Industrial Relations and Technical Change*, London: Frances Printer/Policy Studies Institute.

Daniel, W. and Millward, N. (1983) *Workplace Industrial Relations in Britain: The DE/PSI/ESRC Survey*, London: Heinemann.

Darlington, R. (1993) 'The challenge to workplace unionism in the Royal Mail', *Employee Relations*, Vol. 15, No. 5, pp. 3–25.

Dickenson, M. (1984) *To Break a Union: The Messenger, the State and the NGA*, Manchester: Booklist.

Dickson, T. and Judge, D. (1987) *The Politics of Industrial Closure*, Basingstoke: Macmillan.

Draper, H. (1978) *Karl Marx: Theory of Revolution*, Vol. 2, New York: Pathfinder.

Edwards, C. and Heery, E. (1985) 'The incorporation of workplace trade unionism?', *Sociology*, Vol. 19, No. 3, pp. 345–63.

Elger, T. (1986) 'Affluence, rationalisation and the skilled worker', PhD thesis, University of Durham.

Elger, T. (1990) 'Technical innovation and work reorganisation in British manufacturing industry in the 1980s: continuity, intensification or transfer?', in *Work, Employment and Society*, Special Issue: 'The 1980s: A Decade of Change?', pp. 67–101.

Engels, F. (1974) *The Condition of the Working Class in England*, St Albans: Panther.

England, J. (1981) 'Shop stewards in Transport House: a comment on the incorporation of the rank and file', *Industrial Relations Journal*, Vol. 12, No. 5, pp. 16–29.

Fairbrother, P. (1984) *All Those in Favour: The Politics of Union Democracy*, London: Pluto Press.

Fairbrother, P. (1986) 'Union democracy in Australia: accommodation and resistance', *Journal of Industrial Relations*, June, pp. 171–90.

Fairbrother, P. (1988) *Flexibility at Work: The Challenge for Unions*, Studies for Trade Unionists, Vol. 14, No. 55/56, London: Workers' Educational Association.

Fairbrother, P. (1989) *Workplace Unionism in the 1980s: A Process of Renewal?* Studies for Trade Unionists, Vol. 15, No. 57, London: Workers' Educational Association.

Fairbrother, P. (1990) 'The contours of local trade unionism in a period of restructuring', *Trade Unions and Their Members: Studies in Union Democracy and Organisation*, eds P. Fosh and E. Heery, Basingstoke: Macmillan, pp. 147–76.

Fairbrother, P. and Waddington, J. (1990) 'The politics of trade unionism: evidence, policy and theory', *Capital and Class*, No. 41, pp. 15–56.

Flanders, A. (1975) *Management and Unions: The Theory and Reform of Industrial Relations* (second edition), London: Faber & Faber.

Fosh, P. and Cohen, S. (1990) 'Local trade unionists in action: patterns of union democracy', *Trade Unions and Their Members: Studies in Union Democracy and Organisation*, eds P. Fosh and E. Heery, Basingstoke: Macmillan, pp. 107–46.

Foster, J. and Woolfson, C. (1986) *The Politics of the UCS Work-In*, London: Lawrence & Wishart.

Freeman, M. (1984) *Taking Control: A Handbook for Trade Unionists*, London: Junius.

Friedman, H. and Meredeen, S. (1980) *The Dynamics of Industrial Conflict: Lessons from Ford*, London: Croom Helm.

Fryer, P. (1984) *Staying Power: The History of Black People in Britain*, London: Pluto Press.

Goodman, J. and Whittingham, T. (1973) *Shop Stewards*, London: Pan.

Goodrich, C. L. (1975) *The Frontier of Control*, London: Pluto Press.

Gramsci, A. (1977) 'Unions and councils', *Selections from Political Writings 1910–20*, London: Lawrence & Wishart, pp. 98–102.

Green, P. (1990) *The Enemy Without: Policing and Class Consciousness in the Miners' Strike*, Milton Keynes: Open University Press.

Guest, D. (1987) 'Human resources of management and industrial relations', *Journal of Management Studies*, Vol. 24, No. 5.

Harman, C. (1987) 'The working class after the recession', *The Changing Working Class*, eds A. Callinicos and C. Harman, London: Bookmarks, pp. 53–81.

Hawkins, K. (1985) 'The "new realism" in British industrial relations', *Employee Relations*, Vol. 7, No. 5, pp. 2–7.

Heaton, N. and Linn, I. (1989) *Fighting Back: A Report on the Shop Steward Response to New Management Techniques in TGWU Region 10*, Barnsley: Northern College and TGWU Region 10.

Heery, E. and Kelly, J. (1990) 'Full-time officers and the shop steward network: patterns of co-operation and interdependence', in *Trade Unions and Their Members: Studies in Union Democracy and Organisation*, Basingstoke: Macmillan, pp. 75–106.

Heffer, E. (1991) *Never a Yes Man*, London: Verso.

Hill, S. (1974) 'Norms, groups and power: the sociology of workplace industrial relations', *British Journal of Industrial Relations*, Vol. 12, No. 2, pp. 213–92.

Hinton, J. (1973) *The First Shop Stewards' Movement*, London: Allen & Unwin.

Hinton, J. (1983) *Labour and Socialism: A History of the British Labour Movement*, Brighton: Wheatsheaf.

Holton, B. (1973) 'Syndicalism and Labour on Merseyside: 1906–14', *Building the Union*, ed. H. R. Hikins, Liverpool: Toulouse Press.

Hyman, R. (1975) *Industrial Relations: A Marxist Introduction*, Basingstoke: Macmillan.

Hyman, R. (1979) 'The politics of workplace trade unionism: recent tendencies and some problems for theory', *Capital and Class*, No. 8, pp. 54–67.

Hyman, R. (1984) 'The sickness of British trade unionism: is there a cure?', *The Political Economy of Industrial Relations: Theory and Practice in a Cold Climate*, Basingstoke: Macmillan, pp. 166–87.

Hyman, R. (1987a) 'Rank and file movements and workplace organisation 1914–39', *A History of British Industrial Relations*, Vol. 11, *1914–1939*, ed. C. J. Wrigley, Brighton: Wheatsheaf, pp. 129–58.

Hyman, R. (1989a) *The Political Economy of Industrial Relations: Theory and Practice in a Cold Climate*, Basingstoke: Macmillan.

Hyman, R. (1989b) 'The sound of one hand clapping: a comment on the "rank and file" debate', *International Review of Social History*, Vol. 34, pp. 135–52.

Hyman, R. (1989c) *Strikes* (fourth edition), Basingstoke: Macmillan.

Hyman, R. and Elger, T. (1981) 'Job controls, the employers' offensive and alternative strategies', *Capital and Class*, No. 15, pp. 115–49.

Hyman, R. and Fryer, B. (1975) 'Trade unions: sociology and political economy', *Processing People: Cases in Organisational Behaviour*, ed. J. B. McKinlay, London: Holt, Rinehart & Winston, pp. 150–213.

Industrial Relations Review and Report (1993) *Employment Trends*, No. 535, p. 16.

Industrial Society/Ford Motor Company (1990) *Opportunities for Change*, London: Industrial Society.

Jefferys, S. (1979) 'Striking into the '80s: modern British trade unionism, its limits and potential', *International Socialism*, Vol. 2, No. 5, pp. 1–52.

Jones, B. and Rose, M. (1986) 'Re-dividing labour: factory politics and work reorganization in the current industrial transition', in *The Changing Experience of Employment Restructuring and Recession*, eds K. Purcell, S. Wood, A. Waton and S. Allen, London: Macmillan, pp. 35–37.

Kelly, J. (1987) *Labour and the Unions*, London: Verso.

Kelly, J. (1987) 'Trade unions through the recession 1980–84', *British Journal of Industrial Relations*, Vol. 25, No. 2, pp. 275–82.

Kelly, J. (1988) *Trade Unions and Socialist Politics*, London: Verso.

Kelly, J. (1990) 'British trade unionism 1979–89: change, continuity and contradictions', *Work, Employment and Society*, Special Issue: 'The 1980s: A Decade of Change?', pp. 29–65.

Kessler, S. and Bayliss, F. (1992) *Contemporary British Industrial Relations*, London: Macmillan.

Lane, T. (1974) *The Union Makes Us Strong*, London: Arrow.

Lane, T. (1978) 'Liverpool: city of harder times to come', *Marxism Today*, November, pp. 336–436.

Lane, T. (1986) 'We are the champions: Liverpool vs the 1980s', *Marxism Today*, January, pp. 8–11.

Lane, T. (1987) *Liverpool: Gateway of Empire*, London: Lawrence & Wishart.

Levie, H., Gregory, D. and Lorentzen, N. (1984) *Fighting Closures: De-industrialization and the Trade Unions 1979–1983*, Nottingham: Spokesman.

Littler, C. and Salaman, G. (1982) 'Bravermania and Beyond? Recent theories of the Labour process', *Sociology*, Vol. 16, No. 2, pp. 251–69.

Liverpool City Council (1984) *Liverpool Budget Crisis: The Story of the Campaign*, Liverpool City Council.

Liverpool City Council (1986) *Success against the Odds*, Liverpool City Council Public Relations and Information Unit.

Luxemburg, R. (1977) *The Mass Strike, the Political Party and the Trade Unions*, London: Merlin Press.

Lyddon, D. (1977) 'British Leyland: the shop stewards and participation', *International Socialism*, Vol. 1, No. 102, pp. 20–6.

McIlroy, J. (1988) *Trade Unions in Britain Today*, Manchester: Manchester University Press.

MacInnes, J. (1987a) *Thatcherism at Work: Industrial Relations and Economic Change*. Milton Keynes: Open University Press.

MacInnes, J. (1987b) 'Why nothing much has changed: recession, economic restructuring and industrial relations since 1979', *Employee Relations*, Vol. 9, No. 1, pp. 3–9.

McIntyre Brown, A. (1991) 'Myths and misconceptions', *Business North West*, Vol. 23, No. 4. pp. 38–41.

Marchington, M. (1992) 'Managing labour relations in a competitive environment', in *Skill and Consent: Contemporary Studies in the Labour Process*, eds A. Sturdy, D. Knights and H. Willmott, London: Routledge, pp. 149–83.

Marchington, M. and Parker, P. (1990) *Changing Patterns of Employee Relations*, London: Harvester Wheatsheaf.

Marks, M. (1974) 'The battle at Fisher Bendix', *International Socialism*, Vol. 1, No. 73, pp. 11–15.

Marsden, D., Morris, T., Willman, P. and Wood, S. (1985) *The Car Industry: Labour Relations and Industrial Adjustment*, London: Tavistock.

Marsh, D. (1992) *The New Politics of British Trade Unionism*, Basingstoke: Macmillan.

Martin, R. (1992) *Bargaining Power*, Oxford: Oxford University Press.

Martinez Lucio, M. and Weston, S. (1992) 'The politics and complexity of trade union responses to new management practices', *Human Resource Management Journal*, Vol. 2, No. 4, pp. 77–91.

Marx, K. (1970) 'Wages, price and profit', in *Selected Works*, Moscow: Progress Publishers.

Matthews, J. (1972) *Ford Strike*, London: Panther.

Merseyside Socialist Research Group (1980) *Merseyside in Crisis*, Manchester: Manchester Free Press.

Milliband, R. (1989) *Divided Societies: Class Struggle in Contemporary Capitalism*, Oxford: Oxford University Press.

Mills, C. W. (1966) *The Sociological Imagination*, Bletchley: Open University Press.

Millward, N. and Stevens, M. (1986) *British Workplace Industrial Relations 1980–84*, Aldershot: Gower.

Millward, N., Stevens, M., Smart, D. and Hawes, W. R. (1992) *Workplace Industrial Relations in Transition*, Aldershot: Darmouth.

Morris, T. and Wood, S. (1991) 'Testing the survey method: continuity and change in British industrial relations', *Work, Employment and Society*, Vol. 5, No. 2, pp. 259–82.

Mortimer, K. (1990) 'EDAP at Ford: a research note', *Industrial Relations Journal*, Vol. 21, No. 4, pp. 309–14.

Nichols, T. and Armstrong, P. (1976) *Workers Divided*, London: Fontana.

Nichols, T. and Beynon, H. (1977) *Living with Capitalism: Class Relations and the Modern Factory*, London: Routledge & Kegan Paul.

Nicholson, N. (1976) 'The role of the shop steward: an empirical case study', *Industrial Relations Journal*, Vol. 7, No. 1, pp. 5–26.

Nicholson, N., Ursell, G. and Blyton, P. (1980) 'Social background, attitudes, and behaviour of white collar shop stewards', *British Journal of Industrial Relations*, Vol. 18, No. 1, pp. 15–26.

Nolan, P. and Marginson, P. (1990) 'Skating on thin ice? David Metcalf on trade unions and productivity', *British Industrial Relations Journal*, Vol. 18, No. 2, pp. 81–92.

Oliver, N. and Wilkinson, B. (1990) 'Obstacles to Japanization: the case of Ford UK', *Employee Relations*, Vol. 12, No. 1, pp. 17–21.

Parkinson, M. (1985) *Liverpool on the Brink*, Newbury: Policy Journals.

Partridge, B. (1978) 'The activities of shop stewards', *Industrial Relations Journal*, Vol. 8, No. 4, pp. 22–42.

Pedler, M. (1973) 'Shop stewards as leaders', *Industrial Relations Journal*, Vol. 4, No. 4, pp. 43–60.

Pollert, A. (1981), *Girls, Wives, Factory Lives*, London: Macmillan.

Price, R. (1989) 'What's in a name? Workplace history and "rank and filism"', *International Review of Social History*, Vol. 34, pp. 62–77.

Purcell, J. and Sisson, K. (1983) 'Strategies and practice in the management of industrial relations', *Industrial Relations in Britain*, ed. G. Bain, Oxford: Blackwell, pp. 95–120.

Purcell, K. and Wood, S. (1986) 'Restructuring and recession', *The Changing Experience of Employment: Restructuring and Recession*, eds K. Purcell, S. Wood, A. Waton and S. Allen, London: Macmillan pp. 1–17.

Roberts, G. (1976) 'The strategy of rank and filism', *Marxism Today*, December, pp. 375–83.

Rootes, P. (1986) *Collective Bargaining: Opportunities for a New Approach*, University of Warwick Industrial Relations Research Unit Paper, No. 5.

Royal Commission on Trade Unions and Employers Associations (1968) *Report*, Cmnd 3623, HMSO.

Saville, J. (1973) 'The ideology of Labourism', *Knowledge and Belief in Politics*, eds R. Benewick *et al.*, London: Allen & Unwin.

Schuller, T. and Robertson, D. (1983) 'How representatives allocate their time: shop steward activity and membership contact', *British Journal of Industrial Relations*, Vol. 21, No. 3, pp. 330–42.

Smith, J. (1984) 'Labour tradition in Glasgow and Liverpool', *History Workshop Journal*, No. 17, pp. 32–56.

Spencer, B. (1985) 'Shop steward resistance in the recession', *Employee Relations*, Vol. 7, No. 5, pp. 22–8.

Spencer, B. (1987) *Post-war Trade Unionism: Its Role and Significance*, Studies for Trade Unionists, Vol. 13, No. 52, London: Workers' Educational Association.

Spencer, B. (1989) *Remaking the Working Class? An Examination of Shop Stewards' Experiences*, Nottingham: Spokesman.

Starkey, K. and McKinlay, A. (1989) 'Beyond Fordism? Strategic choice and labour relations in Ford UK', *Industrial Relations Journal*, Vol. 20, No. 2, pp. 93–100.

Storey, J. (1988) 'The people-management dimension in current programmes of organisational change', *Employee Relations*, Vol. 10, No. 6, pp. 17–25.

Taaffe, P. and Mulhearn, T. (1988) *Liverpool: A City That Dared to Fight*, London: Fortress Books.

Terry, M. (1978) 'The emergence of a lay elite? Some recent changes in shop steward organization', *Industrial Relations Research Unit Discussion Paper*, No. 14, University of Warwick.

Terry, M. (1983a) 'Shop steward development and managerial strategies', *Industrial Relations in Britain*, ed. G. Bain, Oxford: Blackwell, pp. 67–91.

Terry, M. (1983b) 'Shop stewards through expansion and recession', *Industrial Relations Journal*, Vol. 14, No. 3, pp. 49–58.

Terry, M. (1986a) 'How do we know if shop stewards are getting weaker?', *British Journal of Industrial Relations*, Vol. 24, No. 2, pp. 169–80.

Terry, M. (1986b) 'Shop stewards and management: collective bargaining as co-operation', *Technological Change, Rationalisation and Industrial Relations*, London: Croom Helm, pp. 161–74.

Terry, M. (1988) 'The development of shop steward organisation: Coventry Precision Tools 1945–1972', *Shopfloor Politics and Job Controls: The Post-war Engineering Industry*, eds M. Terry and P. K. Edwards, Oxford: Blackwell.

Terry, M. (1989) 'Recontextualising shopfloor industrial relations: some case study evidence', *Manufacturing Consent*, eds S. Tailby and C. Whitson, Oxford: Blackwell, pp. 192–216.

Terry, M., Brown, W. and Ebsworth, R. (1978) 'Factors shaping shop steward organisation in Britain', *British Journal of Industrial Relations*, Vol. 16, pp. 139–59.

Thompson, P. (1983) *The Nature of Work*, Basingstoke: Macmillan.

Thompson, P. and Bannon, E. (1985) *Working the System: The Shop Floor and New Technology*, London: Pluto Press.

Towers, B. (1989) 'Running the gauntlet: British trade unions under Thatcher 1979–1988', *Industrial and Labour Relations Review*, Vol. 42, No. 2, pp. 163–88.

Trotsky, L. (1977) *History of the Russian Revolution*, London: Pluto Press.

Turner, H. A., Clack, G. and Roberts, G. (1967) *Labour Relations in the Motor Industry*, London: Allen & Unwin.

Undy, R. (1978) 'The devolution of bargaining levels and responsibilities in the Transport and General Workers Union 1965–75', *Industrial Relations Journal*, Vol. 9, No. 4, pp. 44–56.

Watson, D. (1988) *Managers of Discontent: Trade Union Officers and Industrial Relations Managers*, London: Routledge.

Webb, S. and Webb, B. (1920) *History of Trade Unionism*, London: Longmans.

Werther, W. (1985) 'Job 1 at Ford: employee co-operation', *Employee Relations*, Vol. 7, No. 1, pp. 10–16.

Willman, P. (1980) 'Leadership and trade union principles: some problems of management sponsorship and independence', *Industrial Relations Journal*, Vol. 11, No. 4, pp. 39–49.

Willman, P. and Winch, G. (1985) *Innovation and Management Control: Labour Relations at BL Cars*, Cambridge: Cambridge University Press.

Winch, G. (1980) 'Shop steward tenure and workshop organization', *Industrial Relations Journal*, Vol. 11, No. 4, pp. 50–62.

Zeitlin, J. (1989a) ' "Rank and filism" in British labour history: a critique', *International Review of Social History*, Vol. 34, pp. 42–61.

Zeitlin, J. (1989b) ' "Rank and filism" and labour history: a rejoinder to Price and Cronin', *International Review of Social History*, Vol. 34, pp. 89–102.

INDEX